Elise Spencer-Hughes currently lives in Cheshire with her four rescued dogs from Cyprus and her daughter who lives close by. This is the first of several manuscripts that Elise is working on; the sequel to *Military Wife* is well under way!

Elise covets a life on the coast, with an acre or two of land to allow her beloved dogs to roam freely off their leads, she would also like a few chickens and a Lama! Because Elise just loves animals.

Her one wish in life would be to see her daughter happy in whichever way that may be. Her daughter is her whole life and reason for breathing. Elise would also love to help her close friends to achieve their dreams. Today's world is tougher than it used to be, and the necessity to work does not allow time to make dreams become a reality. In most cases, people work to live and never achieve what they would really like to do in life. Elise would love to help in some small way to give back and help her friends. One friend would like her own dog rescue sanctuary, another would love her own craft barn, a recently acquired friend simply wants to do painting and decorating, but the need to work gets in the way of their dreams becoming reality. If Elise can give back and help them in some small way, that would give her the most pleasure in life.

Having lived a varied and busy life with some bumps, and indeed, major cracks in the road, Elise retains a good sense of humour and strong character with a no-nonsense attitude. To publish her books successfully and live a quiet life is all she would like to achieve by the time she reaches sixty, which gives her a time limit of ten years!

She is an inspirational, truthful and down to earth type of person who has learned to live alone after a long marriage. She hopes to find love again but is certainly not in a hurry, she believes that true happiness starts within, and that it is not a necessity to be with someone to be happy. She does not see the 'moving on' part as having to be with someone. Moving on simply means leaving dead wood behind and letting that shit go. Elise chose to be single until she finds Mister Right, not Mister Right Now! Although, book three is a testimony to the few Mister Right Nows and some fun along the way! It will be eye opening and well worth the read!

Peace and love come to those who wait long enough and work towards it…this is her belief, and she is looking forward to a writing career that she has always dreamed of.

My first dedication is to my beautiful daughter. The past few years have been difficult, and through no fault of our own, it impacted you in ways that I hoped would never happen. I had hoped that you would never have to experience the pain that you have endured and overcome. You have been an absolute legend and an emotional support beyond your years! Wow! We have been through it, haven't we? But we are still standing, and we are two strong women whom people may have underestimated!

You and I are like Tree-Beard, our roots are strong, we stand firm together and we weather any storm that comes our way. Your loyalty and love are the ingredients that drive me forward in my quest to make a better life for us. I will always be there as your Rock-Biter should there ever come a time when you need to be shielded from harm, and I will NEVER let go!

We are mother and daughter with an unbreakable bond and no one will ever take that away from us. My limitless love for you, my girl, will never falter until the day I leave this earth. I love you to Jupiter and back…well everyone says the moon, so I thought that I would aim higher and go for the big one! It is, after all, the biggest planet with a fire that burns eternally.

I love you eternally always and forever. x

My next dedication goes without a doubt to my DP. My Denise. I do not know how I would have got through the last years without you! It goes without saying that we are like mirror images when it comes to our personalities; there is no other that can match one hundred percent. Thank you so much for your eternal friendship, trust and belief in me. Our paths were meant to cross in 1995 because here we still are with our minds and marbles fully intact! For now, anyway!
It may be a different story when we end up in the same care home with a few marbles rattling around, and we are entertaining the other residents with racing our Zimmer frames up and down the corridors!

Wubba Du, my best friend forever. x

To my Maverick family! Louise, Andrew, Pippa and Wilbur. Working for you guys meant more to me than you can ever imagine.

Yoh! Mav! Louise, I will forever be in your debt for the knowledge and guidance that you generously offered so freely every time that you could see me tripping up, or indeed, falling!

The day I met you in my red coat was the start of a journey working alongside you in your beautiful home, and a lifelong friendship that we formed. I can only thank you for all the mind tools that you gave me to help me see things from a different perspective. I am calmer, and my ability to control my emotions stems from the lessons that you taught me. [I was paying attention even if I appeared not to be ;-)]

You and Andrew gave me the platform, and the time and space to allow myself to heal, repair and rebuild from the rubble. Your friendship and generosity, along with your understanding will remain with me always. Working alongside you and becoming a part of your family was always something that made my job so much easier, and even though my body started giving up, my friendship with you will always be. This book was made possible because you both believed in my capabilities and ambition to succeed. Again, this is another of the qualities that I cherish as your friend, and former housekeeper.

But! That does not mean that you are rid of me. Ha! Ha! Oh no! You and the winkles are stuck with me for life!

Love as always…C-bear xx

Now, I must at his own request mention the man behind the scenes, and indeed the man who my lovely Louise is married to! Andrew is a staggeringly good-looking, six-feet muscle man with a character to match his physique!
How was that, Andrew? Was that convincing? ;-)

Andrew is five-foot or five foot nine at most depending on what shoes he is wearing! But Andrew…you are bloody awesome the way you are, and dynamite comes in small packages! Do not underestimate the power of being vertically challenged!

Thank you both for helping me with the publication of this book. xx
To all the other families that I have worked for, I thank you for your patience with me while things were proving to be a challenge in my personal life, and in the last stages of

my housekeeping job when I was in so much pain that I could not work to the pace that I had previously.

And I thank you all for the support and help through the pandemic of 2020/21.

To all my family members. We have never lived in each other's pockets due to the nature of my nomadic previous lifestyle. But we all remain close regardless of how much time passes and wherever I live. Thank you all for waiting so patiently for this book, and although you may read some things that you did not previously know, please know that without these events happening that I would have a shorter word count in this manuscript!

My unconditional love to all my family members. x

To my mum and dad, despite them not having been together for a great many years, it would be rude to leave them out after they brought me and my siblings into the world.

Mum, thank you for being my ear for the last few years, and for your endless support. Just having you on the other end of the phone is sometimes all that I have needed. Much love and here is to new memories!

Your daughter xx

Dad, nothing changes with regards to our relationship. The lack of communication was, is and always shall be the same. I understand why, but it does not excuse the fact that you could have made more of an effort for your only daughter.

Your only daughter who needed some support from her father after the loss of Darren, and all those times that you said that things would be different. You once said that you had lost your son, and that you were not willing to lose your daughter. But you allowed the ravine between us to deepen with every year that passed. You allowed one person to stand between the love of a father and daughter for the sake of a peaceful life even though there could have been room for both of us women. So, I let go. And you did eventually lose me because I simply gave up the fight to maintain closure, I could not sustain a one-way relationship.

You are my dad, and I will always love you to bits, but I will no longer put you on the pedestal that you once were for many years.

Delores…GFY.

My final shout out goes to all my friends. Denise, Ajay, Julie H, Dilys J, Jacob and Sam, Denise#2, all the fab friends that I have made past, present and future.

Tina H, Kim, Bianca, Sarah (aka JM), Helen S, Nicole and Hayley, Hayley P, Michelle F, Tracy A…the list could go on forever!

My friends, you know who I am, and I know who you are, and if I have missed anyone, then it simply means that I would run out of time and blank pages to name you all. But rest assured that you are always in my thoughts and on my social media. I have some amazing friends and I value each one of you dearly. Stay safe, stay happy and healthy.

Lastly, to all my friends that I have not met yet, buckle up, it will be fast and furious but so worth the ride!

Lastly, I would like to thank my publisher; it has been a rocky road but I really appreciated everything that you did and for your guidance throughout the publication of this book.

For Carl,

For Shelley,

And for John.

Note to the reader:

You own everything that happened to you.

Tell your stories.

If people wanted you to write warmly about them, they should have behaved better.

I am not responsible for the way other people have behaved; they wear their own crowns for their actions and achievements. I am only in charge of my own personal decisions in life and I will not allow anyone to dictate to me how they think I should live it!

If someone looks bad on account of the things that they have said and done, then that rests on their shoulders. But please be aware that everything I have written is based on the truth. I have no reason to lie to make myself look better, and we all must take responsibility for our actions eventually.

This book, and indeed the follow on, is from my perspective alone.

I will no longer allow anyone else to write it.

And I do not see why I should stay silent, so that anyone can stay comfortable.

This is the story of my life. I am a nobody. If you dislike it…write your own!

This book is based on true events that happened to me and I write from my heart.

I was asked the key to my happiness. And my reply was "I unfollow people in real life". How you treat people tells everything about you, integrity is everything.

THE TRUTH SOUNDS LIKE HATE

TO THOSE WHO HATE THE TRUTH.

Elise Spencer-Hughes

MILITARY WIFE

AUSTIN MACAULEY PUBLISHERS

LONDON • CAMBRIDGE • NEW YORK • SHARJAH

A CIP catalogue record for this title is available from the British Library.

ISBN 9781528992671 (Paperback)
ISBN 9781528992688 (ePub e-book)

www.austinmacauley.com

First Published 2022
Austin Macauley Publishers Ltd®
1 Canada Square
Canary Wharf
London
E14 5AA

Thanks to all who have waited patiently for this book and are now waiting for the second! Love you all.

Rome was not built in a day!

Synopsis

This is the story of my childhood and of how I became an army wife, with the unpredictable and emotional experiences that came with that kind of existence. No one could prepare you for it no matter how hard they tried. It also includes the wonderful birth of our daughter, and the tragic and devastating loss of my Brother.

I hope to enlighten and inspire people's perception of how an army wife feels when her husband is on operational tours, and the fear of what could potentially happen.

I hope to walk the reader through step by step and see through my eyes. Although there was much content that I was forbidden to write, because it would have been crystal clear that certain circumstances and incidents were brushed under the carpet. Not just by the fact that I signed the official secrets act, but because the man I was with does not want to be portrayed as a bad person. I write the truth, and the truth alone will portray it how it was, and indeed still is.

Of course, I will reiterate that the content of this book is from my perspective and how I felt personally. It is not a story of how other people lived their lives, nor is it stereotypical of a military life. My closest friends from my days of being 'wife of' have however, related to my description and they cannot wait for this story to be told on behalf of them too.

Like most people, all I hoped for in life was a marriage that lasted and a family of my own. But after I married into the army life and we started our journey together, it soon became apparent that I would never be enough for him. The constant moving and changes of address were something he relished. My gut instinct told me that his daughter and I would eventually become a thing of his historic past. In time, it would come to pass that we would be casualties of our own family war.

Ten years after the loss of my brother, my marriage broke down irretrievably with a nice side dish of divorce to follow. I am surprised it lasted that long!

The 'moving on' part was easy because he had made it so difficult in the last two years of marriage that I was glad to be free. I saw it as a blank canvas, a chance to write chapters of my creation and to paint the road I wanted to walk without the confines of marriage. I was done!

After the initial emotions, feelings of loss and being unaware of the full reasons why it had turned so sour, I embarked on a shiny new life path as a single lady. A clean slate. I embraced it as a chance to reinvent myself, and to rebuild my life the way that I wanted to live it! As you will read, sometimes the end of something stagnant can be seen to be a blessing in disguise.

I have used fictional names to protect those whom I care for the most in this world, and even those whom I really do not, but they matter not to me in any case which sounds very harsh! But having been repeatedly treated badly by the same people, I learned from the patterns and became a product of their making. I stopped giving second chances a long time ago.

Chapter 1

My Heart Will Always Be in the South of England

I arrived on this wonderful planet in April 1971 in a town just to the north of London. My parents are Lynn and Leo. I do not really wish to mention my original surname as it is not of any relevance, I have not carried that name for years now and I fashioned myself a new one later in life.

My Brother Darren followed on 10 July 1974, a proud moment and I loved and cherished him as a sister should do. We had a lovely dog named Paddy, he was a Labrador Alsatian cross bred and he was absolutely the best dog a child could wish for. We also had a cat named Whiskey. She was a black and tan tortoiseshell, a beautiful cat that Auntie Karen (Mum's sister) had given to me for one of my birthdays. I remember her fondly. The animals were aptly named as Dad's side of the family are from Irish descendant and once lived on Narrow boats on the canals. (Mum recently corrected me for calling then Barges)

Darren and I have six cousins on Dad's side, and four on Mum's and as kids we saw all of them regularly, it was great fun.

Fullerton Road was where we called home, and it was conveniently located close to our infant and junior school. Mister Gibson was the headmaster. He took no crap from anyone about anything, although he was secretly a big softy under his tough exterior. On the one and only occasion I was sent to him, the fear of walking to his office struck the appropriate amount of fear into me without physically being stood before him!

The crime that I had committed evades me, but I remember him towering over my small frame with his wide eyes and red face expecting him to release a booming angry voice. Instead, he stood in front of me and bent down so that he was a little more at my eye level to say the words, "So tell me, young lady, for what reason did I have to stop drinking my hot tea?"

I replied with a touch of my cheeky personality thinking that it would soften the blow, and to offer my most sincere apology in advance, "Sir, I think that I had said the word bloody, aloud. Instead of it staying in my thoughts, it unintentionally and unbeknown to me had crawled out of them. Before I could zip my lips together, it had jumped out of my mouth. It was like the fairies crawled in and grabbed the sentence which contained the offensive word and forced it from me. Before my brain had registered what had happened, it was already too late. I am so sorry!"

This honest reply seemed to amuse the big burly man whom I had feared for the duration of my attendance at the school. He said with a grin on his face, "Well...please don't let that word escape from your lips again, and I would advise that you ask your mum to gently remind you when you are at home so that the opportunity for those imaginary fairies to crawl into your mouth and steal your words does not happen again!" With that, he gave me a wink and told me to behave myself. As I turned on my heels to return to my classroom, I heard him telling me that he could now replace his warm cup of tea with a fresh one, and that he would be adding a custard cream biscuit or two.

I turned my head to smile, and Mister Gibson threw a little wave as I hurried along the corridor. He had always reminded me of a younger Father Christmas...maybe he was his son! Junior school was full of the innocence of childhood. A time when life was so much simpler. The bad things in life were not so prevalent in my mind, I was only five years old and I was too busy enjoying my days attending my little red bricked junior school to worry about what the world was like outside of it. After my initial induction that is!

My first day in the infant's school had not gone well. Granddad had to come and collect me from assembly as I had screamed the hall down! At age four, I simply did not understand why I had been abandoned with all these strangers. Of course, I did eventually learn that I was to go every single day as we all do. My worst memory of infant school was always the little dreaded milk carts that were wheeled through the double doors for the nine o'clock gathering in the assembly hall. The milk was always tepid, and I would drink it very reluctantly. I always left about a quarter of the milk content in the bottom with the hope that the teacher who came to collect the bottles did not notice I had left some, or simply did not say anything if they had. I did not like the smell of the full fat milk and still cannot stomach it to this day. That milk experience scarred me for life!

We were sometimes served with semolina at lunch break, I refused to eat it so many times that the dinner ladies eventually gave up trying to put a heaped spoonful in my bowl. I have never even considered eating semolina because I remember the texture of it, yet I absolutely adore rice pudding. Thankfully, I have a lactose intolerance, so I do not have to smell milk in any capacity, I blame it on the thick, white, warm liquid that we were forced to drink in the infant's school!

When I was aged four, I made a friend called Larissa. Our mums knew each other and she lived just around the corner that joined our streets, so we walked to school each day and remained good friends into senior school and beyond.

My other friend was a girl a year younger than me; she only lived five doors along and had three sisters and one brother. She was named Angela, and we spent a lot of the time hanging out together.

When I was eight years old and Darren was five, my dad had been acting strange and seemed not to be at home as much as he perhaps should be, or indeed used to be previously. It was that age-old scenario that kids pick up on, even though the adults think the kids are too young to understand and cannot guess that something is amiss. I used to ask him where he was going out to, and could I go with him, and the reply was always "to see a man about a dog" or "there and back to see how far it is". I may have been eight years old, but I knew that there was another party involved, and I later classed the first statement to be true except there was no man, only the dog. I was not stupid enough to know that it had to be another woman based on how he was treating my mum. I watched her deteriorate as she developed into an angry and sad person that cried behind closed doors.

The news was broken to Darren and me one morning over the phone. As Mum handed the phone receiver for me to hear, she said the words, "NO, you can bloody tell them yourself because this is your doing!"

Dad's words "I'm not coming home anymore" still ring in my ears to this day. I remember it like it was yesterday because Darren and I were standing in our school uniforms sobbing our little hearts out.

We could not understand whether we had done something wrong, and we were excused from school for the day. We spent the following days crying, as did Mum, and to think he could not have sat us down and told us properly face to face. What difference would it have made? But having recently heard it on the phone for a second time in my life, I know now that it is the coward's way of announcing something and not a very fair one.

We had good neighbours before all this happened, but that was soon to change as it became apparent that they knew about the affair my dad was having and had met the woman in question. Dad had worked and was friends with the male who lived in the adjoining house, therefore, he had obviously confided in the man.

Understandably, Mum was bitter about the whole thing, as Dad had left her with debts to clear, two kids and two pets. Things became very desperate. Back in those days, the man was responsible for paying child maintenance, it was not yet known as CSA, and according to Mum, he had failed to pay it on several occasions, and despite Mum having three or four cleaning jobs, times were extremely tough!

Mum would collect her social security every Monday morning and by Wednesday, it had all gone. Firstly, on the bills, and then on whatever food she could get with what was left. We had fifty-pence meters for the gas and electricity (there was no central heating until I was aged 14 when the council finally installed it after Dad left. Before that, it was a coal fire in the living room and the back dining room) and it was always expected that one, if not both would run out of money on the weekends. We had a gas fire that was eventually fitted to replace the coal fire in the living room, and we used to huddle around it if the electricity ran out. I also used to wash my hair with cold water and dry it in front of that gas fire as best I could before school. It was absolutely freezing in winter with frost on the playing fields whilst I walked to school with wet hair. I also did not own a hairdryer until I was aged fourteen when the neighbour next door took pity on me and gave me one. It was a terrible way to live but Mum did the best she could with two grumbling kids who constantly complained that they were cold and hungry. We were all fed up with sitting in the dark every weekend, and Darren and I wondered why we could not have a life like the other kids. My cousins were living further up the street. They lived in the same situation with the bloody fifty-pence meter only going so far before it ran out. It was awful being so cold and I have no idea how previous humans before our generation survived!

I could only imagine how hard it was for Mum until I recently hit tough times myself, and now I can relate to how she must have felt. It is hard to cope with the financial burden of running a home, mouths to feed and paying the bills on time after you have been fucked over by someone that you trusted. It is difficult in today's world when you live by yourself with no one around to support you because the one person that you trusted is now supporting someone else and his/her kids instead of honouring a promise that they made to their own flesh and blood, and to the people that they once claimed to love.

Mum would send us to borrow fifty pence pieces from the neighbours, or from Granddad (Dad's father). He lived locally and was within a short walking distance. Darren and I were always mortified at having to ask him if we could borrow and his answer would sometimes be "no, I am so sorry. I don't have any", but we had done as we were instructed. Granddad was always in the pub behind our house, but of course that did not necessarily mean that his loose change would be given in the fifty pence pieces that we needed to heat and light our house.

The winters in this situation were unbearable. Darren and I had been sent to Sunday school in the mornings after getting out of our beds into a freezing cold house! This was so that we were not in the house freezing any longer than we had to be, and Mum could monitor and reduce the amount of complaining that she had to endure. This was then followed by a hurriedly cooked, cheap and cheerful lunch which usually consisted of chops, some form of vegetable and potatoes. Mum literally did the best that she could with what little resources she had to hand, but it was always against the clock as to whether the electric ran out! Half cooked became the norm as did the 'BURNT PAN PORRIDGE'! Which to this day sends shivers down my spine!

Mum had a specific pan which was only used for porridge, and it had burnt attachments on the bottom that were (allegedly) un-removable, nothing a bit of elbow grease and wire wool would not cure! Mum and I laughed about this recently!

We dreaded the burnt pan porridge mornings; they were absolute torture and it tasted foul! Imagine if you will the faces that Darren and I pulled whilst trying to force it down our throats, it would resemble that of a person eating half a lemon…yuck! The mere thought of it still makes me cringe even now.

Life with regards to the adjoining neighbours became increasingly difficult for them. My dad had put them in such a shitty position; he was the lucky one to have moved away and did not have to deal with the wrath of my angry mother. Mum can be very vocal if someone pisses her off or does her a wrong; she is only human, but they eventually moved away after the abuse and comments continued and some new (victims of torture) tenants moved in straight after. It was a council estate although a nice enough area to live and so the houses were never empty for long.

Another of Mum's ways of getting us out of the cold house we lived in, was to take us on a long dog walk which usually filled about three hours of a Sunday afternoon. She took us through a lot of streets towards the towns largest park. We always walked into the park along the canal and I loathed the narrow towpath because I was scared to walk too close to the edge for fear of falling in. I am afraid of deep water that you cannot see the bottom of, but years later I recently embraced the fear! But I will tell that story in the second book…I was so proud of myself and declared it a demon that I had smacked in the mouth and put it to bed! In the second book I smack quite a few demons and put them in their box!

On one of our extensive Sunday afternoons walks, we had taken a short cut through the thick wooded area on the edge of the country park. We had experienced torrential down pours the night before, so Mum made us wear our welly boots that Nan and Granddad had brought for us. Darren was walking just up ahead of Mum and I, and we watched as he stepped into what he believed to be a small puddle, which incidentally turned out to be quite a deep, small puddle! His foot completely disappeared with a sound that resembled quicksand suction. To our absolute hysteric's, he had put his left foot forward to step out of the puddle, but the foot was minus his welly boot!

Stroppy knickers kicked in and his anger turned to rage the more that I laughed, but I could not stop! It was an involuntary reaction to the ensuing sight just up ahead! I nearly wet myself from laughing so hard! It appeared to be such a natural reaction in his stride that resulted in him having to walk home with one welly boot squelching because it was full of his muddy sock after he had ended up with his foot in the mud. This was despite his best effort to stand on one leg for as long as it took for us to reach him and try to save his foot from landing in the mud, but we clearly failed to get there in time. There was no saving him, he was too far ahead of Mum and I, so we were unable to prevent the whole scenario from happening. If he had been walking alongside the two of us, then maybe we might have been able to prevent the foot from being immersed in the mud by supporting his weight whilst he could not maintain his balance! I still chuckle about it to this day, but my word he could sulk…and he did so for days after. Retrieving the welly boot was cause for more laughter and I simply chuckled to myself all the way home although I did feel a little remorseful about it, I just could not help myself…it was only mud and would wash out! But his mood would not!

Despite his sulky moody temperament, my brother and I were close, and we looked after one another while Mum worked her evening jobs. Our Nan looked after us straight after school until things changed and it became known that Granddad was seriously ill, he had bowel cancer. Darren and I had never experienced this word before, and we did not fully understand the full impact that it was about to have on the family. We both believed that our granddad Arthur was tough and that he would be okay. How wrong we were.

We lost Granddad not long after Dad had left to go live with his new woman and her kids. Nan also became unwell a few months later and looking after us two kids did not help. Our lovely Nan who we cherished passed away nine months after Granddad. She had a heart attack in the kitchen, which from what I remember was followed by more. Nan had been the glue in the family, the one who knew the answers to my questions, and the lady who we all loved very much. Her loss was one that none of us ever really recovered from, and the family were somewhat divided. Everyone learnt to live with her loss, but we grieved for a long time and my heart still flutters when I bring up memories of her.

Nan had once reprimanded me quite firmly on one occasion after she had heard me say "bloody hell".

I was watching something on the TV and the words escaped from my mouth before I even had time to think about it. Nan got up from her armchair, casually walked into the kitchen and told me to follow her. She then took out a bar of soap from the cupboard underneath the sink. It was at this point that I knew I was in trouble…but it depended on what she did with that bar of soap as to how much trouble. Nan looked me square in the eyes and without blinking, she said to me, "If you dare say that word in front of me again, I will wash your mouth out with this bar of soap! Now do I make myself clear?"

I could only reply, "Yes, Nan." The sheer smell of the soap made my stomach do a three sixty-degree turn and back again.

Then, she said, "And if that soap does not stop you swearing, I will get the TCP out!"

Now that memory puts a smile on my face because one year when I had a slight toothache, I did indeed swill my mouth with TCP. And I found that it worked, and I have used it for minor things ever since. Bless her I did love my nan.

My last painful memory was unfortunately just before she passed away. One of my favourite aunties on my dad's side of the family worked in a floristry shop on the main high street. On our way to see Nan in the hospital, Mum had insisted that we would stop and purchase a little flower for each of us to give to Nan for her bedside table. I chose purple primroses; Darren chose yellow pansies and Mum got Nan some flowers as a bunch.

I remember the long walk to the other side of town clutching our pots with the little plants in. I was so impressed with how plump and colourful they were. I could not wait to give them to our lovely Nan and give her a massive hug and tell her that I loved her so very much.

On our arrival, she was really pleased to see us, and we gave our little gifts to try and raise her spirits. Nan looked frail. It was an appearance that I was not used to seeing of her, and it caused me a great deal of worry. I asked her how she was feeling. And was she going to be all right. I asked her to promise that she would be coming home soon. She promised both Darren and me that she would be home in a week or so when the doctors said that she was well enough.

We only stayed for a short while because it had taken us an hour and a half to walk to the hospital, and we had run out of time according to the visiting hours. I scanned the room that Nan was staying in. There were around ten more hospital beds, and Nan said she had held long conversations with the occupants of these beds, although the room was not full. I was glad that she had company with people her own age to make friends with. I also remember the colour of the crockery and more specifically the teacup and saucer; it was sky blue because it matched the colour that I could see out of the window. There were the current day's newspapers lying open on the lap tray that was wheeled down to the end of the bed, and people rustled in and out of the room to use the bathroom.

I did not have a sense of death at this point, because despite the frailty of some of the patients, it was not apparent that any of them were in there because they were about to die. I was only nine years old and had no experience of being in a hospital environment until now. Nan seemed healthy enough and I believed in my mind that she would be home as she had promised at the end of the week or the beginning of the following week, but that she would be home soon regardless.

Within the next two days, Darren and I were being marched at speed back to the hospital. We knew that something had happened, but we were not told what had occurred until we arrived at the hospital. I recall that all of us were ushered

22

into a private room. My brother sat beside me and instantly started chewing his nails. Uncle Alex and Karen were in standing positions until the news that Nan had passed away was announced. Everyone was silent for a time. We were taken to the bed space that had previously been our Nan's, the last place we had seen her, and of course Mum, Karen and Alex had seen their mother. I spotted the pot plants on the windowsill above her bed. I asked if we could take them home because they were dying. It was as if, at the precise moment that our Nan had died, the little flowers had given up and gone with her. I felt so heartbroken that she would no longer be able to see the flowers, or feel the wind on her face, because now…our most treasured Nan had become the wind and had returned to the earth in spirit.

In the last two years, the family had been devastated by the loss of three valued and loved members. Mum's brother, Uncle Alex, stayed in his family home and later raised his own family there. Mum's sister, my Auntie Karen who is more like an older sister was already married and living elsewhere but the siblings were there for each other when needed.

My mum and Karen have had sisterly discrepancies as most siblings do, but I will not speculate as to what about and it really is not my place to talk about it in any case. I would not want to get it wrong, so I stay out of it. It is water under the bridge, none of my business, and between the two of them although they do still converse.

I have no idea how we got through the losses, I just know that like any family, we just did because we had no alternative. Mum grew increasingly grumpy, distant and impatient but under the circumstances, it was unavoidable considering the past and recent events that had such a detrimental effect on her life. As an adult, I cannot imagine the emotional pain that she had endured and was now coming to terms with. Having lost her husband and then both parents within the space of two years. As an adult, I fully understand why her mood swings occurred and I now know that my mum had the mental strength to keep going, and to keep fighting for the welfare of me and my brother. I now understand where my strength was inherited from, and I am extremely grateful to Mum for the guidance and upbringing that we had despite her struggles and hardships.

My mum is and will always be my rock and my go to person.

Auntie Karen is also my rock in a different sense because she has been a tremendous support and loving elder sister type. I adore my existing family members although I cannot say too much about my dad because there has always been a barrier in the way that prevents any sort of contact or closure. I love my dad to bits. But I gave up trying to sustain contact because it is always me that initiates it. I accepted after thirty years, that is how it has always been. He very rarely contacted me, and I was always totally shocked when he did.

The ongoing court cases that Dad had initiated in previous years to try and gain access to see me and Darren had proved futile and costly. From what I can remember, the agreement was that Dad would pick us up from Fullerton Road at 10 am, and then would drop us back at 5 pm the same day and this day was supposed to be every other Saturday.

Dad would arrive on time, only to find the house empty because Mum had already left with us and walked us around to Nan's house by 9.45 am. He would have to drive to Nan's where he would be met by verbal abuse from Mum. She would then be reprimanded by the courts and the whole process would repeat itself. I remember being in Nan's kitchen on one of these occasions where Dad had delivered our Christmas presents. The heads were instantly torn off the Barbie dolls that were for me, and the destruction then spilled over to gifts that were meant for Darren. Mum said that they could have them back and that the gifts were not welcome or appropriate.

Dad was never going to win with her. She was venomously bitter and twisted over his betrayal and there was never going to be any sort of compromise.

After paying for solicitor's time and again, Dad could not afford to fight it any longer and threw in the towel. He was unsuccessful in gaining any time with his own kids, and Darren and I started to believe that he did not want us. Which of course could not have been further from the truth. I presumed that Dad believed that he would never be able to see us, and if he did, it would be made so difficult with all of Mum's bitterness to contend with.

Darren and I were used as weapons and sometimes convinced by Mum's way of thinking. In effect, we were brain washed a bit by the very person who was accusing the other of the very same thing. As a teenager, I decided when I reached the age of sixteen that I would contact my dad no matter what, and that I would meet him and get to know the other woman who Mum despised so much. I decided that I would make up my own mind.

I had often wished that Darren and I were adopted, and that one day, our real parents would come to collect and save us from the war of the roses, but clearly, it was just a fantasy to pull myself through the time of hardship.

My form tutor in junior school was a lovely lady called Miss Sweeney. Shortly after the loss of Nan, she had sent a message to my mum to arrange a meeting with her for a chat. She wanted to understand if there was something going on in my home life that could shed some light on my recent behaviour. I had retreated into what was described as a shell. Miss Sweeney explained that she had noticed a dramatic change in my behaviour and that I had become painfully distant and not my usual self.

Mum sat in my classroom and set out the road map of events that had occurred in such a short space of time. And that she was doing everything to avoid the upset as much as she physically could. But there was no going back to the way things had been. Nan and Granddad were gone, and so was my dad, even if he was only living in a different town. Miss Sweeney was very understanding and had a kind nature that meant she had been observant and patient with me. I was grateful for that because school was the last place that I wanted to be. I wanted to be at home locked away in my thoughts while I sat on my single bed in my bedroom. I wanted to crawl into the shell that I had named Archimedes. I gave it that name because it was the only safe place in my head that I felt was real and stable. I named my shell Archimedes or Archie for short, because I liked the wise owl in The Sword in The Stone. He is wise, and I considered myself to be older than my ten years of life so far. I hoped that one day I too could be as wise, and full of the knowledge that would get me through tough times. I trained myself to retreat when I needed time to process my thoughts, and my shell Archimedes was the only place that I could do this in peace.

Until I found out that loud music in my bedroom had the same effect even if it did disturb the peace of others for a short time! I confided in my friend, Larissa, but she was the only person that I talked to. I do not like to burden people with my problems when they have their own, so I never revealed every single one of my thoughts to her either. I became good at bottling things up and putting my troubles into the little bubbles at the back of Archimedes for future reference, that is if I ever felt like popping those little bubbles to deal with the problem that I had stored inside it. Some of them remain there today. Hence, the reason that I started writing this book, it is cathartic therapy and I found that writing helped me to cleanse my system of these bubbles, and therefore, confront and deal with the problems contained within those bubbles. Now my Archimedes is no longer drowning with the weight and burden of my childhood thoughts and problems, because they are now creating the pages of this book.

By the time that junior school was coming to an end, it became apparent that Darren would be going to a senior school in Kent. When he was six months old, Nan had noticed something 'not quite right' with his sight. He was partially sighted, and it grew progressively worse as he aged. Mum always assumed that it was because she had German measles when she was carrying her unborn little boy. But after investigating further as an adult, and wanting to know why he was losing his sight, it was eventually diagnosed as retinitis pigmentosa. A disease that eats away at the retina resulting in eventual blindness.

I was devastated! I wondered how on earth was I going to see him when he would be in another county. I think that his sight had always bothered me more than Darren, because there was so much that he wanted to do in the world and be a daredevil when I did not crave the thrills that he did because they usually involved something to do with heights! I felt guilty that there was nothing wrong with my sight, and yet he struggled with lampposts and had plenty of up close and personal fist fights with them.

His humour was what made him special. He always wore broken glasses (aka…spectacles) on his face, and he always had a smile to cover up the fact that he had bruises as a result of not knowing that something had not been in his pathway before, and that it had suddenly "jumped out at me that bloody thing did"!

Darren was brought home at the end of every half term and on some weekends for various reasons. We were at home one week after he had arrived on a Friday afternoon with a large holdall and an attitude to match. He became more and more resentful towards me because I got to stay at home while he was sent away to boarding school. What he failed to observe at the time, was that he would eventually be the one that excelled in his academic background more-so than I would. His education was more tailored to his needs to help him achieve whatever he wanted in life to progress into a good job, despite his disability of partial sightedness.

We argued fiercely one evening while Mum was at work. He had a right mood on him and was so nasty and bitter about the fact that it was always me that was offered to go and stay with Karen and Tom in their new home in Milton Keynes. He said that he was angry with me because he saw me as the favourite one. I was mortified, but I could understand where he was coming from and I probably would have felt the same way. We had fought like cat and dog all week and on this occasion, after he had seated himself back down on the floor in front of the TV, I decided that I had enough of his poisonous angry fork tongue and I launched an orange from my hand, it was now in-bound towards his unsuspecting head!

I had thrown the orange that had previously been in my hand, and it had travelled with my full force behind it without even thinking about the consequences! To say that I am impulsive is an understatement, but this was one of my most flawed incidents!

Before I had time to react, and with justified retaliation written all over his angry face, he was up in a split second and bolting towards me with both fists clenched tight! That orange had made full on contact with the back of his head and I was bracing myself for the full impact of his punch. The expected punch did not happen. He changed his tactics at the last second and gave me a boot in the shin that would have made any footballer envious, because Darren would have scored a cracking goal with the effort that he put into that kick!

I screamed like I was being murdered! I could not even walk properly or stand on it! I hated my younger sibling so much that I was not sorry for his resentment towards me for anything. He showed no remorse as I screamed and cried in agony. He simply sat back down and carried on watching TV. Little shit!

I guess the orange attack had hurt just as much, but he had just not cried about it. As the large lump on my leg grew daily, and Mum wanted to know why I was limping, I had to tell her that my brother and I currently hated the sight of each other and were dealing with it.

The lump that he caused remained in the same place for years after; it served as a reminder that I had thrown the orange, and that it was a cause and effect of how he justifiably reacted. Later in life, it came to be a permanent reminder that he existed, and that I once had a brother who meant the world to me despite our silly quarrels and fights.

There were times that I had wished that it had been me who was sent away to boarding school too. Mum had become quite free and easy with her hands, and the discipline that she dished out. These were the days when the lovely Esther was getting child line up and running and I considered calling them on a couple of occasions.

Keeping ourselves and our personal hygiene was of paramount importance to me and Darren. I was always conscious of my hair being greasy as a teenager, so I used to wash it with cold water if we had no hot water, and even if I could only have what we referred to as a birdie bath, I would do that as opposed to no washing at all. I refused to go to school looking or feeling like I was dirty! It was embarrassing enough that I had holes in the soles of my shoes and sometimes the sole had come away at the front.

Mum simply could not afford new shoes in the middle of each school term, so I improvised with the school glue! I could not cope with the front part of my shoes flapping and getting stuck underneath as I tried to walk, it was so embarrassing and I hoped that none of the other kids saw this because it would open me up to ridicule, and I did not want that! I just used to super glue and make do and mend as much as I could. This is the reason that I have so many varied pairs of shoes, boots, Converse (I love Converse!) and trainers for the gym. I am not fearful of the holes developing because I have lots of footwear instead of having to wear one pair of shoes daily, as was the case throughout my senior school days.

I also had a limited amount of clothes and only owned practical clothes that Mum could afford. Being from a single parent family did not bring shame upon me, but not being able to replace things did. I did not have the latest trendy designer names and I still do not bother about it now. I am thrifty because of my upbringing and for the sake of buying one jumper that may cost £100, I would buy lots of clothes for work and still come out with half of that amount in change.

I did not blame either of my parents for the situation as it was. I just became more motivated when I realised that things were evidently never going to improve unless I found work.

We did not have a shower in our house back in those days; it was a downstairs bathroom adjacent to the kitchen. I am slightly ashamed to say that bathing in our single parent house was restricted to once a week, usually on Sundays, with the obligatory birdie baths during the week. We could not afford to heat the hot water with the gas or the emersion heater because it would use what precious little of the credit that we had on the meter. If we wanted to try and heat it up, we always had to ask Mum so that she could time how long it was on for.

My frustration grew the older I got. I started my monthly women menstrual cycle at age twelve. This increased my angst with the added requirements for this occurrence, and I was conscious because it was an added cost on Mum's shopping bill.

We used to walk bloody miles into town once a week to help Mum with the shopping at a store named Presto in the town centre. Mum had one of those pull along wheelie things and I detested handling it because that was the vessel that transported the heavy items such as cans of beans. Darren and I complained about this weekly ritual but of course, he did not have to do it all the time because he was at school.

In any case, Presto was the cheapest place to shop and Mum could get everything on her shopping list with a little left over for the utilities. She paid the bills before we went shopping, and the utilities were last on the list of essentials, hence sitting in the dark and/or cold most weekends. Bless her, Mum was a warrior, and it rubbed off on to us two kids.

Now aged fourteen, and with my anger and frustration growing by the month, I found myself a boyfriend by the name of Karl. Bottom line, he was a Cock Womble! Mum knew it, but I refused to see it at the time, and I thought that I knew better. If only I knew then what I know now, I would tell him to do one before he even got to the stage of opening his pie hole to say hello!

Mum tried absolutely everything to stop me seeing him. But unfortunately, I gave in after a year of him pestering me about letting him have his way. It was a less than romantic setting and I instantly regretted it because of my age, and…because I did it to stop him going on about it. I thought that he would now stay with me because he got his way and I had lost my cherry to him. Disgusting. I felt disgusted with myself and that I had let myself down, and Mum was right about the fact that he would only treat me like crap.

I could not take it back; it was done. I could pretend that it had never happened, but I knew damn well that he would tell all the lads in our group of friends, and that they would know that he had got what he wanted. Nothing changes and it was the same back then as it is now, women are from Venus and men are from Mars and only think with their penis. (This is my third book subject, keep your eyes peeled because it will be true to life and a very revealing insight into the world of online dating based on my own experiences!)

Peer pressure played a massive part, and I was most definitely under pressure from him. But at the same time, it was not life threatening and nobody died, it was only that now I was no longer a virgin and had given my innocence to an absolute idiot. I was naïve and stupid, but who is not at that age?

We think we know better than our parents and we learn the hard way in most instances. My friends all said that I would be the one who would get pregnant first. But on this occasion, they were wrong. I was the one who evaded it because there was an element of common sense and I made him cover it! In fact, I was married a year before I had my first and only child.

Shortly after the incident in the woods and the demise of my innocent cherry, Karl took it upon himself that it would be okay for him to slap me across my thigh with a large paddle hairbrush. Monumental mistake!

After I lost the plot and told him to get out and that I was going to tell my mum, he started yelling at me and told me that one of the other girls at school had recently given him lots of sex. (Well, good for her!) Her name was Caroline, and I had taken no notice of her giggly comment about that fact that someone had really taken an interest in her, and that she liked him a lot. I did not think at the time that she meant my weirdo boyfriend, but she was most welcome to him. As far as I was concerned, she could have the donated toy that I no longer wanted to hang on to. That toy was now used goods and was nothing but trouble, and every culmination of bad boy. I wanted no part of the road that he was walking, and I later found out that he was physically and mentally abusive to a girl who he was living with. A special kind of fucked up he turned out to be, and my mum was of course correct on every level of her analysis of him, which she later relished as I admitted it to her. But…she refrained from saying the words "I told you so!"

On the evening that he had left my house, I called Mum at work to inform her that Karl and I were no longer. She said, "Oh thank God you have seen sense at last! But why have you seen sense and what has happened?"

I told her that he had smacked me one on the leg with a brush and that it was the equivalent of one of her slaps! We ended the call because she was busy, and it was not long until she was finished work so I knew that she would be home shortly after.

Mum had the choice of two routes that she could walk home. One was slightly longer than the other, but it was not by much, and after what I had just told her on the phone, she went looking for Karl on the slightly longer way home because it was on that road that he resided. The chance of him being out and hanging around was slim, but she found him! He was on the corner that we, as a group always hung around. Mum said that he was bumping his gums in his usual confident and arrogant manner and had not even seen her approach. Until she launched her attack!

Karl only cared about himself and his appearance. (I have a habit of choosing this type of guy!) He was particularly proud of his blonde hair and spent time copious amounts of time washing and blow drying it. He was such an arrogant and cock sure of himself young man without good reason for being so. Because underneath his deluded persona, he had the capability of being a nasty little shit who was full of it too! He dreamed of being famous and rode his BMX bike like it was his chariot to stardom. Looking back on how he was makes me cringe! I cannot understand why I was so taken with him, but it was the case that most of the girls wanted him, and it was me that got him through not being so bold like the other girls. He said that I was pretty, and that I did not need to plaster my face with makeup and that he preferred it when I did not wear any at all. (A little bit of control going on there, but I ignored it). We went out with each other for three years. It only went bad after I gave in to him. He had always joked that when we were married that we would walk around our house with no clothes on and shag all day every day. I was not convinced of this, and I knew full well that I would never marry the likes of him. I wanted a man with motivation and a drive to succeed in life. All I envisaged from Karl was a council flat and a boyfriend that wanted to control and abuse me, and not go out to work. You know the sort, cannot be bothered and would rather kick around in the gutter wishing he were lucky like Marty, (Wet-Wet-Wet) no thanks it is not for me! I never wanted a tracksuit chav and that remains to this day.

Yeah, I took a rain check on that whole scenario because I wanted more out of life.

Mums have a canny way of knowing whether a boy or man is wrong for her daughter, Mums just know because they trust their gut feeling, even if the daughter cannot see it for herself. Sometimes, as parents, we need to allow them the opportunity to get it out of their system, and just be there when and if the train wreck happens. Until then, there is not much point in battling with a child that thinks they know best. Mum came through for me time and again. But she allowed me the time to discover for myself what type of boy Karl was, and it is true to say that I used that whole experience with him to see similar traits in other lads, and in my mind, they should have come with a hazardous to health warning label! I knew that was not what I wanted.

Mum suddenly appeared in the living room doorway, red faced and shaking with a clump of blonde hair in her hand! I knew straight away what it was. His beloved hair that he worshipped. Ha! Ha! Ha! She informed me that she had "Got the little bastard! No one hurts my kids and gets away with it"! She proudly spat out at me. I felt bad that I had told her when we spoke on the phone, but the red mark on my leg winked at me as if to inform me that her action was justified.

When we finally went back to school, one of the other lads who had been with Karl at the time that Mum was grabbing his hair and smacking him around the head with her handbag said to me, "Elise, what the hell has your mum got in her bag?"

His name was Gerry, he had lovely, curly, dark hair and beautiful, brown eyes, he resembled Curt Smith from Tears for Fears who are to this day, my favourite band. I adored him, and my knees went weak if he spoke to me with his slightly husky voice. I had always wanted him and not Karl, but he was Karl's best mate. It was too difficult to ask him to go out with me, the same as it was for him to ask me, and he had never even noticed me unfortunately (or so I thought). Gerry was painfully shy…hence, we never got together, and he was the one that got away, my teenage crush escaped.

Mum liked Gerry and saw him as a suitable boyfriend, but it was never to be.

After everything that had happened with Karl and the way it had ended, I thought it was done and dusted. But one early evening just before the start of term, I heard little stones being thrown at my front bedroom window. (Bloody hell this is not Romeo and Juliette! These things only happen in movies!) I opened it to find him standing on the grass with a red face and puffy eyes. Quite evidently, he had been crying a lot by the state of his face and snotty nose, for which I threw some toilet tissue down to him because it was a tragic sight to say the least. I asked what he was doing here! He begged me to come downstairs and talk to him at the door and said that he would not touch me. He said that he was sorry for hitting me with the brush, but it was too late as far as I was concerned and there was no going back.

I told him that if Mum saw him out of the living room window that there would be hell to pay! He said that he did not care if she caught him standing there, and that he was at my house trying to make amends to get me back. I had absolutely no remorse when I said to him, "So what has happened? Did Caroline dump your ass and now you think that I will be stupid enough to go back there with you? I am sorry, mate…but it is not happening. We are done!"

As I predicted, and with the noise and commotion that the drama queen himself was performing under my window because he could not have his own way, Mum opened the front door and told him to fuck off and get off her property!

He exited the garden in a hasty fashion as if the devil were chasing him (in effect she was!) Karl remained on the footpath across from our house and stood there shouting and crying at me while I was watching the event unfold. I could not understand why he was so hell bent and so adamant that when we got back to school that we could see each other, and that my mum could not stop us. I had to go and tell him the facts face to face before he would leave me alone. I persuaded Mum to let me go and tell him the truth because that was the only way we would get rid of him.

I went over to speak to him and calmly told him the reasons that we were done. And to his horror and delusional bubble fantasy that he had created for himself, he thought that we were forever and that he had done no wrong. I told him that the decision to finish it was not because Mum was forcing me to, it was because of his actions and the way that he had treated me. I was not willing to accept his bullshit and arrogance any longer, and that my mind was my own and the decision was based on my unwillingness to be smacked around by anyone. I pointed out that this time it was a hairbrush, next time it might be his fist. And I reminded him that he was just an insecure boy that saw fit to shag another girl while all the while telling me that he loved me, like I believed that bullshit anyway.

We were young. It was done. He finally walked away with what dignity he had left. And a bald patch for the trouble that he had caused.

With the lack of money in the house, I decided that helping Mum with work (cleaning jobs) would maybe help provide me with a little income for shoes and hopefully some trendy clothes. I wanted to take the pressure from Mum a little bit, and so I persuaded her to have a word with her boss and see if she could get me in somewhere to help. I wanted to fit in with what other kids my age wore, but we just could not afford the named brands. If my clothes were clean and fit for purpose, then that was all that mattered, there was no alternative anyway.

I had a paper around at age thirteen, but obviously, these do not last long.

I started working with Mum at a brewery in town and it was a 5 am start so we had to be out of the house by 4.30 am. We would clean until 7 am, and then walk back home where I would get ready for school. I was fourteen years old but not far off my fifteenth birthday. After school, I would go with Mum to her evening cleaning job in an office building and helped empty the bins and vacuum. The people who were still sat at their desks working took no notice of us, but I hated it. It was degrading and I always felt like maybe they thought that they were better than us cleaners! Which was obviously not the case and only my issue to deal with not theirs, the chip was firmly planted on my shoulders.

Every day was the same, and then on Saturdays, I found myself a little job in a sweet shop in the middle of the town centre which was good, and it smelt divine in the back storeroom with all the various sweeties stacked floor to ceiling! But I was undeniably hopeless at getting to grips with the vintage cash till, I ended up leaving because I disliked embarrassing myself with so many mistakes of giving people the wrong change and looking at their angry and confused faces as to how I had managed to mess up so monumentally.

Chapter 2

My Dad Re-Enters My Life

While the saga with Karl had been going on, and I was being a completely uncooperative little cow with Mum, she had been in contact with my dad somehow. She decided that after he had offered no help with me, that a social worker would be introduced with the hope that it would make me see sense with regards to my boyfriend being a bad influence, and then maybe my dad could be given supervised access on the condition that he was not permitted to take me and Darren to his new place of residence with his "slapper", as quoted by my bitter mother.

I will rephrase the first line and tell it exactly how it was. I was being a total selfish little bitch, and I thought that I knew what was best for myself. What I would never have known at the time was that there were underlying issues of abandonment and a need to be loved. These issues had been stored in Archie for dealing with later. I went about finding acceptance and love in all the wrong ways because I was still in my teens, and what I realistically knew about life was a grand total of nothing.

I only knew that I was making my mother's life harder than it should be.

The social workers name was Hazel, and she was kind. But with regards to Karl, I had been defiant! I had not been willing to forego the boyfriend just because Mum hated him. Instead, I had once arrived home with spite written all over my face and a nice big love bite on my neck. Well…you can imagine the proverbial crap storm that had created, and this was brought up for discussion with the lovely Hazel who told me all the stuff adults say about love bites and having sex at my age. I vehemently denied ever having sex of course because I did not want Mum to know I had lost it in the woods for my first time! Which I hasten to add was one of my biggest regrets, but unchangeable…shit happens, and lessons are learnt.

Mum knew. I did not have to admit or deny anything, because she just knew. I did not need a banner on my forehead announcing the dispersal of my cherry; it was evident on my face for my acutely aware mother to read the signs.

Supervised access had been granted to Dad, and after not seeing him for nearly five years, I thought that he might understand my predicament. But he agreed with Mum, which made me aware that the problem had been me all along. I had been awkward, stubborn and rebellious. I was immensely ashamed of myself and saw the error of my ways, and not before time my mum would cry out!

On one of these supervised visits, Dad was permitted take me to a small park which was a short walk from Hazel's office. Darren was at school in Kent, so he saw even less of Dad than I did. It transpired that it had been discussed on Dad's side that I could go and live with him and Delores (I shall call her that after the despised lady on an incredibly famous witches and wizard's film).

Delores is, in my opinion, a want to be snob. Her parents had money and originated from an affluent town a little further up the M1, but that was in the past and she still lived in it! Over the years, I had tried to get on with her, but I cannot abide someone who talks the language of bullshit most of the time. Residing in a purchased ex-council house does not sit well with someone who likes to think she is still living a luxurious lifestyle; suck it up, buttercup. It is what it is, and you chose to stay there.

In the early days and despite my mother detesting everything about Darren and I visiting Dad, I made every effort to understand why Dad had left us for Delores. I had lost sight of the fact that Dad deserved to be happy too, but the term 'frying pan and fire' constantly sprang to mind. I have always felt that Delores could never accept that my dad was fully capable of loving her as well as his kids equally. Anyone with this level of paranoia and feeling threatened by the kids has something to be worried about deep down. In recent years, I have backed off as the tension between Delores and I became too much to deal with. I will explain more on this as we go through my story, but there were numerous occasions that we fell out and contact with Dad was limited, if not cut off for prolonged periods of time altogether because of these fall outs. And to make matters worse, my dad allowed this to happen instead of standing up to her. I feel that in all the years they have been together, she has adopted narcissistic ways to control my dad by making it so difficult to live with her. If Darren or I tried to remain in contact I felt that he just gave up and gave in to her, even for the sake of his own flesh and blood. He lost his backbone and became a slave who jumps every time she dictated how high. "Darling, could you go and get me a vodka from the kitchen downstairs?" I mean…what the fuck? Was slavery not abolished years ago? Especially as they were sitting on the same couch and I never saw her fetching my father anything except a barrel of her opinions and bullshit about something she had read in a magazine, oh and her mood swings! Let me not forget those bad boys!

But Dad has made it worse for himself by doing what she wanted. If Delores wants a vodka, she gets it. But not because she has got off her ass and gone to get it herself!

The thought of her infuriates me, and it only got worse as the time went on, because of her ways, I now refuse to accept her as a part of my life any longer. Cut contact…enjoy the silence!

It also infuriates me that Dad could have left years ago; he chose to stay because he believed that he would never find anyone else at his age. He chose his life, and Darren and I witnessed our own father become exactly what he said that he never would, he became his father. His father (our granddad who we borrowed the fifty pence pieces from) lived with a horrible woman after Dad's mum (our Nan Rose) died. Granddad replaced Rose with a complete waste of human air space and intelligence, and he took in an old battle-axe! Dad had now turned into our granddad, but he will never see that.

Delores is a stout woman who is always on a diet that never works (the vodka will not help). She reads all the latest magazines and takes everything as fact not fiction. She once told me that she had read that drinking out of plastic bottles was bad for your health! If it is not out of the tap, then it is bottled as in 95% of cases surely! And what about the millions of sports bottles that are sold every year! These need sterilising or washing out obviously, but if they were bad for your health, they would not sell!

The only difference with my sports water bottle is that it does genuinely contain water, vodka does not count as a sports drink, Delores, and you cannot get drunk on a bottle full of water whether it is pre-bottled or out of a tap. My cousin Mark will laugh his head off when he reads this! This topic is not open for debate, and only used as an example of the kind of thing that I was up against. I try not to get involved in stupid debates with anyone who has convinced themselves that black is white, and that white is grey. I could not be arsed with it and had no more desire to try.

Again, my sarcasm knows no boundaries and my brain has no filter to stop the words projectile vomiting out of my unwilling mouth. My brain and mouth are always in conflict, and the chimps on my shoulders have regular fights too! (Jeez, I crack myself up!) It is free entertainment for me, and I observe my chimps while I wait for the winning party to come forward so that I can proceed in whichever way I see necessary. My mouth is usually the loser by the way and gets me in trouble all the time. My chimps do not run my life, but they used to play a massive part in causing so much trouble!

I can envisage the comments that would have exited Darren's mouth with regards to the plastic bottles. He would have probably laughed until his sides ached, and his comments would have been legendary!

The mind boggles!

Delores had always bragged about what all four of her sons have achieved in life, and how wonderful they all are. But being ashamed to tell someone that one of your kids is gay is surely not a show of support? I figured that news flash out when I was in my teens because it was not rocket science. Personally, I did not care what his sexual orientation was, I still liked the guy for the person he was/is, and his sexuality had no effect on that. In any case, the point I am making is that she has always tried to make me feel inferior to my stepbrothers. If I am brutally honest, they have no influence on my life whatsoever, they never have, so why would I let what Delores thinks of me get to me. It used to, but with age comes wisdom, and having put up with the way she has been with me over the years, I have learnt not to let it bother me. I am true to myself, and I too have things I have achieved that I am proud of, including my latest capability…discovering that I have a collection of books in my head that I am determined to get published. And fair play to my four stepbrothers because every mother has the right to be proud of her kids, including mine. And I will add that I do adore them because they are not their mother!

To be fair to them, they are cool dudes. I never had any reason to dislike any of them and got on with all four of them. It was only their mother that was the problem, mainly because she breathes.

It bothered me that the difference between Darren, myself and the stepbrothers was that they had the privilege of going to private school. It was always claimed that this was funded by the father(s) of the boys, but it must have been great having the extra financial support from my dad being there. We went cold and hungry while she rubbed my face in it telling me how well they were all earning money in life. Bloody bitch always belittled Darren and me. We tried to pretend that we were happy for them, and to a degree, we were, but we felt we had missed out on something that was possibly a better start in life.

Quote "Do your best, and rejoice with those who do better."

One of these childish fallouts that Delores had instigated came about one night when I was visiting at age sixteen. I was told to go and make myself comfortable in the lounge after dinner and so I did as I was instructed. After a short while, Dad called me back down to the kitchen. I sat down wondering what was going on as I was faced with a tearful Delores. Had I said something out of context?

Actually! What I was really thinking was "for fuck's sake here we go again, what now? She had obviously cooked up some delusional bullshit to stop me seeing my father YET AGAIN."

In his soft mannered tone, my dad said, "Delores thinks you are going to ask for money!"

Yep! She had done it again! And brought my dad down that road with her bullshit!

See…narcissists are renowned for making up shit to suit their requirements. Psychopath.

To say that I was shocked and stunned was an understatement! I had no intention of asking to borrow or be given money and I could not understand where this had come from. It was decided that Dad would drive me home to whatever address I was residing at the current time as I had moved so many times and slept on a few floors. I wanted to get the hell out of there, and not have to deal with her any longer on this occasion. I accepted that this was another ploy to keep me away from Dad, and that he would have to face an argument when he returned. She got her way again.

I cried all the way home and although Dad was kind and understanding, I just could not comprehend where she had produced the idea. And again, as predicted, I did not see my dad for months after that misdemeanour. These were the years that I considered to need both parents the most; they were very influential years where I needed the guidance and advice from both of my parents. Darren had thrown in the towel and told me that I was pushing an elephant uphill when it came to matters with Dad, and that it was futile. Of course, my younger brother was correct.

When I was fourteen, Dad had asked me if I wanted to go and live with them, but my initial excitement faded quickly after I asked the question as to whether Darren would go too. Dad said that he could only take me, not the both of us. I may have fought over certain things with my younger sibling but there was no way I was going to leave him! I was totally horrified that Dad would even consider it to be totally honest, and for me, it was not an option even though it still meant facing the wrath of Mother now and then. But I would rather deal with my own mother than deal with Delores. My decision was one that I made based on the volatile relationship with her as opposed to staying with Mum. I chose the lesser of two evils.

The reason for this as I mentioned earlier was that Mum had become free with her hands, the trouble was that she also used whatever was to hand at the time too, and although it was not too frequent, it was emotionally scarring when she did blow a temper tantrum. Once when my friend Angie was with me in my room and were listening to my twelve-inch vinyl's, one of Mum's temper fits erupted! It resulted in my being whipped across my back and head by a fishing rod that Dad got me years ago when I went down the canal with him to catch crayfish. It was only a small child's fishing rod that was blue metallic in colour, and on this occasion, it had served as an effective whip. My friend Angie witnessed my mum's temper, and I was left crying and mortified that she had seen it happen. Mum was shouting and screaming at me to "go live with your fucking father and that old tramp." This was to become a regular saying in our house with a few swear words (sentence enhancers) thrown in for good measure. I had no idea what had sparked this outburst, but I had clearly said or done something that displeased her.

Another time after I had clearly said or done something to provoke her. I ran up to my room two stairs at time. Moments later, Mum came bursting into my room and picked up a snooker cue. I have no recollection of where this item came from, or why it was in my room, but nevertheless, it was used to hit me over the back and on my hands as I tried to defend myself. She broke the bloody thing in the end after hitting me for so long it just snapped. I was emotionally broken.

I hated the fact that she saw it as acceptable to use such weapons on me, but I hated it even more when Darren was home one weekend and she used a wooden clog. We had friends who had moved in across the road. While we were all stood outside talking one afternoon, the boyfriend of one of the three sisters had commented that if Darren scratched his precious car, he would not be impressed.

Darren was only standing by the car, but Mum overheard the boyfriend and flew into a complete psychopathic, angry rage! She started chasing Darren back over the road into our house! While he was running, she was swinging at him and shouting. But Darren could not get up the stairs quick enough before she caught up with him, the clog came off the foot, and it was used to beat him around his legs and bum. I stood watching it unfold absolutely numbed to the spot, unable to speak and unable to believe she was doing it just because of Gary's "if he scratches my car" comment! It was only a second-hand Rover for Christ's sake not a fucking Bentley!

There was no scratch. There was no mark at all, but Darren could not walk properly for about four days.

The big 'no, no,' was always 'DO NOT' hit Darren around the head! Despite the 'DO NOT', there had been quite a few smacks around the head that he received, and it drove me nuts to witness it! He had forgiven me for the orange by this time I hasten to add.

Darren had met a girl at his school and had fallen in love, and Maggie was to become his future wife. He was aged thirteen and she was fourteen. Mum did not like Maggie, and she always said there was something about her that reminded her of Delores. Mum could not put her finger on why, but it did not sit well. I brushed the comments aside and thought nothing of it because I did not think that it was fair to compare Maggie to the lover that Dad had chosen over us lot. I just wanted to see my brother happy and Maggie apparently did just that. If it turned out that Maggie was a bad lot, then that would be for Darren to find out for himself.

Point to note, in later years, I renamed Maggie venomous femme fatale (VFF) on account of the crap she gave my brother.

But for now, I had not seen him so happy in for a long time. Maggie was a girl who had lost her sight completely after a wardrobe had fallen on her at age five. She had long, dark hair and brown, glassy eyes that reflected her confident, if not arrogant persona. Darren loved her for that reason, and her witty charm. He would pick her up and throw her around like a rag doll during their play fights, he was a strong, young man, and she was slim and petite, there was not much to her so elevating her over his shoulder was of his favourite past times.

When I was sixteen, we lost Paddy on a summer's day after he had a heart attack in the front garden. The veterinarian came and collected him, but we inevitably said goodbye to our beloved pet who had always been there. I disappeared on an extremely long walk for hours. I recall vividly it was a blisteringly hot afternoon and I had nothing to drink and no money to buy one. All I could feel was my heart breaking at the loss of Paddy, so being dehydrated was not on my list of concerns.

We never knew what happened to Whiskey but there was a car dealership at the back of our house with the garage in the rear, we think that she could have jumped over the back fence and could possibly have been struck by a car, or that maybe she just went off to die on her own. She was sixteen years old and it was a devastating blow straight after losing Paddy.

Shortly after our pet losses, Mum met a man at her work called Simon. After eight years on her own and a few failed dates with previous men, this one seemed to be working, and Simon moved into our house. Darren and Simon never really saw eye to eye, and I was out with my friends or finishing my last term of school when he moved in because I wanted to stay out of the way as much as possible and not get under their feet.

There were numerous arguments in my house for whatever reason but one of them resulted in my black bag that I had hidden under my bed being put on the doorstep! I never really planned to run away from home but a phone call to a friend meant that I had secured a bed for the night. I will be honest I was still running alongside the rails not knowing what to do with myself or where I was supposed to be heading in life. I ended up staying at my friends for seven months, but was eventually forced to move back to Mum's. The friend in question was an ex-army wife and she took great pleasure in telling me what an ass her ex used to be and only ever put his career first. Wise words from someone who knew. She seemed exceedingly strong willed, although a little bitter about him.

Before I moved back to Mum's, I was babysitting for another friend while she went to her evening job. I had met her former partner a few months previously, and I felt uneasy with the way he looked at me with lust in his eyes. It had been an unnerving experience and I felt intimidated by him. He phoned the friend's house on the evening that I was babysitting claiming that he wanted to see his son while his mother was out. I was shitting myself! They were both parents to the youngest boy so I did not feel I could say no as it was his son! I did not have a contact number for my friend to check and see whether it was all right to let him see the boy, because there were no mobile phones in 1987, and I knew that she would not be able to talk at work anyway.

I had seen evidence of his temper in the form of a black eye on my friend, so I was terrified of him, and I was alone in the house with the kids in bed. I opened the door and let him in, but to my absolute horror, he had brought wine and joints to smoke! Oh my God! The real reason for his visit was not to see his son at all, and now, I was stuck in the house with him. I was terrified of what he was capable of.

While it was happening, I removed myself from my body. I pretended that I was with Gerry and that we were walking through my favourite country park. I prayed that it would end quickly, and that this monster would just leave. He was too big and strong for me to fight him off, I should have run out of the house, but I had the kids to think about and did not know what to do!

I will spare you as the reader the gory details because it was horrendous. It was a demon that I put to bed a long time ago and reliving it will not change what happened. I know that there are millions of women out there who have encountered the same sort of thing. You know what happened, I do not need to spell it out. As a result of his action, he gave me a virus from his total lack of consideration for anyone other than himself and his own gratification. There was no condom involved. I was devastated and scarred, but I never reported it to the police because I did not think they would believe me, I had let him in the door under false pretences for heaven's sake!

He was foul and I felt so unclean for months despite constantly scrubbing my body's plumbing parts and trying to erase the whole horrible memory. I hid the disgusting secret because I could not believe that it had happened to me. I just wanted to forget about it.

I left school having not sat any of my exams. I had missed a crucial theory test before the Art exam. My plan was to go to college and study to be a Graphic Designer. But as I had missed the theory test my art teacher informed me that I was unable to take the main exam…I was devastated because that was the main one that I had my heart set on, now my hope of going to college was gone. Truth be told before I was booted out of home at sixteen, I had been working the Saturday job in the sweet shop, cleaning with Mum in the mornings and evenings, and going to school.

This all resulted in my lack of concentration and focus on my exams, and I had lost track of where I needed to be to make forward progress after school term ended. I was exhausted all the time. The devastating news from my art teacher had just been the cherry on the top. I gave up for a while and resigned myself to that fact that I just had to go and graft while I considered my next plan of action for my life.

Chapter 3

A New Start

After moving back into Mum's, my friend Larissa got me an interview with The Department of Employment. She had been working there a couple of months and she loved it, so I was very keen to make a good impression and thankfully, I found myself in full time employment as a Civil Servant. Larissa worked in a separate office but we both did administration and we both loved our jobs. It meant that we had each other for company to walk home with and our friendship was back on track.

When we were both seventeen years old, Larissa was battling with Bulimia and Anorexia, she became ill and in truth, I did not fully understand why or what this disease was. I am ashamed to admit that I did not know how to help. We still walked to work together but we became distant, it was emotionally scarring, I just could not handle it. I had no idea of how detrimental it was to our friendship. I felt that I had my own demons to cope with and regrettably, I was not there for Larissa anywhere near as much as I should have been. But I think in my defence, I was backing off in case she passed away…which makes me sound an awful friend, but I had lost my nan and granddad, I could not bear the thought of losing Larissa too.

I was in my Civil Servant job for six months when it transpired that in order to stay in your role, you were required to take a test at the main office situated in London. I made the journey on the day that my appointment was booked and prayed that I got the 100% pass rate. I loved my job, and the people I worked with and really wanted to stay, but I failed by four points which is worse than failing by forty. Devastated, absolutely devastated!

They moved me into a different department which I did not like, and so I found a new job closer to home which was due to start at the end of October 1988. In the week that I had left my job and was due to start the new one, I caught the flu! Full on, could not eat and did nothing but sleep, flu! I remember it clearly it was the worst case I have ever had in my life!

With my new job as shop floor assistant on the wines and spirits aisle in Asda, came the opportunity to make new friends and earn some money. Although back in those days the pay was not fantastic, and the hours were long (or so they felt!) but I really enjoyed it. My work colleague was called Amanda and department manager was Melvin, they were great, and it was a good laugh. Things at home settled down for a brief time but Mum and I did not seem to get along if I was living there. We just dealt with it. A couple of weeks into working at Asda, Mum had also joined the workforce on a different department, she only stayed a couple of weeks and then left so I never received the 'introduce a friend bonus' because she was not there the whole month! By this time though, a certain security guard had caught my eye and I discreetly enquired to my manager as to who he was. I was swiftly told that I would never be allowed to date a member of the security team as it was deemed too much of a risk to the store, and that it was company policy that shop floor assistants would be sacked if it came to light of any fraternising going on!

That was like a red rag to a bull. I liked this security guard and he had already spoken to me. I was busy putting bottles of red Chardonnay on a shelf with Amanda just a little further up the aisle putting out her designated bottles, when a message was announced over the air waves for a member of wines and spirits to go to Customer Services. Amanda and I looked at each other wondering which one of us would make the short journey, and after she laughed and flatly refused to move from the spot, I knew that person to do the walking would be me. I was completely oblivious of who was at the end of the short walk as I was nursing a papercut on my finger that was bleeding, and how much it suddenly hurt now that I had noticed it! "Bloody boxes," I was cursing as I looked up and came face to face with the excessively big, brown eyes of the security guard!

5' 9, slim but muscular, he had a slightly receding hairline but was gorgeous with a smile to die for! I was taken with him but tried to hide it. I failed to do that very well as it turned out. Apparently, I pulled a face that nearly put him off me (that could have been viewed as an early warning sign for me, but I missed it).

Oh, my days! I had been called to customer services under false pretences! There he was stood before me in all his glory and in that uniform! Until now, the uniform thing that women go for had not been of any interest to me. This soon

46

changed of course, and we started exchanging little notes through our very covert friend's delivery system so as not to make it blatantly obvious that we were seeing each other.

In one of his scribbled notes, he asked some difficult questions to answer like "Why are you interested in me?"

"Do you think we would last?"

"Would you want us to last?"

Clearly, a very insecure young man, but I overlooked it and went about seeing him anyway.

My word…I had not expected to have to pass the Spanish inquisition just to be seeing him! Insecure did not even cut it, and I answered as much as I could without feeling like I was justifying why I liked him. I did not understand why he could not just go with the flow and see how it developed.

Even his boss Len was in on it and had conspired with my boss Melvin, they knew what we were up to! Jack (JB, I will explain this abbreviation further in the story) and I became nigh on inseparable, and I fought off the opposition of girlies who thought that they still stood the chance of winning him over. One girl even wrote him a love poem. I ran into her in the warehouse shortly after reading said poem, and I politely (not!) asked her to "Back off." To my knowledge, she adhered to my request and no more was said, bless her…ten out of ten for trying.

Within two weeks of dating, we got engaged, and at 5 am one morning as Jack was leaving for work, I sleepily found myself saying the words, "I love you." Our first couple of weeks had been a complete whirlwind romance, and we had been wrapped up in each other, so it seemed like a natural thing to say as it slipped out of my mouth!

His response was a welcome one, and he had watery eyes when he replied, "That's the best thing anyone has ever said to me." I had no idea at the time if those words were love, lust or whether I was 'in love'. I had never been in love, and I did not know the difference yet. I did not say the little three words lightly because I did genuinely love him, I just did not know in what capacity and thought that it did not matter at this time.

We spent the next few weeks including Christmas together when we agreed that I would move in with him. He had booked a taxi for me to pack my few belongings and bring it to his large bedsit. It was magical, and I was on cloud number nine for the first time in my life. I felt wanted and loved and it was a very welcome sensation.

We decided that the commute was both time consuming and proving to be hard work, so we relocated to a shitty little bedsit closer to where we worked. It proved to be a really bad decision. Jack found work in the opposite direction of our current jobs. I carried on at Asda for a while and then decided that the walk to the business park was less foot mileage than the one I was doing every day. For convenience, I too found work in a family run card-printing factory. It was Monday to Friday, so I got the weekends off.

One night while we were out for a drink in the town centre, we passed a couple of girls on the high street, one of which I recognised from the Asda checkout team. She proceeded to hurl abuse at me calling me a "Slag". As Jack was practically pushing me away from the onslaught of her verbal bullshit, he started to explain why I was under attack. He said that at the same time he had asked me out, he had also asked this other girl out. "Just in case you said no" was the term that he used. And now, I was taking the abuse because I said yes, he had even asked my mum for her permission to ask me out! Another warning sign I ignored. That girl had a lucky escape.

What had probably occurred was that he had asked more than one out to keep his options open so that he would not be left without a girlfriend. He always has a back-up plan and is never without a woman in his life; he does not know what it is like to be single and has not had that status in all the time I knew him. Another of the girlie staff called Christina apparently walked home with him one night and kissed him in the subway near our bed-sit, but he used the term "would not touch her with yours!" I tried to ignore my jealous side. There were so many red flags, but I was willing to work at it and keep going. It would prove to be hard work for a total of twenty-seven years.

I became part of the card packing team and made a particularly good friend who is to this day still in my contacts. Cathy and I hung out and got on well, she was a listening ear when things were not going well with Jack and I, she despised him and still does to this day.

Jack had moved from job to job and was very restless and moody and I could not cope with him or his temperament, he treated me like shit. He took a bar job in a local pub and became distant and quite nasty with me. I was trying to maintain a healthy relationship with him, but it became increasingly difficult and he would sometimes criticise me for doing certain things, and for what he considered things that were wrong with my body.

"I wish you would dry the back of your hair!" he exclaimed one time as we were getting on a bus. My hair is naturally wavy, and it is more beneficial to let it dry on its own sometimes.

One night after we decided to have some bedroom fun, I was heading for the southern region when he suddenly blurted out, "That does not turn me on you know!" Bloody hell! I was mortified at the timing of his outburst, how insensitive. I started feeling that he was nasty and cold because perhaps he had found a different lover. Something just did not sit well; the ice that was in his tone could have powered a Mr Whippy ice cream van for weeks.

He also really shouted at me once because I was apparently "watching him", and why was I watching him? I thought that was sometimes part of the process and it was completely normal. To be able to look at your partner and know that it is right and that you love them, is that not normal? I concluded at that point he was very naïve and inconsiderate, but I did not say anything and kept my thoughts to myself to avoid yet another Mister Frosty argument. I also really felt he was treating me like a piece of meat at his disposal, he would be nice when he wanted sex because it was not love making, it was sex…then after that, he would be a moody miserable sod again, he was capable of sulking for hours and sometimes days, it was mentally exhausting. The arguments were fierce, and I felt that I was losing my identity whilst trying to please him in order to keep him, when realistically, I should have given up. His ability to be cold with me and completely unfeeling left my heart aching because I wanted to make it work, but it seemed that everything I did was wrong or not good enough. The fact that I was breathing seemed to be enough to inconvenience him sometimes.

Eventually, I decided that I would go and sit in the pub while he was working just to try and chill out and be a little closer to him, but it backfired drastically. I was chatting to a man named Steve who apparently had observed the closeness of Jack and the barmaid whose name I chose to forget a long time ago. Steve told me that Jack and the barmaid were clearly more than work colleagues, and the more he spoke, the more things ticked over in my mind. Jack had claimed that the 2–3 am arrivals at home were due to the lock ins that the pub landlord insisted on having. The sex between Jack and I had dissipated, and that again aroused my suspicions and of course as far as I was concerned, everything Steve told me added up to the fact I was being cheated on.

After a brief altercation outside the pub, Jack told me to get my stuff and leave.

It was late, and the result was Jack and Steve having a fight outside the pub. I had to go back to our shitty bedsit and pack some of my stuff not knowing if I should stay, or do what he said and leave, that meant going back to Mum's and I really did not want to. So, stupidly I stayed and waited…and waited.

He came back in the early morning when the birds were chirping. I had cried most of the night because he was just being such a shit. His coldness froze my bones, his demeanour screamed that I repulsed him, but we talked for hours and somehow managed to sort it out. I did not trust him and that immediately put up my barriers. My gut instinct was telling me that I was not the only one that he was sleeping with, but I knew that he would never admit it if he was. It was very strained for weeks after, argument followed argument and he was cold and unfeeling and at one point I told him to stay away from me, which to my horror he did for a couple of weeks. And! It was me that begged him to get back together. He made no attempt to patch things up except make me work for his attention. What a fucking mug I was at age nineteen. Now, as I approach fifty years old, I would not bother with that kind of bullshit. Everything about him meant drama and stress.

We made the decision to temporarily move into Mum's dining room until we could find another cheaper bedsit. It was not ideal, but the one we were renting was extortionate and we were struggling for money.

We had not been at Mum's for long, and one day while I was at work, I had a sort of sixth sense feeling that all was not well, the previous evening we had viewed a room in an Indian family's house and given them a small deposit. I called Mum at home during the morning to see if Jack had any luck finding someone to move us in. Simon answered the phone and said that Jack had already gone and had left our small fridge freezer and a few plants. I asked who had moved the stuff, Simon said that a young lad and another older man had come and loaded Jack's things onto a van, but that all my clothes and things were still at Mum's!

I cycled in the biggest hurry I have ever pedalled to the new house where we had left the deposit for the room. I was told by the Indian man that he had not seen Jack, I knew deep down what had happened but hoped it was not true.

When I reached Mum's house, the hammer blow was too much. I searched the house for any sign that would tell me why he had left me with nothing but nine months of bad memories, there was nothing but heartache to follow. I stood outside Mum's unable to comprehend or process why, or what I had done to deserve this desertion. He had left me with the fridge freezer and a couple of plants. No note, and no explanation, just gone.

I collapsed on the ground sobbing as the heartache gripped every bone in my body.

The comment that came out of Mother's mouth had not helped either. "Simon, it looks like we are lumbered with Elise again!" Like I had planned it! I mean, there was a serious lack of feeling in that statement.

So, Jack had been in touch with his long-lost mother, a mother whom he had explained was very cruel and uncaring enough to have him put in care aged seven because his parents could not cope with the little troublemaker that was Jack. It was his younger brother and stepfather who had helped with his escape in a van. He had gone to live with his sister back in their hometown, the prodigal son had returned. I obviously knew nothing of the deception that had been planned, nor of how callous someone could be by just doing a bunk like that!

It tore my world to pieces.

He had done a peculiar thing the day prior, I appreciated the gesture at the time, but I could not understand why he had brought half the stock of flowers home from the garage where he worked. (He had changed jobs four or five times by this time.) Even while he was handing the flowers to me, he was cold and distant, and there was a look on his face I could not have deciphered, it was his impending abandonment.

I stayed in my job because I needed something in my life that was stable. But I moved out of Mum's into my friend's house across the road. I could not forget or forgive Mum's comment and did not want to be in the same house.

I lost a lot of weight, but I carried on with my broken heart and Cathy was there for me every step of the way, she put up with all the tears and tantrums for three months. Then suddenly, one day whilst I was working, the office phone rang, and I was called in by my supervisor Mary. Every one of my work colleagues witnessed what I had gone through, Mary was kind of a mother figure to the three of us girls packing the cards.

I answered the phone not having a Scooby doo clue, assuming it could be my mum. I had never heard Jack's sister's voice before, but she said, "Jack wants to know if you still have the engagement ring?" I was gobsmacked! He had the audacity to get his sister to ring me at bloody work!

I replied, "NO," which was a total lie, as I had buried it in a box somewhere out of my sight.

51

The next sentence was that Jack would ring me in the next few minutes. I obviously looked shell shocked as Mary came into the office and I was completely rooted to the spot, and terrified as to what I would say when he did ring IF he called at all!

The first words out of his mouth were "if you start screaming and shouting, I will hang up and you will never hear from me again!"

I just said, "Okay." (If this were a call I received now, my reply would be "Fuck you, mate, I will hang up first and you can do one".) Who the hell did he think he was?

I did not know what to say to him because I had no idea why he was bothering to call. I wanted to tear him to pieces! Everything always had to be on his terms! And if he had his way, it would still be that way to this day! To say I was angry does not even cut it!

We agreed to meet after work on that Friday. Unfortunately, for me, my bus arrived before his. I had arrived first and I was a bag of nerves, all I wanted to do was smack him one in the head! I wanted an explanation, and then I was going to tell him to go live his sad lonely life and leave me to get on with mine.

He walked in with badly bleached hair and he reminded me of an eighties singer that sang *Too Shy* (Google him), except more pitiful. He looked tired and bedraggled. I had made the effort and bought a leather jacket a few weeks earlier to cheer myself up, so I wore this to meet him. He had said, "You look good." *Well*, I thought to myself…I was hardly going to let myself go completely, was I?

He was not the centre of my universe after leaving the way that he had, I may be temporarily weakened when my heart is trampled on, but I will always make the bloody effort! I did not want to appear like a weak young lady who had crumbled too much after his dramatic exit. We chatted a while and decided to get the bus to where he was staying so that we could talk and decide if we had a future or not. The bus came to a halt in his town and we stepped off, and as soon as my feet touched the concrete, he blurted out, "Oh by the way, this may make a difference as to whether you want to be with me or not, but I joined the army!"

I was in a strange place, and it was late. I was really annoyed at the timing of this deliverance of news and wondered why the bloody hell he could not have told me this before I agreed to try and talk about things. Yet again, it was on his terms, as I had no clue where I was or how to get back. I was NOT happy!

Chapter 4

Another New Beginning but Hard Times Ahead

After Jack's surprise announcement, we got a bag of freshly cooked chips and went to his room in his sister's house to talk. No one was home and the inevitable happened when two people who have been together, and still attracted to one another are now sitting in a small room trying to piece together some sort of normality.

I was hurting emotionally, and extremely angry, but I still loved this young man sat in front of me. This man who clearly craved love and attention but was emotionally scarred for a couple of reasons. One of which was just about to enter the room!

Thank God we were not having sex! Because in the room were suddenly standing Jack's mother and stepfather! They must have had stealth mode on or something because neither of us had heard any movement in the house prior to their appearance. She was looking me up and down like I was some sort of bad smell up her nose, she announced that Jack's sister wanted him out of the house! Now! Tonight! And that they were there to enforce it. Now it made crystal clear sense as to why I had been called in the first place. I reiterate that he always has a back-up plan. Quite clearly, he had been too much for his sister to handle and she no longer wanted him there. Hence the reason for passing him back over to me! Like I wanted this crap all over again.

Oh, my days! That shit had most definitely hit the proverbial fan, and I was now caught in the middle of it. In fact, it felt like I had been positioned directly in front of that fan! I was involved in whatever was unfolding before my eyes. Two shocks in one night, I mean come on! Seriously? Was this really happening? My thoughts turned to, *I should have just punched him and got back on the bus to the safety of my hometown and got the flock out of there!*

After hastily packing a few things, Jack made a phone call to his granddad who thankfully took us in. The bus back over to where this drama had all started was the last one of that evening, so I stood no chance of getting back to my hometown until the morning. I stayed until Sunday, when Jack and I once again parted company and planned to see one another each weekend whenever possible. His granddad took Jack under his wing having been a military man in his hay day and it was his pleasure to get Jack prepared for his military life. I visited most weekends and we just hung out and spent our weekly earnings on crap and tat from the shops.

Granddad however did not like me as much as he had pretended to, I had stolen the heart (even if it was cold) of his beloved long-lost grandson. He always passed comments to belittle me, although still being quite sweet some of the time. I never knew what sort of verbal abuse I was going to receive from him, but Grandma was an absolute gem who I adored, and I spent a lot of time with her.

The time came for Jack to go up North for his training. I was crushed, but I knew it was what he wanted and by this time, I knew I wanted to be with him, even if that meant spending months apart while he played his soldier game.

There were few visits and not much of seeing each other, but we kept in contact by pay phone and letters. We did arrange to meet on one of his weekends off, but one of the recruits in his intake had done something wrong during that week which resulted in all of them being confined to camp. I waited at the train station for hours with no word as to why my boyfriend had not walked through the ticket barrier, and it was another week before I knew the reason, I was devastated. I should probably remind the reader that back in those days (1989) there were no mobile phones, so contact was limited.

Jack always had very neat and tidy handwriting, so I loved getting the letters telling me how he felt and what he had been up to. I had also moved another three times due to people not being able to accommodate me for one reason or another. I was a bit lost too, and just made sure that I was working so that I did not fall on my ass completely.

In 1989, Darren lost the sight in his right eye. I took it hard and was hurt for him, although he said it changed nothing apart from the fact he would be "kissing a lot more lamp posts", as he walked down the streets. His humour was his main character, and he took everything in his stride knowing that the Retinitis Pigmentosa would claim his left eye in time, but for now, he had five percent tunnel vision in it.

I eventually moved in with a lovely lady for whom I had babysat on numerous occasions and I was given my own room in Hayley's house! She worked nights, so I was there for her young daughter Nicole who was around five years old at the time. We would get Nicole ready for school and her Auntie across the alley would take her so that Hayley could sleep, and I went to work.

I had relocated to a nice village just outside of my hometown to live with Hayley, so my journey to work was a lot longer. I would either catch the bus, or if the weather were good, I would cycle the twelve miles there and twelve miles home. On a couple of occasions, Cathy would drive me.

I still worked at the card factory and Darren would come and stay when he had transport up from Kent because he hated going to Mum's so much. We would get the bus out to somewhere or other just to spend quality time as brother and sister. We had our favourite place that we would get the bus to, but because I am now rewriting this with the location restriction in place, I cannot say where. It is a lovely town with a Cathedral and is surrounded by a park and a lake; it is simply stunning in the summer. Darren and I used to go there as kids when Mum could afford the bus fare for all three of us; we always took a picnic when Mum took us. But as we were older now and I was working, Darren and I would get some food whilst there.

I took my old camera on most of these occasions, the old-fashioned phone calls were our way of making our arrangements, and the house brick camera was the tool to capture the moment. I have treasured photos of him when he was sixteen years old at a bus station with him stuffing his face full of his main weakness, Walker's cheese and onion crisps. It is a common connection that we shared.

Living with Hayley was an arrangement that worked well as she was so awesome and good fun! I loved being there and I never felt in the way. She was so accommodating and allowed Darren to stay on the couch when he visited, Hayley was such an inspirational bundle of energy to be around, and I adored Nicole. Still do, to this day.

One day, news came that Jack was to be heading off to his Regiment in Germany, and that now he was fully trained, he would then be heading straight out to Saudi Arabia. The first Gulf War 1990! I cried for days as I had already gone for weeks without seeing him, and I felt my heart crack when he told me this news. But obviously, this was what he had trained for.

That Christmas was a very lonely one, but I spent it with Hayley and the little girl I adored so we got through it despite my heart aching for the one person I wanted to be with. The letters kept coming so I knew that Jack was okay.

When I say letters, I mean the folded blue envelopes that were free to send to military guys on operational tour. They folded in three sections like a secretary would fold a formal letter. The inner bottom section was cut slightly smaller so that it would fit in the other two sections easily. But it meant that if you are a person that could write a lot (like me), the end section of writing would be squeezed in as small text so that you did not run out of enough space to say the obligatory "I love you" at the end. You could not insert anything into the envelope, so if it were an exceptionally long letter you intended to write, then it was easier to write on normal paper and post in a usual envelope.

At the card factory, we used to do collection boxes, they contained sweets and toiletries and paraphernalia to send out to the lads in that sandy place halfway around the world. These were always gratefully received and shared out by Jack, as he was obviously my point of contact. Even he did not need all the sweets and disposable razors that were enclosed, and the lads really enjoyed receiving the big boxes. Today the packages that you can send to the military personnel is restricted to two kilos, but back then, we sent bigger boxes provided courtesy of the card factory.

We, in return kept the letters of thanks sent from the recipients, it was heart-warming to know they had a little piece of home now and again.

In October 1990, I went on holiday to Tunisia with Dad, Delores and two of her sons. I had saved the money to pay for it, and Dad sorted me out with some spending money. The first week was good apart from the sandstorms on the beach and we had managed to arrange a day trip to the historical site of Carthage, that was a nice day out. But the second week was made extremely difficult due to a silly (if not predicted) fall out with Delores. (It was only a matter of time!) I had commented to one of my stepbrothers that I was "pissed off with the weather".

Which he then repeated to Delores, who then had a go at me and told me to "go sit with Rose and Vera if you are so pissed off!"

Rose and Vera were two elderly sisters who we had met at our hotel and I thought they were awesome! I got on with them because they thought that I was cheeky and liked my witty humour. I was horrified that my comment about the weather had been taken so far out of context and blown completely out of proportion! (Mountain and molehill, she is a nut job that woman!) Dad was sitting outside on a bench chatting with me at the time of Delores's outburst and we were both taken aback. He did not want to leave me sat there, but he said he had better go and see if she was okay and find out what was going on. I was ignored by her for the last week of the holiday, and I was only able to sit with them at mealtimes in the restaurant. It was ridiculous and childish, but that was/is her nature, and it drove me crackers to the point that I wanted nothing to do with her. Dad came to the shop with me at one point; he was a bit lost as to what to do and did not want to piss her off by spending time with me. I was nineteen years old in a foreign country on my own. It was devastating and I never forgave her. Maybe Dad should have sold me for the thousand camels he was offered!

I arrived back at Hayley's after Dad dropped me off first from the airport. No one in the car had uttered a word for the whole return journey, we travelled in an air of frosty silence. Delores had not spoken to me for a week and a half (no loss there). Childish to say the least, but I accepted it was how it was, and I knew I would not be seeing Dad for as long as it took for her to pull herself out of her pathetic mood that she had with me. I was forced to say "thank you for taking me", to the miserable cow as I exited the car, my thank you was met with the ignorance that I expected. She simply stared out of the window and said nothing. In my mind, and despite her elderly years, she behaves like a five-year-old child with zero manners or consideration for anyone but herself.

Hayley was at home and I just fell into her arms as she hugged me while I cried my eyes out. I just could not believe it was such a normal comment which resulted in the fact I would not see my dad.

Truly pathetic. Writing this now brings back all those feelings of despair and frustration that I endured on account of Delores's actions. In today's views, and the way I see her now, I feel sorry for her because she was fighting so hard to keep my dad away from me and Darren that she was willing to cause so much damage and destruction to get her own way. She eventually succeeded. Because at age forty-five, I wrote a letter to explain why I was no longer interested in maintaining a relationship with her. And although I know Dad only ever wanted her and I to get on, it was never me that built the brick wall with an iron padlocked gate. But at the time I wrote the letter, I simply did not give a shit and cared nothing for her bullshit anymore, I was done.

The silent treatment went on until the following February when I plucked up the courage to call Dad and see what the current situation report was, hostile was the reply. But Dad did not say those words, it was what he did not say, and I just read between the lines. It was a further three months before I could see him. Totalling seven months.

I had Hayley and Nicole and they were a great source of positive energy and motivation to get me through, plus I had Cathy and my work colleagues. Mum and I had rebuilt a bond because I no longer lived in her house, which meant that we got on better.

I focused on dealing with the situation at hand. The fear of the unknown and the thought of losing Jack gripped every ounce of my being; it was all new to me. I knew I loved him and wanted to marry him, so I suggested it in one of my letters. We planned it loosely, but we stayed focused on just getting him back to the UK first.

Jack's return happened after what was described as 'The Four Day War'. I am sure people will remember the name of this one because it was Storming Norman's time to shine! Therefore, I will not edit my description of this section as there were hundreds of British soldiers out there, and I will not be dictated to by one solitary person about what I can write! Operation Desert Storm was over, the boy that left, had returned a man. He had seen things that made him appreciate life a whole lot more, but this is not my story to tell. He had seen death and things he carried with him for the rest of the time I was with him, with other tragedies that piled on top. Jack had seen the worst horrors that war has to offer, but plenty more was yet to come in later years. Again, these stories are not mine to tell, but they affected the whole family. Not just the men who returned!

After a long, seven-month stretch of time, he arrived back in the UK around the middle of April 1991 after promising in his letters that he would be home for my birthday on the seventeenth, and he stood true to his word. We met at the train station, and he was walking out through the main station doors as I stepped off the 348 bus.

It was very romantic, only he and I knew why we stood there holding each other for the longest time with no need for conversation. I loved him so much and now that he was stood in front of me, I did not want to let go of him. We stared at each other like we could not believe the time was finally over. It was the best feeling in the world that my man had come home.

We celebrated his safe return and my birthday in the town centre with our joint friends Dan and Lily, and my friend Cathy. (She still detested him but made an allowance) We also announced that we planned to marry. It was a celebratory occasion whilst eating pizza, and I felt that my heart would burst I was so happy. In the two weeks that he was home in the UK, we planned as much as we could and we asked Jack's uncle for help, which he gave willingly. The registry office was booked for May 1991.

Jack returned to Germany, and in the days to come, I busied myself arranging the big day. Hayley helped tremendously as we only had two weeks to sort everything out, so the pressure was on! Hayley knew someone who owned a wedding dress shop, and the lady was selling everything off as she was closing the shop for good, so I got my dress for £50.00 and I borrowed everything else. Hayley did my hair and makeup, and then drove me to the registry office in Nicole's father's posh BMW. Nicole was my beautiful little bridesmaid. I love them both dearly it was an immensely proud and nervous day. These two ladies are still very much a part of my life and both still beautiful souls who I will cherish forever. xx I love you guys. xx

Jack was nervous, as I had arrived fifteen minutes late! He had travelled from the south coast that morning after staying at his best man Dean's house, and Dean had brought along his wife to be Louise. But my friend who had picked them up took them to his greasy bike shop to get changed and I do not think it went down too well as Louise had a lovely dress to change into, and the two lads were going to be dressed in their number two dress (uniform) which was the green one. They are all very meticulous about their uniforms being perfect, they must be, it is their career after all.

It was a special day, followed by a small party for whoever wanted to attend at Hayley's because that was still my home. Of course, the obligatory rice and bottle tops were planted in my bed! But we caught my friends in the act, so it was averted in time!

Mum and Simon attended, but my dad refused point blank as he did not want to be in the same room as Mum and would not put himself through that ordeal. His absence upset me greatly, and I would have been happy even if he had just watched from the car park, just to see his only daughter get married, and maybe given me a little wave while we had the photos taken outside. But it was not meant to be, and I knew that I was expecting too much of him. Darren was also absent due to being busy with the venomous femme fatale (Maggie) and could not afford to come up from Kent. That broke me emotionally more than Dad's refusal, but I understood and just got on and enjoyed my day.

I later studied our body language in the photos at the registry office. We looked more like good mates than a new husband and wife. Or maybe my judgement was too harsh, but I should have seen the difference in our pictures, to that of other people. Because we stood with our hands at our sides and there were no pictures of the "you may now kiss the bride" moment, maybe I was being too harsh. Or maybe I saw the shape of things to come.

Jack and I waited a month for a married quarter to become available for us, which is about average. And in the meantime, Dean and Louise were also getting married on the South coast so we enjoyed their big day in a lovely church, followed by a fabulous reception in a seafront hotel. It was a beautiful ceremony and the sun shone for them the entire day. We finally had the news that army accommodation was ready for us in Germany. I prepared for married life in a foreign country, knowing that the bride Louise was also following close behind me. I had a friend to look forward to and the knowledge that I would not be completely alone was comforting.

Chapter 5

Setting Up Our First Home

I had travelled with Mum and Simon by train to Victoria station, to catch the coach to my new beginnings. It had been arranged that I would travel back with Jack's best man Dean who was travelling back to the regiment after taking his leave to get married, Louise would be following a couple of weeks later when their accommodation was ready.

I said my goodbyes to Mum who gave me her last £5.00 note to get a drink, (Yes, Mum, I do remember, and I was incredibly grateful but spent ages feeling guilty). It was a weird feeling knowing that Mum was not going to be as accessible by bus anymore. But I was married now and had to take control of my life and take responsibility of it.

After sixteen hours on a coach, Dean and I arrived at the camp in Germany, and we had a further thirty-minute walk to reach the ground floor flat which was located on the far side of the camp. We walked through the camp, and out of the far side gate onto a range road that stretched on as far as the eye could see! The road dragged on for miles in the July heat in Germany…it was stifling! It seemed to take forever to put one foot in front of the other after being on the coach for so long.

On arrival at the flat, I set about finding the tea making essentials because I knew Jack would not go without his cup of tea. Dean finished his drink and just as he was leaving, Jack came in from work. They shook hands as Jack thanked Dean for delivering his five-foot three package who was now his wife, and then Dean took his leave and closed the front door. Having not seen Jack for a month again, it was lovely to finally be in our own space. It was so exciting because this was our first home together, and after three years of dating and making do with the scraps of time that we had, I thought that we deserved to be a bit more settled, and that maybe our relationship would be less volatile now that we had a roof over our heads.

Jack had already bought a stereo and TV, and all my possessions were on their way over on a removal lorry from England. I say all my possessions, there was so little that I owned and the guys who packed my little boxes were mocking me because it hardly made a dent in the allocated space on the lorry. I had brought as many clothes as I could to see me through. Jack had bought a second-hand washing machine and installed it. Bless him he had spent the week before my arrival making the place homely.

When he was 'marched in', there had been what they called a get you in pack. This comprised of an army sofa and a couple of chairs, a double bed, an army dining room table and chairs plus the coffee table and the necessary cutlery and plates etcetera in the kitchen along with some pots and pans. I think there was a kettle, but it is that long ago the memory evades me.

Soon after my arrival and having settled after a couple of weeks, it was suggested that I should look for a job, as we would need the money. Bloody hell I had only been here five minutes! But I did as I was instructed and found out where I should look for a job, and although I was quite nervous and no friends yet, I made the best of it.

Becoming the wife of a serving soldier was exciting and at times exceptionally scary. I had left all my family and friends back in the UK, and I could not just get on a bus and be at my mum's in twenty minutes. Despite Mum and I having our stupid disputes as all mother and daughters do, we now had the English Channel and four countries in between us. And phone calls would cost the earth!

Jack and I used to make the walk into camp to the NAAFI as neither of us could drive. On one of these walks, Jack suggested that I should pick my face up off the floor, and that was probably the reason that I had a double chin! Devastated and hurt by that comment…I was so hurt that I did not reply. But it was another of his little put downs I never forgot. I was isolated in a foreign country and married to a man I had been with for three years. But a man who felt the need to control me in little ways such as putting me down about my physical appearance. Probably to hide his faults and insecurities, and the first signs of the controlling ways that became apparent over the years.

Now living in Germany, I secured a full-time job in one of the cookhouses. We were earning money and paid in Deutschmarks. It was bloody hard work!

And the hours dragged on as if there were no end to the day. Pots and pans bashing, as it was known, was the job I hated the most because the pots were huge! They were used for cooking for lots of lads at one time after all!

I still cringe at the thought of the scrambled egg pots…they made me heave when I became pregnant. It was the smell as well as the fact it was always stuck to the bottom; it was ghastly! I loved the flat we lived in although it was reputed to be haunted; I never experienced anything that made me uneasy. The only thing that I did feel uneasy was when someone had followed my neighbour home, she lived in the flat above me. And she worked in one of the smaller NAAFIs on the camp. Some Squaddie had followed her home and watched which flat she went into. Then, he climbed onto my ground floor balcony and stood on one of the plastic chairs to climb up to hers! But he did not make it because the wall of her balcony hung over too far and it defeated him, thankfully!

It was not the flat that was the problem, it was the fact I was being singled out at work by one of the other wives who had taken a total dislike to me. I had never done or said anything to bring this on, and nothing to antagonise her. I chose to stay as far away from her as possible, but she was relentless, and it totally ground me down for the months I was there. She would sit glaring at me and giving me the evil looks that meant if she could kill me, I would be six foot under and then some! According to another lady who befriended me, the offending person (Sally) did nothing but complain, calling me "that fucking thing". And complaining that I was not working hard enough and shirking my duties. This was completely unjustified as I was working just as hard as the others, but she just took a dislike and that was that. Nothing I did ever made an ounce of difference and I even sat and listened to her sob while she was telling me that her father was dying.

I cycled home on the last night I was there in floods of tears. She had broken me, and I just could not take any more of the way she was with me. Jack arrived home from a week on the ranges (firearms and weapons training) to a distraught and broken wife. He was raging but there was nothing I could do until the morning. I called the Master Chef to explain my reasons why I could not come back, he told me to leave it with him and that he would be in touch shortly. The Master Chef was named Mark; he was married with children and fiercely dedicated to his job and family. He also took care of his staff and was very understanding.

To my knowledge, he called the offending person (Sally) into his office after putting down the phone. And when I say called her, from what I was told by my other friend, he had screamed for her to "get your fucking ass in here now"! The master chef had seen for himself and been told previously of the things that she had said and done, and he had already given her a warning after overhearing her comment something about me in the staff room.

He sacked her on the spot! Declaring that he would not tolerate bullies in his cookhouse! I was relieved, but I felt bad that she had been dismissed. As far as I was concerned, I had decided that I was not going back, and that I would look for another job. But the master chef had other ideas and asked me to, he said now that she was gone that all would be well. I did return as we needed the money, and I did not want to sit around in the flat all day especially as we were setting up home and needed to buy things for the flat.

I had been advised just before I married Jack by my ex-army wife friend, that military wives had a bad reputation for being bitches and they could be particularly cruel to the newcomers. I had just had my first taste of it and decided I would have to toughen up or I would not survive if it were to happen again. Although I did not want to see army wives as stereotypes. I did hope that this sort of thing was only a one off. After all, the women are only the same as the women on civilian street and we would all be going back out to civilian street in the end. Women are women, I do not think that the reputation as told by my friend could be seen across the board, or in general. I assumed that she was advising me from her own experience, but I did take her advice on board and put it in Archie for future reference should I need to draw strength from it.

Shortly after all this, I became pregnant as we had been trying for around seven months, and I was absolutely delighted when I went to the medical centre on account of my boobs being exceptionally sore, and a missed a period that was two weeks overdue. Jack was away for a couple of weeks on a training exercise when I found out, so I wrote the news in a card announcing, "You are not a Jaffa." (As in not seedless, which I thought was hysterical!) I gave it to him on his return; he was overjoyed too! It was magical I was so excited and could not wait to be a Mum! I was twenty years old, but I did not want to be a mature Mum…I wanted to grow up with my child. Plus! I was terrified of the pain of giving birth and if I did not do it now, I would bottle it later!

They say that being pregnant makes you glow from the inside. I was extremely fortunate to not have morning sickness, although I was not spared the heartburn or the pressure on my bladder, but not much of any drama and everything went fine for the nine months duration. We prepared for the arrival of our daughter. I had wanted to know the sex and found out at one of the scans so that we could buy the essentials and choose a name.

Our beautiful bundle of joy was born in January 1993 after a bit of a traumatic Caesarean section and a scare due to pre-eclampsia.

She had jet-black hair, there was so much of it and it covered her forehead and a lot of her neck. She was an angelic baby and the German ladies used to see her in the pram and comment and say that she was sweet in German. Faye was turning heads from the start of her life and continues to do so now. I am extremely proud of my beautiful girl.

Mum had travelled over to spend the last month of pregnancy with me as Jack was away in Cyprus for six months, she was a welcome companion although I remember making her cry for some reason or another and felt bad about it for a long time after. But I was really pleased my little mum made that dreaded coach journey over to be with me and see her granddaughter straight after birth.

I was out of it for three days after the massive operation I just had, and the shock to my body had wiped me out. So, I just slept and was very unwell for three days. Jack had passed his driving test by this time and was on leave (R and R, or rest and re-cooperation) from Cyprus for the birth of Faye. He was making the journey up to the military hospital having borrowed Dean's Volvo; the drive took an hour each way. He also was bringing Mum and complained that she was driving him nuts and that he was sending her home. The next thing I knew he followed through with this threat and my mum was no longer going to be visiting anymore, I was gutted. Oh my God my poor mum! He had put her on the coach and sent her back! I had no say in this matter. It was done.

The look of pride on Jack's face as he held his daughter was a look of love that I will never forget. It was a treasured memory and a massive smile on his face, probably the one and only time I ever saw him at peace with his life. And the only time I saw that look of love on his face for anyone.

I spent ten days in that military hospital. I left with bedsores on my butt and a scar across my tummy that made me walk with a bit of a stoop. They had opened the sunroof because Faye was in distress, so an emergency caesarean was performed, and my daughter was born! She was beautiful and had a full head of black hair, she was our little miracle created by two people that came from nothing and built a little life together, we were a family. A week later, Jack returned to Cyprus to finish the United Nations peacekeeping tour they were on and I was left with our new-born.

Shortly after Mum's return home, she became pregnant with my half-sister Eva. Mum was aged forty-three at the time and it was a bit weird because Faye would have an Auntie that was a year younger, but it is what it is, and we would not change it.

Some of the wives went out to Cyprus to visit their husbands before the end of the tour in April 1993, and I had been invited by one of these wives with three kids to an Ann Summers party that she was hosting. It would mean that the women had nice surprises for their long-awaited husband's arrivals back home, which incidentally sparked another baby boom ;-).

This was to be the first time I had been a bit drunk in the army life, and my next-door neighbour who had very kindly offered to babysit a new-born Faye said that I was hysterically funny when I got back in the flat. But the next morning, I remembered the conversation with Ann Summers party lady. She had said that while she had been in Cyprus, she was being hounded by some Cypriot locals and "oh Elise! Your Jack was my hero and came to my rescue". I turned it over in my head and set it aside for the time being. After a couple of days' thinking it over, I had decided to store it all in Archimedes and not think about it. Until I received a phone call from Jack's best mate Dean in Cyprus who said, "There is a rumour that Jack is having an affair, but it's not true I can assure you." I lost the plot! And now, the doubt was in my head after what Ann Summers lady had said. I cried a lot and wondered if it could be true, I mean I had just given birth to his child! It rattled around my head why had Jack not had the guts to tell me of the rumour himself. It was the same scenario of getting his sister to make the phone call a couple of years previously…the coward's way!

April brought about the lads return from Cyprus, and Faye was three months old. She initially cried at this strange man who was trying to kiss her, but she soon got used to his presence after the gifts he had brought back with him had been dispensed and she had something to occupy herself with. She did not take kindly to the black man who was in the regiment at the time, and screamed if he came anywhere near her, he took it in good humour though bless him.

Darren and Maggie (the poison-compact) made the coach trip over to Germany for Christmas 1993. (Bearing in mind Darren was partially sighted, and Maggie was totally blind, so this was a big deal!) Faye was eleven months old and walking, and it made Darren's whole year to meet his cheeky niece and they adored each other from the off! Jack repeatedly played *The Power of Love* by Frankie G to H and it drove us all bloody crackers! It makes me cringe even now and I cannot listen to it at all.

Saying goodbye when they left was bittersweet, because Darren and I were closer as adults, and he was now married too. We were adult brother and sister and not the kids we had been when we last saw each other.

But there was a bitter taste in that Maggie had made a pass at Jack one night whilst they were staying. Darren and I were asleep already, when Jack came to bed in a shocked state and whispered to me, "You are never going to believe what has just happened!" I could not understand why she would have done this in our own home! I heard Darren get up and go into the living room, he said he had heard her flirty little laugh and knew what she was up to.

We sat up most of the night while Maggie tearfully explained that due to her lack of sight, she could not read Jack and found him very intimidating. After she had consumed some wine, she had adopted some bravery and thought she would try to connect with him by being flirty. She had been suggested to Jack with her "you know you want to" line. It made things bloody awkward to say the least! But the four of us worked through it, we had to! We were family after all.

A year after Faye was born, I decided that after the caesarean experience and the healing process, I did not want any more children at this stage, and I made the decision to have my tubes clipped (sterilised).

After I had the keyhole surgery, I felt a bit more at ease, because now I knew that although I would have loved another child, I was too much of a coward to go through that kind of pain again. I was extremely grateful for the healthy beautiful little bundle of cheeky joy that I had, and that I was still breathing and able to raise her and give her everything that we could to give her a good start in life. I have never regretted my decision not to have additional children, despite knowing that Faye would have loved a sibling and quite often felt alone as an only child.

I found a little morning cleaning job right next to a kindergarten so that I did not have to travel too far, and it meant that Faye was not left for hours with a childminder we could ill afford. Faye was getting some social skills, as was I. I had made a couple of friends in the little NAAFI where I worked and was seeing human faces whilst Jack was away, which was ALOT! Faye and I made our journey into camp on a German bike that Jack had surprised me with one night on his return from work. It had an awesome child seat attached on the back so that I could take her anywhere with me! It was great and we loved it! I used to cycle into camp, show my identification and go and get some shopping with Faye quite happily sat behind me watching the world go by. She was a happy child and even liked the transfer as I lifted her out of the bike seat into the trolley one. She was always singing in her little bedroom and was happy running around the flat with only her nappy on whilst jumping from the sofa to the floor as far as she could and from a great height too! She was a fearless little warrior.

Our bike meant that I was getting exercise which I was more than happy with as cycling is something that I have always enjoyed.

The NAAFI carrier bags hung off the handlebars, but we managed very well unless I needed lots of shopping, in which case I took the buggy and walked. I loved the times when it was just me and Faye. I know that sounds bad, but we were so much more relaxed and there was no stress and we just did things in our own time and pace.

One of my favourite memories with Faye is picking her up from the Kinder Garten one bright, summer's day, we went back to the shop where she chose her desired ice cream and we walked across the square of grass which was surrounded on all four sides by the military buildings, so it was very safe. We sat on the grass outside and we spent over two hours picking daisies to take home with us. We dry pressed them and put them in Faye's keepsake baby day's book. Which is where they remain. We still have the little daisies, and it is an exceptionally treasured memory that I possess with my innocent little one-year-old.

The summer of 1995 came around and the whole regiment was in full preparation for moving back to the UK. I could not wait as the journey was so far to visit relatives and I missed my family. Coupled with the fact that I could not yet drive and spending four years in Germany in a remote area, where the nearest decent town was a half an hour drive was enough for me! I was more than ready to move! I also suffer seasickness on the ferry crossing from Dover to Calais; it is not a pretty sight in the mirror after that hour on the boat I can assure you!

Chapter 6

Vows Are Spoken...to Be Broken

Faye and I flew over to the UK in the summer of 1995 while Jack got the married quarter in Germany painted and finished the cleaning, which I had already started to make it ready for the march out inspection (the white glove treatment) to hand the keys back to the estate manager. I felt awful leaving him to do this. (He did throw it back in my face later.) He would then drive back to UK by himself in our first brand new little car which was a left-hand drive. But he was happy (or so he said) that we were out of the way so that he could crack on with it.

Faye and I got off the flight, and then caught the train from Stansted Airport to Kent where Darren and Maggie had a small flat. Faye screamed for no reason most of the train journey despite every effort to entertain and pacify her, nothing worked! The looks and sighs that I received from the commuting people on their way home were relentless. But I was more understanding that they were tired after their long days in the Capital of London or wherever they worked, they were less understanding of my plight that I had travelled from Germany and had been up since the crack of dawn to do so with my screaming child because she was tired too!

Jack arrived a week later, and we hung out at Darren and Maggie's for a further week which caused a couple of tense moments. Jack could cause an atmosphere in an empty room! Darren and Maggie went out for hours one day for some headspace even though it was their flat; they just could not handle it.

We were glad to leave when our married quarter up north was ready, but again I was sad to say goodbye to my brother, I know that they could not wait for us to leave though on account of the atmosphere...and I resented that.

The house way up north had two bedrooms and a bigger, more modern kitchen. The back door led to a nice and easily maintainable back garden. That in turn backed onto fields, and the view was absolutely breath taking on a cold morning with the mist rolling gently across! I settled in straight away and before Jack prompted me to do so (because I knew he would), I applied for a job on the nearest camp which was a thirty-minute walk up a substantial hill. But I had piled the weight on in Germany and quite frankly I needed the exercise!

Fortuitously, there was a Kindergarten right opposite the camp too, which was an absolute Godsend for Faye. I secured a place for her and began work as a domestic assistant from 9 am – 12 pm in the mornings; the pay was shockingly low at only £2.55 an hour! I only came home with £125.00 a month! Nowadays, I would not even set the alarm for that but at the time it was better than nothing, and I planned to learn to drive so that potentially I could look further afield. Meanwhile, it was cheap budget shopping and no luxuries.

Having dropped Faye off at Kindergarten a few times, I quickly became friends with another woman called Denise who had a daughter the same age as Faye, and they were in the same class. Denise and I instantly clicked like we had known each other in a previous life or something, it was bizarre! But she was a most welcome addition, as was her daughter Louise. I did not take to her husband and thought he was a dick. She is more than aware of my feelings on this matter, but it is also none of my business and I just do not have anything to do with him. It was so nice to have a friend who was on the same wavelength as me. She worked on the same camp, and her dad had been in the army, so she had been brought up in the military life and her daughter Louise got on well with Faye. It was just meant to be, our paths were meant to cross and as my best friend forever, she remains a monumental part of my life to this day.

Personality wise, Denise is like a mirror image, we have shared a lot of laughs and my family became hers and Louise's.

We spent the whole time talking and going to each other's houses so that the girls had time to play together with the Barbie dolls and the games that the girls made up for themselves. We laughed about the things that we had in common, as we are both from South of England and have a similar warped sense of humour; we find things funny that others do not. And we are not afraid to laugh at ourselves or each other! I was alone a lot of the time with Jack training and hardly ever home, so having someone to hang out with was great.

It was a bit humiliating at times having to clean the accommodation blocks on camp, but I had to get used to it, as there were no other jobs that were so locally convenient. Denise, my new best friend, worked in block C and I was in B block. Mine was the smaller block with only two floors and three staff, but in

Denise's block, there were lots of domestic assistants as it was considerably bigger with three floors.

We used to clean what were referred to as 'The Wets'. This simply meant the bathrooms and toilets that the recruits used. It was disgusting sometimes! But the permanent staff took responsibility for getting the recruits to do their block jobs so that we did not walk into complete gut-wrenching, stomach-turning stuff of nightmares! I would throw lots of blue urinal blue blocks in to make them smell half decent after the recruits had done their block jobs. It was only the corridors and bathrooms that we cleaned, and we never went into their rooms because we did not have to.

Seeing recruits running along the corridors with only towels wrapped around them became the normal thing, but we took no notice. They always were in a hurry and usually had a permanent member of staff shouting orders at them. We also had to use floor buffers and polish up long corridors that were time consuming, but this was my favourite job. I could drift off into a world of my own and dream of a sandy beach and a holiday one year. I used to strip the old polish off the floors first, and then renew it, so they were shiny and looked like glass with no boot scuffmarks. Until the next onslaught of footfalls as the recruits entered the building. I liked it when it was empty because we could get so much more done without feeling that it needed going back over. (I had worked there three years in total, and by the time I had left, my blue uniforms were faded in colour).

It was at this point I experienced my second helping of another army wife taking a dislike to me; she had worked in the block for a while and was a short plump woman with short strawberry blond/greying hair, not particularly attractive and a surly approach to everyone. I do remember her name, but I do not feel it is necessary to give her the recognition or the humiliation. She took an instant dislike to me because I was taller, and I had a nicer personality which the permanent staff accepted me for, and they appreciated a woman that did not walk around with a face like a baboon's ass that was about to explode any second! I was easier to talk to than she was, and it was quite clear that there was jealousy involved. I had started working in the block and because I was the new woman, the attention was suddenly on me and not on her. I had obviously undermined some sort of role that she had adopted for herself as chief whip! It was embarrassing because she tried to mock me in front of the permanent staff on our side of the building, and when they defended me and told her to shut up, she did not like it. On one occasion, one of the guys said that she was bloody pathetic and that I was the Mascot of permanent staff and could do no wrong, he went on to tell her a few home truths about what they knew that she was doing with guys in the block, AND that everyone knew about it.

After a few months, she was moved to work in a different block much to my relief, but man all mighty she gave me rock all before she went! She had noticed that one man was always talking to me as we got on well. But I was shocked when she delivered the news (and it was only her opinion) that I would end up having an affair with him…and that I was a bitch if I went down that road. She said that he was "ripe for an affair as his marriage was breaking down". Bloody hell how naïve she made me feel, not to mention that she was judging me before I knew what she could clearly see, but I did not.

She had set about giving free ventures of pleasuring a couple of the permanent staff with blow jobs and she assumed that no one knew that she was doing it, but loose lips sink ships as I learned later in life. After the dressing down the cheeky cow gave me, she was completely hypocritical. She started wearing more makeup and perfume and was overly flirtatious with any bloke with a pulse, but they used to refer to her as 'Jimmy Cranky' and she was not very well liked.

This next part is extremely difficult to write, but I must write it as it is a significant part of my life. It is the one time in my life that I should have followed my heart, and not my head that talked practically all the time! My chimps on my shoulders had a field day with this one, believe me!

One of the permanent staff in B block was extremely attractive, and yes it was the one who was always talking to me. He had always spoken to me as a human being, and his smile and beautiful, blue eyes were totally addictive to immerse into, and he was such a nice a man to top it off. At first, his stare intimidated me, and I could not look at him for long because I knew that I liked him. Then, as time went on, I became aware that it was not a look of lust in his eyes. He was staring at me because he saw the woman inside of me. He saw the person that I could be, but I had become someone else because I was part of a marital unit. I think he saw that I was withholding the real me and not showing my full potential. He would say that Jack did not deserve me, and that he did not know the gem of a woman that he had in his possession. I did not agree with the comments at the time and tried to ignore them. But when I was alone at home, I did consider it, and I wondered if that was why I was even questioning the way that Jack was with me. I dwelled on the little things he had said that had slowly

72

eroded my confidence over the past years. And I knew it was the reason why I was thinking more and more about the Corporal.

I dreamt of him holding me with his arms around my shoulders. And of what his kiss would be like if that were to ever happen. I so wanted to feel this way about Jack and have the butterflies in my stomach like I did with the Corporal. The butterflies and excited joy had stopped after Jack had started with the belittling comments.

Corporal and I started with fleeting conversations. These conversations turned into long talks and heart to hearts. But I was married, and I had to resist any sort of advances from anyone. Although I felt that there was a distinct lack of something in my marriage, I did not understand what it was until this man arrived on the scene, and things changed forever.

As time went on, working in the same vicinity as the Corporal (who will remain anonymous for obvious reasons, and because I will always respect him and want to protect his privacy!) became increasingly difficult. I was facing the fact that Jack had been training to deploy to Bosnia for six months. I had to try and resist the temptation that I was attracted to the blue eyed Corporal. He said nice things and was very complimentary to me. This was always lacking from Jack who would only ever say "you are pretty in my eyes", which was not exactly a confidence builder and essentially, made me feel like I was a consolation prize that would perhaps be replaced when he had time to look for what he considered something better. (Funny how the future can be predicted!)

The Corporal noticed things about me that no one had ever commented on, like how I have a darker spot in one of my blue eyes, and that I had nice nails for a domestic cleaner. He had this regular and daily habit where I would catch him staring at me and the look went deeper than lust, we both knew that we were falling, and falling hard. There was a chemistry between us that was so transparently obvious that one of the other permanent staff eventually caught on and complained that he was the last to know and we should "go get a bloody room will you, you two oh my word". But! We were on opposite sides of the room and had not even so much as kissed yet! Just our stares gave a clear indication of where it was going.

It was like there was electricity in the room, and everyone felt it!

Yeah, it took Stevie a while to cotton on that something was happening because the Corporal and I avoided being in the same room together for too long. He saw me for the woman I was, not 'wife of'. He constantly told me that Jack did not deserve me, something I now know years later to be true, and lots of people said the same thing through the years.

The Corporal was going through his own marriage breakdown because his soon to be ex-wife had gleefully admitted to seeing a DJ called Dwayne. I did not want to be his distraction as a way of coping on the rebound, but the chemistry was mind blowing and I eventually gave in to it. Much to my shame and I have no explanation of why I did not stop it before it started but consequently, it did start. And I wanted him.

A week later, I had tearfully said goodbye to Jack for six months, although he would be home on R and R (rest and recuperation) for two weeks mid tour. This time apart would be difficult as Bosnia had been a war-torn area for quite some time, and anything could happen to any of the soldiers who were deploying.

The build up to deploying on operational tour started with training, which was sometimes weeks away on Ranges. There were weeks and days before they left when they would be so focused on the task ahead that they were exhausted each day. It felt like my heart ached constantly with the knowledge that very soon it would be the night before he would go into camp and not come home. I must have cried more than a few rivers over the years like all the other wives and children. It was sometimes gut wrenching to know that this was his job, and there was nothing I, or anyone could do to stop him going on tour, it just was the way it was. I wondered if I was cut out for the constant six-month tours that stretched on for eternity. Eventually, I had enough of crying those tears and wanted more out of life, I grew tired of wishing my days away for someone who was never really at home, even when he was there.

Jack would pack his bags a couple of days before and take them into camp so as not to upset Faye and me. But on the days before he left, it was absolute torture knowing that we would not be seeing him for six months with only two weeks R and R that went so bloody quickly. No sooner had they come back for the two weeks, then they were gone again! And of course, they always needed to go into camp for various reasons, which left me feeling like I had been robbed of time I could not get back with him. I so wanted a normal life where my husband came home every night and enjoyed doing so. He used to have a look on his face that indicated it was only temporary, and that it would soon be time to depart on whatever tour or training exercise he was due to go on again! "A soldier before a husband."

I spent a lot of time crying for the man I wanted to have a normal life with, but I hoped that at the end of his twenty-two years, we would buy our own house and settle down. Well, that was what I was always led to believe by the man I was married to and I hoped that it would be true. All I ever wanted was the one thing that Darren and I never had, a stable home life and a family that stuck together through thick and thin, for better or for worse. Yeah right! Little did I know that delusional bubble would burst, and our daughter would no longer have parents that were together. The reason I named him Jack in this book is because he was always a Jack Bastard! Everything was always about what he wanted, and he hid behind the excuses that "if it were not for the army, we would not have…XYZ…"

I was at work in one of the ground floor bathrooms wiping down tiles behind the sink. The lads on this corridor were away so I thought I was alone and had decided that I was going to hose the whole bathroom down and give it a good clean.

The door opened gently, but I was too busy thinking about my life and the fact that Jack had gone and how the time always seemed to drag, and six months is so long! I had to be strong, but I now had Denise and little Louise to keep me and Faye company. The doors were quite often caught by the wind in the draughty old building and it was blowing a gale outside so the doors rattled profusely!

But the door opening was not the wind…

The Corporal was stood behind me, and I was not stupid enough to not know the reason why. It was the moment I prayed would not come. I prayed because I did not trust myself, and I prayed because I genuinely loved Jack and I had Faye to consider in all of this.

When I turned around to face him, I knew that I was in so much trouble. I wanted him to do nothing and say nothing as we stood staring at each other. Yet I so wanted him to kiss me so that I could experience that 'first kiss' feeling again. My tummy had elephants trampling through it at this present time with a brass band in hot pursuit! Leprechauns were marching through my head singing, "We know what you are doing, and you are going to get it!"

He stepped forward; I backed away slightly. But my bum touched the sink behind me, and I could not back away any further other than move to the side of him to get away. But before I knew it, he was against me. And I no longer wanted to fight it, I no longer wanted to resist that look in his eyes and the feel of his hands on me.

He placed his hands on my waist as we moved closer. Then, his kiss was as gentle as I had imagined it to be. It was a romantic kiss from a gentleman, not a mouth open and stick your tongue out and hope for the best type of kiss! This was a kiss to die for! He knew exactly how to do it properly. It was a knee trembling, knickers wetting, passionate kiss that set my whole body on fire! It was a goosebumps and hard nipples kiss! I could feel his hardness pressed against me. And I knew that eventually the inevitable would happen.

I wanted what was to follow, and I wanted it now. It was not a kiss that one would forget in a hurry, and he had set the bar high for any future men, and I doubted that anyone could match it…ever!

He finally let go of my waist, that sensation alone had me hooked on him as I had never experienced a man who clenched my waist in that way. I liked it.

We cuddled in the bathroom and laughed because I was leant against the sink, and on glancing around the room, the location of our first encounter was hardly under a blanket of stars! He said, "I will be around tonight."

I said, "No, you will not! And you do not know my address anyway!"

"Yes, I will, and I will bring wine, and I know exactly where you live. I have a mate who lives on that street."

I found this to be a true statement as I got to know him. I had never seen him on my street visiting his alleged mate and I assumed that he had followed me home. But his friend did live further along, and it was just a coincidence that he had seen me long before I had seen him, because he drove, and I did not…yet! It was a genuine and true kind of love. We could not stay away from each other even though we tried to. We ended it a couple of times but went back. It was impossible to finish it while we were in the same town. I used to use the chalkboards of his classroom in the training wing to leave messages telling him that I loved him. We snuck kisses and exchanges of lusty looks in the car park. It was a forbidden obsession.

We met more after I had passed my driving test; he was the third person to congratulate me after I had told Denise on the walk into work. But the first person to know that I had passed had been Jack.

The first time that we were intimate was like nothing that I had ever experienced. It was the same as the scene that Maverick and the civilian contractor Charlie Blackwood had in Top Gun. In her flat, up against the wall. It was passionate and performed by two people who were forbidden to be doing what they were, which made it more exciting! I had never known the difference between sex, and love making. Until now.

I will have to spare the details as it would not be fair on anyone and it is irrelevant in any case. But we fell in love that very first time. We even talked about how it just happened, and it was unavoidable. I was unfaithful with someone that I came to have a different love with. The kind of love that I had craved but had not known what I was missing until he gave it willingly.

It was a love that had I have been single, would have resulted in marriage further down the line. He was serious about me, but I did not know how to leave Jack despite wanting to and spending countless nights staring at the wall. Every waking minute was spent trying to decide what I should do for the best. Not just for me, but for Faye! I could not bear to put her through the same thing that went on between my mum and dad, and I did not want Faye being a part of a hostile feud. That would be a given with the type of person that Jack was, it would be inevitable. I would defend myself and not just stand there and take his dirty looks and foul comments, he could be bitchier than a ten-year-old girl at times.

I knew that the relationship between Jack and I would be a volatile one if I left, especially if I left him for another man. He would play the victim for the rest of his life and would never see that he had a part to play in all of this. I accepted the love of another man because I had never received it wholeheartedly from Jack; he was too focused on his career and himself. I do not think that he is capable of a full and complete love that can make someone feel that they are fully immersed, and that he is totally in it with them. I never blamed him for the way that he was; it is in his genes and his unfortunate upbringing. That was why I was struggling with my decision so much because I deserved happiness, but not at the cost of Faye and Jack's. And Jack did not deserve to live with me in a lie. Most men do not seem to know or bother to comprehend that if they do not elevate their woman, the woman will seek someone who does. The same is true of the opposite, we all need to know that we are wanted, and that the partner still values us and finds us attractive. Pretty in my eyes does not even scratch the surface, let alone cut it.

It was a love that I never truly forgot as it was how I wanted to be treated by someone. Being with him made me feel like a woman, not just 'wife of' or an accessory. The Corporal taught me lots of things about myself, but most of all he taught me real and true love. I believe that had I left to be with him, that we would still be together today. It was a complete absorption of body and minds. I can say that I was wholeheartedly in love with him beyond any doubt.

And I also doubt that I will ever find that kind of love again, it was too special and real. But I let it slip through my fingers.

Hindsight is a wonderful thing, and not going with him was a decision I always regretted. I know he would have looked after us and loved me the way that I wanted it to be. But everything happens for a reason.

The affair went on for as long as he was there, two years in total. It eventually ended when the Corporal was posted back to his Battalion in another county. I turned off my feelings and mourned in silence. I looked for any reason I could to detach myself from him which was extremely difficult, as I had never felt this way. I was so confused and torn. Once he had left, I felt remorse and guilty. Jack may not have been perfect, but he did not deserve the betrayal. Although in the back of my mind, I was still convinced he had been unfaithful to me in the past, but he always denied it, as you do! It does not justify what I did, but I learnt so much from the Corporal and I felt that I had been wholeheartedly loved for who I was. Jack was always in love with his career first and foremost, I resented being second best, but I had learned to live with it.

In fact, I always felt that Jack only loved himself, and he was only ever worried about being portrayed as a good person. Because heaven forbid that he was ever seen as a bad one! We all need to take responsibility for our actions, I accepted mine, but a narcissist will never see any wrongdoing on their side. It is always the other party, and woe betide that you try and tell your side of the story. They are always the victim and they cannot see what they have done to you or why you have acted the way you did.

I had to detach myself from my feelings and pretend the affair had never happened so that I could be normal at home when Jack returned. I felt so many emotions in one go that it was difficult to know which one to deal with first. The guilt was the main one. I had an amazing experience of electricity just from the looks that the Corporal and I exchanged. I had the knowledge that I had never had the same butterfly feelings with Jack, not even when we first started dating, he never looked at me adoringly. That made me feel ugly and that I "would do for now".

Once when we were in the pub after work in the first days of knowing him, we stood with some of his work colleagues and one of them exclaimed, "So!

How the fuck did you manage to get her?" Jack just laughed but I knew that he was taken aback by this question.

I was once told by the Regimental Welfare Officer that Jack was "a soldier before he is a husband". Which was never a truer word spoken. I was heavily pregnant at the time. I had walked the long camp road which took me an hour, to collect any mail from the post bunk and enquire if Jack would possibly be arriving home in time for Faye's birth. To be told that he would "arrive when he arrived", and that it was not guaranteed to coincide with the arrival of our first child. The Welfare Officer's words resonated in my ears every day of the military life and served as a reminder of where I stood in the grand scheme of things.

My friendship with Denise was very welcome because she made me see things from a different perspective, and that my trivial complaints were not that bad at all. I had everything that I wanted, but I was being selfish and could only think about the wrong I had done to Jack. Now I had to live with my guilt and the knowledge that I had loved the other person. I did consider leaving Jack and run away with the Corporal as he had tearfully begged me to. But I grew up without my dad and I did not want that for Faye, I wanted a stable home life where her parents grow old together. So, I buried my emotions and got on with it.

I feel that I have explained my reasons for the affair, and I have accepted my responsibility for it. I had never really forgiven Jack for the desertion a few years previously, then there were the little criticisms about my body. I was not feeling the love at certain stages of the marriage, so when someone comes along and says the things that you have longed to hear, it can be the turning point. Some people will probably think, *Oh my word what a bitch, how can she cheat on someone who is away doing his job?*

Everyone is capable of being unfaithful. Whether we choose to admit it or not. The circumstances are irrelevant.

I would ask you to bear in mind that I had my suspicions of his infidelity over the years, more than once! That does not justify the one affair that I had. And I would merely point out that there was no proof as to whether he did or did not, only my gut instinct and the things that people had told me.

Sometimes the not knowing and having no clarification can be worse. In this type of life where the saying goes "what happens in the field, stays in the field", it is difficult to trust anyone. And while they were away, who knows what they get up to, and they are loyal first and foremost to each other.

I once made a joke that I was juggling five blokes. It was not a serious joke and I was not shagging five blokes, but it was taken that way, not that I care what Jack thought at that point anyway. I joked because I had been propositioned by a further nine blokes who were all in a habit of telling me how unhappy they were in their marriages, I felt like Clare Raynor the agony aunt! I was joking with four of them and basically letting them think that they were one day going to be in with the chance. It was harmless fun, and they knew it to be as such, nothing serious to be taken by it, it was banter.

The affair was not planned, it just happened as these things do, I am not proud of myself but until you are put in a similar situation where you are left frequently for months on end with little quality time in between with the person you are married to, it is hard to judge how you would handle it. I felt like a single parent most of the time and learned how to run the house by myself. Just as well, because in a few years, I would need this ability.

Do not judge until you have walked in my shoes as the saying goes!

I had decided to move to another house. There were bigger rent-free houses on the other side of the Garrison. Rent free because they had no heating upstairs, and they all needed renovating, which was apparently under way, but we saw no evidence of this claim all the time we lived there.

Denise stayed frequently with Louise and we managed to keep warm with a couple of paraffin heaters that I had bought, but once we had turned them off at night, it was absolutely freezing! I woke up one night with icicles on my nose. I took to wearing a hat and thick pyjamas to bed with my dressing gown as well sometimes. The winters in Yorkshire seemed particularly cold, but I guess it was no different to anywhere else in the country.

We spent two years in that house, well Faye and I did as Jack was never there!

Faye started a little junior school just a stone's throw from the house which was predominantly army children. It was the only school she attended where she was not subjected to any sort of bullying. It was a proud day the first day to see her in her little school uniform and white ankle socks, brand new shoes on her feet and a big smile on her face. I did not want her to grow up!

I had been scared when Jack was in Iraq in 1990 on Operation Desert Storm, but the upcoming tour of Northern Ireland was a different level of fear. I was terrified and had nightmares that played out scenarios in my head of what I would do should I get the dreaded knock on the door from the RMPs. I did not know, and I tried not to dwell on it, but I was lonely and scared with a young daughter to look after, so I had to get on with it and get through this tour. The ceasefire had not yet been put in place as it is now.

In effect, as an army wife, you play the role of mother and father and you learn to become a single parent to a degree, as Dad is away a lot. This is not the case for everyone, but I felt like I was married to someone who volunteered for extra work, as he did not want to be at home. He liked the missing the family part and enjoyed coming home because he had missed us. But I felt that a life apart was not worth the constant waiting for him to return and I grew tired of being on my own.

I wondered how this would play out when there was no more going away, when there were no more operational tours after the army life. Only time would tell when his years were up. I wondered if I would become a casualty of divorce as a lot of military couples do after the farce of the army life. My brother used to say it was a false life and that we would come down to earth with a massive bump after the time was up. Little did he know at the time this was one of the most accurate things he came out with, but unfortunately, I never got to tell him.

Jack returned from Bosnia and was a different person to a monumental degree. He had witnessed things that were nothing short of inhumane. He told me that there was a young girl around the same age as Faye who had been murdered. They had found her in a barn, but I cannot divulge more because of the restrictions that have now been place on my writing of this book. He described what had happened to the mother and father of the little girl, but it was something he would tell me another time. He could not tell right now, and I did not need to know, as he put it. It haunted him, and there were restless nights and bad dreams that followed the tour. I was told the full story in later years. But right now, he was unable to disclose any more and quite frankly I did not want to force the issue, he was too disturbed…I needed him to talk when he was ready, but not before.

We focused on enjoying life in Yorkshire. Denise and I used to bundle the girls and our gorgeous female Collie cross that we had adopted in 1995 into the car and go off for walks along the river Swale. As my confidence grew with driving, we went further a-field and I used to make the drive to Scarborough! Denise and I would take the girls to eat chips by the beach while the wind was blowing a gale! I do not think we ever picked a warm day to go, but we loved it and the fresh air did the girls and the dog Lara the world of good.

In the three years I lived in North Yorkshire, it was a standing joke that when you saw one of us, the other would not be far behind! Denise and I were a double act and we liked it that way. After our days out with the kids, we would bath them and put them to bed, then we would sit and do our hair and nails in our fluffy white dressing gowns with crap on the TV in the background, and we would put our worlds to rights according to Elise and Denise! We just generally had a laugh despite never having much money, we made our own fun. I really miss those days. I guess we were both lonely as Jack was away all the time and so was Denise's man, but we had our friendship, and it was all that we needed. Denise is to this day my best friend and we know if something is wrong without either of us having to say anything. She lives in Northern Ireland now and we only see each other by the traditional social media ways and video chat. But we are still together at heart, and always will be.

In the three years we lived in Yorkshire, I spent seventy to eighty percent of it with Denise. Jack had done the Bosnia tour, and was now training for the tour of Northern Ireland for six months. I sat outside my house on one occasion unable to go inside because I did not know how I was going to cope with the fear of this one. Jack came out having heard the car pull up ages ago and wondered why I had not gone in. I just sobbed, I was absolutely dreading this tour and had lots of sleepless nights trying to prepare myself for the months apart again and the fact that the ceasefire was not yet in place as it is now. There was still unrest. I feared that knock on the door from the RMPs every day he was out there.

The six months operational tours were taking their toll. I loved Jack and wondered whether I had what it needed to carry on as an army wife. Clearly, I did, and the time rolled on, but I really struggled. There were so many times that I wished that I had taken other pathways of life, but I hoped that one day I would find a way to make something of myself whether that included Jack or not. It would always be with Faye's future in mind, and here I am…writing these books.

After the return from the N.I. tour, I noticed a further change in his behaviour, only slightly, but I felt that every time he had been away, that he had left pieces of himself in whatever country he had been to. I did not understand why as he would only give me snippets of information on what had happened. I know this was to protect me and avoid any worrying on the future tours, but I also wanted so much to understand why the man I had married had chunks of his personality missing. One day there would only be a shadow of his former self-returning, an empty shell that was no longer recognisable to me; he was becoming a different person from the one I had married. Things were changing, and I felt different and I was less inclined to believe that he would ever be around.

Shortly after his return from N.I, he was gone again; this time on a very crucial course that was part and parcel of furthering his career. It was seven months on the south coast. I lost the plot a little bit as I just could not cope with the lack of quality family time. No sooner than we had tried to settle for a few months than we were separated again.

I was monumentally bored with my life! I could feel a rebellion coming on! I started going out to the pub/club on the main road in town with Denise and sometimes the other girls from the camp we worked on. I never came back sober after completely kicking the crap out of the cheap booze called WKD blonde! Befitting of my nature, blonde, fruity, full of fizz, with a wicked side that spelt naughty fun and trouble of the mischievous kind!

It was like drinking apple juice and eight to ten bottles later, I had drowned my sorrows but also had a laugh as I was out with my best mate. We looked out for each other and ALWAYS had each other's backs. We usually got egg-fried rice with a pot of sweet and sour sauce to dip our chips in on the way back to mine, and after stumbling through the front door, we would put the babysitter in the taxi we had come home in. One night, we were on top form and had managed to completely convince two of the very drunk permanent members of staff that we were driving away to perform a Thelma and Louise. They were so drunk that we could have told them anything and they would have taken it as gospel! We also told them that we were lesbians and had no need for their sexual advances because we had the double-ended vibrator waiting on charge for us at home! God we had such a good laugh it was the best time of my life with her because we mocked the drunk squaddies and completely let our hairs down!

We had a language of our own and just enjoyed our time that we had while I was living there, because we knew that one day it would come to an end and that one of us would be posted away. So, we made the most of it.

These shenanigans went on for about eight months until I realised that it needed to stop because it was not the best way to spend my wages. It also did not help my health. I was in the NAAFI one day just before Jack and I were about to move on a posting, when suddenly I had a pain in my lower stomach that rivalled the caesarean! I doubled over much to my embarrassment, but it was agony.

After a trip to the medical centre, I was told it was colic, which was a totally wrong diagnosis as I later found out it was irritable bowel syndrome. Probably brought on by worry that Jack would find out what I had done and end the marriage. But of course, the excessive weekend drinking was the trigger, my body was simply not used to alcohol because I am not a drinker, I never have been.

Chapter 7

Saying Goodbye to My Best Friend

After three years in North Yorkshire, 1998 brought about a posting down to Hampshire, our time in Yorkshire was over. I had tried to detach myself from Denise in advance of the move as I knew that leaving her meant that I might not see her for a long time or if I ever got to see her at all! We swore to do our utmost to stay in touch.

After a very emotional goodbye to my best mate who had technically become my sister (even if it was not by blood) we moved to a training camp, Jack had been promoted to Lance Corporal and was to train recruits, and our house was outside the fence. Most people envisage that when you move, you automatically are in army quarters on the camp or behind the fence which is rare and not always the case.

I struggled to settle and finding a job was soul destroying as I still had no qualifications or skills and could only get cleaning work again; the same as I had been doing in the previous camp. I resigned myself to the fact that I had to do it and it brought in a little bit of money.

I could hear the voice of my husband on the other end of the camp sometimes and he was very dedicated to his job, so much so that for the first year I hardly saw him and threatened to leave. I had had enough of being ignored and lack of conversation. We never really did anything as a family, it was always me who walked Lara and took Faye out, so one day I packed the car and started driving out of the estate. At the back of houses, there were garages for the properties around ten in a row on each side, so there was only one way in and out. As I started driving between these garages, Jack appeared at the end of them. His work colleague had alerted him of what I was doing as he could see out of the window of his house (he lived three doors down) and called the office they worked in.

Things were just too tense, and I could not take it anymore! I knew Jack was working hard but it was the age-old complaint that he had no time for me or his daughter. Sex was not on the agenda and conversation was always about what he had done at work and we lost sight of 'us'.

It was also rumoured that Jack was 'going with' a female recruit, but I ignored this because it came from an unreliable source who had a habit if using a wooden spoon to stir the shit pot to deflect the attention from himself. But I already suspected something was going on with someone, because he was behaving the same cold way he had done on previous occasions. No sex, no conversation, lack of patience with me or his daughter and he did not want to go anywhere or do anything! Which was not a bad thing because even if we did, it was more stress than staying in. I regret not going off with the Corporal. I wonder why the hell I did not react to all the signs that pointed to what would happen in the future.

Faye was also being bullied at school by a girl called Victoria, so I started taking her in the car instead of putting her on the school bus to drop her at the door so that the contact was limited. I said a few choice words to the mother who flatly refused to accept that her little angel could do any such thing! Oh…the rage I felt! I wanted to smack the woman into next week! She was totally oblivious that her daughter could do any wrong and offered no apology or suggestion of asking her daughter whether she had acted this way. Bloody people!

I found a domestic job with a Warrant Officer from the camp who was female, and she happened to be looking for someone to 'take control of the mess her house was in'. She had young twin boys and a Nanny to care for them but still needed a housekeeper. It was fantastic as it was walking distance from my house.

I left the camp job and went to work for her, and she paid more an hour than minimum wage. Any extra was a bonus! This was to be my first role as a private housekeeper, and she gave me a good reference for future employers.

I got to know the Nanny and we became incredibly good friends very quickly. She once told me that if she was not in the house on a regular basis when I was working there, it was because she did not like the housekeeper! Consequently, I feared the worst after not seeing her for a few days! But she had simply been out with the twins and there was nothing to worry about, and so entered another of my best friends Anne. She became another Denise, and she joined the family as Faye's Godmother. The second year of the posting was a bit better but financially, we struggled terribly. Jack took an extra job at the weekends doing security, I felt awful as again, he slipped into tiredness and it was because I earned so little.

Darren and Maggie came to stay with us a couple of times, but their marriage was now on the rocks. Maggie's flirting had changed completely; she was acting like a little siren and was flashing not just her eyelids at potential men and anyone willing to look her way. Darren had lost a lot of weight on their last visit and his eyes were sunken with dark rings due to the worry and lack of sleep. I took Maggie off to the shops one day so that Darren could chat to Jack, and we could find out what had been going on and to see if there was anything we could do. No sooner had Maggie got her seatbelt on that she blurted out that she was seeing a bloke called Kevin! Kevin apparently liked her in stockings and suspenders, and she obliged in wearing them for him with great pleasure.

I listened in horror at what she was telling me in the car! And all the way around the supermarket like she was proud of herself! If this were being written in text talk there would be a red angry emoticon following that last sentence, my blood was boiling! On the way back to my house and without even thinking about it, I had heard enough and asked her whom else she was shagging! She claimed there were other interested parties, and she was absolutely glowing with the knowledge of this. In a split second, I shouted at her, "Shut up! Do not tell me anymore!" I was raging and I wanted to punch the life out of her smug face! The only thing that stopped me was the fact that she was blind. She was destroying my brother, I know this is hypocritical of me, but my brother was my life! He was the fourth pillar in our family, and I could not cope with what she was doing to him knowing that it was not just one man that she was seeing! Darren worshipped her, and she was breaking him little by little.

We had to watch Darren deteriorate more and more knowing that he knew what was happening. His marriage was failing at a rapid rate of knots and he felt that he was never going to be enough for Maggie, she clearly wanted the attention of other men and relished in the fact that Darren was so unhappy.

The whole situation was infuriating, my brother was in so much emotional pain that it tore my heart to pieces, but I could not do or say anything as he had asked me not to. He wanted to try and save his marriage. He had known her since he was thirteen and he could not bear to lose his one true love and would do anything for her, even be her doormat.

Whilst we were living in Hampshire and before Maggie revealed her sordid secret, my brother did something that scared the absolute life out of me! I picked Maggie (Poison-compact as she was now known) up from Kent and drove up to Leicester. Despite his eyesight or lack of it, Darren had volunteered to do an abseil down a two hundred foot building for charity; his fear knew no bounds!

My uncle took his video camera to record the moment and my dad and Delores were there to watch. But Dad offered no conversation to speak of with his ex-sister-in-law although Karen used to get along with Dad when he was married to Mum. Such is the hold that Delores has over him that he could not even have a conversation with an old mate. But I could not force them to speak, and it is only in recent years that I understand why Dad could not. A jealous, paranoid woman who pretends to be nice is a force to be reckoned with. But we were all there to cheer Darren on and support his achievement, it just would have been polite if Dad had said something.

Darren was immensely proud of his monumental achievement and rightly so! I was terrified because I hate heights. I asked the obvious question: what was it like? His initial reply was that the worst bit of the experience was climbing over the edge, then said, "But even if something had gone wrong, at least I could not have seen the floor coming up to meet me!" We all burst out laughing because it was his eternal sense of humour that was his greatest asset. I worshipped him and adored his bravery, no matter what life threw at him he would run at it like a bull in a china shop. His eyesight did not stop him being a daredevil. I was so proud of him beyond words and so was Faye because she witnessed it too.

Darren was an eternal larger than life character who loved Phil Collins and Dire Straits. He had taught himself acoustic, bass guitar and drums and we used to sit listening to him play when we visited. He would sit on his knees on the floor until they went dead. Then he would flail his long legs about whilst complaining that he had pins and needles in them! He was funny and predictable. But while he was sat on his knees with his guitar of choice on his lap, he would zone out. He adopted a certain look when he was concentrating and tilted his head slightly to the side and stare into his own oblivion. He would only lift his head a fraction if he heard his name mentioned, or that he decided it was tickle time for Faye. If crisps and/or chocolates were brought into the room, it was game over and he abandoned post whilst he consumed whatever was on offer and stuff the wrappers into his jean's pockets.

He was awe inspiring to watch as he strummed his chosen guitar and he went to town on it if it was *Hotel California*, or, *In the Air Tonight* by Phil! We used to laugh and talk into the small hours about everything and anything. Darren was aware of my infidelity, but he did not judge or reprimand me because he knew how I had felt for a long time and agreed that I was not being appreciated.

He also did a tandem parachute jump a couple of years later which my dad attended again, there are photos of that day and they are one of the things I treasure the most.

My brother was not the only person going through a hard time with a partner. Anne and I had been having lots of conversations over the past few months about her relationship with a man she had been with for ten years. He was very controlling and did not like her hanging out with 'the army people' and he tried to stop her coming to army functions with us. But we as a family had grown to love Anne's company. I told her my opinion one day after she had asked me what I thought, and what I would do in her situation. I could only put forward my perspective, but it was her life, and I did not want to advise because I did not have the answers. I did say that in my opinion he was suppressing her, and not allowing her to be an individual. (Pot this is kettle. I am a fine one to talk.)

I had consciously started to withdraw from Anne a couple of months prior to leaving Hampshire in order to avoid so much heartbreak when the time came to say goodbye, but my attempt failed to work. She was fully aware of what I was trying to do because I told her that I had done it with Denise, and that leaving her had hurt...a lot! Anne was at our house helping us pack and spending as much time with us as possible, so the inevitable happened and the tears flowed before we had even put our belongings on the removal truck. She was having such a hard time and it was devastating to know that we could not do anything to help, as we were no longer going to be there.

We said another emotional goodbye to yet another best friend. I remember driving away from the farmhouse she shared with the twit that had his foot on her head and we promised to stay in touch, and that I would call her as soon as I found a phone box in the place we would be living. (We still had no mobile phones.) Moving to Germany again was not up for debate, we had to re-join the Regiment.

The March out of the married quarters involved the total cleaning blitz of the accommodation. We kept the cleaning essentials including the Vax carpet cleaner, and cleaning products that I always used, along with the cloths for buffing taps and the floors. After the furniture had been packed and loaded on the removal trucks, I would start in the main bedroom and work my way around the room ensuring that there were no items that had been left behind and that it was spotless, then I would move on to Faye's room.

The bathroom was always left for cleaning until last for obvious reasons, but no one was allowed in any other rooms upstairs once I had cleaned.

We sometimes had to go and stay with someone after leaving a married quarter or timed it so that when we had finished the cleaning, the Estate manager could come and do his inspection and we would hand over the keys. With the relevant paperwork signed and the keys handed back, we literally drove away and on to our next quarter in whatever location we were posted to. It felt a bit like being homeless for a short time.

We did not always have two cars, and on this occasion, we were crammed into the Racing green Escort that we were currently driving, along with our possessions. We stayed at Darren and Maggie's for a night or two before departing once again for Dover.

The posting was over, the march out was done, and we returned to Germany. We were allocated a first-floor flat that was extremely spacious compared to the little house we had just handed the keys back for.

The only thing that was a little bit questionable were the Rose colour pink carpets, I mean oh my word! Neutral colour in a living room is always advisable in an army quarter but at the end of the day, it falls to the person that is occupying it at the time the carpets are due for renewal, and they do not tend to think about the future tenants. I too was guilty of this when the carpets in our first flat became due. I chose blue as it went with our colour scheme of the time. It looked lovely with the furniture that we had managed to obtain at a very reasonable price after a colleague had split from her husband. She was selling everything off and going back to the UK.

Married quarters were never up to the standard that you would have as your own home, but you had to make do with what was allocated to you and be done with it. Repairs were carried out as opposed to renewing stuff, and carpets had to be kept immaculate as much as possible. A candle wax spillage can be potentially hazardous as well as a pain in the butt when it comes to the march out! But you had to deal with it!

Our new accommodation was a half hour drive from the camp, and we were amongst a couple of estates that the army occupied with a few flats and a few houses. But it was predominantly in a German neighbourhood. It meant we were like a mini community that was intermingled with German civilians. We had a small NAAFI and a medical centre, but the bulk of the food shopping was done in the German shops, as it was cheaper.

I secured a job as a cleaner in the NAAFI in the early mornings and it got me out of the flat to earn a little bit of a wage so that I felt I was contributing to the household. I did want to feel crap about the fact that we were struggling for money anymore. Jack always made it abundantly clear that we would never have any spare money, and I was so used to being told that throughout our entire married life.

There is a bigger picture as to why I had never earnt a great deal and it is partly because we moved every two bloody years! It sometimes took that amount of time to settle down and find any decent jobs, and then we were off again! I never had time or the money to train for anything that would set me on a career path, so I had to make do with shitty cleaning jobs. If you have a qualification or skill in something for example hairdressing, office or admin, then you stood more chance of getting a better paid job. But because of my lack of skills apart from being a cleaner/housekeeper, it meant that I took what I could get.

By this time, I had another job with more hours on our camp, but I tried to make sure I was there when Faye came home from school or that I picked her up. She was responsible enough but at aged seven, I would never leave her to fend for herself for more than half an hour while I travelled home, so I worked part time wherever we lived so that she had at least one parent who was around. Kids need someone who is their staple, my daughter came before anything else, as did Lara dog.

Jack went back to the UK on another crucial course, this time I went with him and he dropped me off at my brother's after I decide that I was going to live with him and try and get on the council list. I had enough of moving and being away from my brother.

The other reason I made such a drastic move which also upheaved Faye from her school, was because stupidly I had confided in the young woman who lived on the ground floor about my affair with the Corporal. We had become friends although she clearly thought she was better than me, as she was thinner and more attractive. She would boast on how many men stared at her if we walked into town, and she always flirted back and made a monumental deal out of it. She also boasted of her affair with a PTI guy on their previous posting back in the UK.

She joked in front our husbands once that if she fucked me that I would never need Jack again, his reply to this was "can I watch?" Her husband laughed, but I was hurt and horrified by the pair of them! I felt that if I were ever to leave the two of them alone that she would make a play for Jack despite her being married. We fell out after she said that I was taking her for granted by her picking Faye up from the school bus, but this was a childish statement because Faye was perfectly capable of walking past the two blocks of flats from where the bus stopped so she was doing me no favours at all. I was literally driving straight home from camp at 3 pm so I would only be fifteen minutes in the door after Faye and she had her own key. It was not rocket science, but the blonde bimbo then took it upon herself to fall out like a five-year-old! In fact, her son was more grown up than she was! And he was five!

The last time we spoke face to face was when she was at the front door and had evidently been crying as she spat out at me, "Aren't you going to tell him, Elise?"

I just told her to go away! Which to my surprise she did, but of course Jack wanted to know what the hell she was on about and I spent the next couple of days with a very intense bout of IBS due to the worry and stress of whether she would blurt my affair out at Jack. So, I packed up and left with him because I could not be bothered to have this battle with another bloody army wife who liked stirring the shit pot. I should have made her lick that spoon!

It turns out I need not have performed this evasive action because her husband had put in for a posting back to England due to her constant nagging that she hated being in Germany. Truth was she was missing the PTI that she had been shagging back in England and from what I understand a few years later, she had another affair with someone on returning to the UK. I had only done it once, but I spent years feeling remorseful over that time let alone a repeat performance.

After many telephone fallouts, Jack had to buy a second-hand vehicle so that I could go back to Germany in the family car with Faye and Lara dog. On his last visit at my brothers, it had not gone well at all. I could not find work and we had no money. I had tried to get on the council list in Darren's hometown, to be told that I had not been in the country long enough and therefore, I could not apply because I would have to literally declare myself as homeless!

Jack's anger got the better of him on this occasion and after a heated argument in the spare bedroom Faye and I were sharing, he put me up against the wall and shook me. I understood the situation and I knew what I had to do, but there was no need for the hands-on approach. I needed to go back to Germany and settle my daughter back down because trying to get accommodation and a job had proved futile. I was trapped and I had to do what was best for Faye. I know that I should not have left, but I had to try, I just had never imagined that it would be so difficult.

Again, I felt remorseful because we could not afford the cost of another car or the running of it. If I had not run to the UK, he would have the family car. I would not have been able to get to my job in camp though. Swings and roundabouts.

After being at my brother's for two months, I borrowed fifty pounds from Maggie and drove to Dover from my brother's house in Kent to catch the next ferry to Calais. I drove the six-hour journey through France, Belgium and Holland into Germany without a satnav and a primitive printed out map. I tucked the girls up after feeding and watering them and drove through the night with my sleeping girls Lara dog, and Faye in the back seat. While I drove, I focused on what I needed to do next. I was disappointed in myself for confiding in her and the events that unfolded straight after. I was disappointed that I had let her get to me and drive me away from what little I did have. I had to stop worrying about the blonde bimbo and grasp what was my reality. I was stuck in this life, and it was me who had made the choice to marry into it, so I had to get on with it. But secretly, I was desperately unhappy, I just developed a coping mechanism for covering it up because it was not so much the life that made me miserable, but who I was married to, and the way he treated me, like I was a noose around his neck.

I went to ground for a week and ignored the house phone because I did not want to speak to anyone. I wanted to get my head around the fact that he had shaken me. I know that he was fearful and worried. And that his reaction would have been a result of the frustration over the things that I could not change whilst I was still in the UK. It was when I drove over to camp the following week to collect any mail from the post bunk when a friend that we knew came running out of the guard room asking where I had been, was I okay? And that Jack was frantic with worry as he had no way of contacting me and his daughter!

He cried down the phone when I finally answered it to him. Stating how worried he had been, I replied, "You will never put your hands on me like that again!" I was angry because it was the actions of both of us, not just me. To this day, I will always get in the car and just drive. I go off radar completely and I retreat into my Archimedes, as it is safe there where no one can hurt me. Archimedes was my refuge while I set about finding a job and getting Faye settled back into her school in Germany.

That was the worst part about my actions in trying to leave, I had upheaved her little world and I took it on the chin and claimed the responsibility when the head mistress took pleasure in telling me how detrimental it would have been on her. As if I did not know that but Faye had been to school while I was in the UK and she had settled in well.

I went back to my job as a chambermaid in the officer's mess and focused on not making any waves or saying anything to anyone, I just kept my head down and worked. Then I would go home and walk Lara before locking myself and the girls in for the evening. The money I was earning was good so I could finally sleep at night without fretting over that.

Meanwhile, the block of six flats we lived in became empty. The bimbo had gone, and the other couple who were in the flat opposite me were allocated a house they had applied for. Which meant that I was left in the block with Faye and Lara alone. It was not a comfortable feeling and I too applied for a house after I voiced my concern to the Estate manager. One night, I was convinced that someone was breaking into the cellar door at the back of the building! And then, I heard boots walking the length of the cellar! I did not imagine this as Lara was going nuts at my front door and barking continuously, so I knew someone was in the block and I was terrified!

The Military Police were based in the main Garrison which was half an hour away on the other camp near where I worked, but I rang them regardless. They in turn rang the German Police, who arrived about 20 minutes later and searched the cellar. The internal cellar door was locked, I had checked before I went up to the flat after collecting Faye. I went down there to investigate with them, as I needed to see for myself that there was no one there and the police said that I had imagined it, or that it had been a rat. I felt that I was being taken that piss out of so my reply to that stupid comment was "well, it must have been a bloody big rat with hobnail boots on! I know that someone was down here because I heard them, and so did the dog who never barks at anything!"

I felt like a fool, but to this day, I know that I was not safe in that block on my own. The house that I had applied for became available quite soon after and I did the march out of the flat myself. The Estate manager on this site was very understanding and had the wife and kid's best interests first and foremost in mind, because we were the ones left behind when the guys went away. He was a good guy like that and had good banter to go with it. He had asked me if I had anywhere in mind I wanted to live on the estate because there were so many empty houses due to the camp next door having been derelict for some years now. Where we were located was an overspill of quarters when there were not enough on the main Garrison. I had help to move the furniture courtesy of a few of the regiment colleagues who volunteered on the understanding that they got cups of tea on tap and bacon sandwiches with biscuits to follow.

I chose one of the little two-bedroom houses right next to the Estate Managers building because it was where the school bus stopped, it was so close to the flat that I was vacating that the guys could have carried my furniture up the street! And they did with some of the smaller items. It did not take long, and I was in and arranged everything before too long and more to the point I felt safer.

The Estate manager said the flat was 'too clean'! I had scrubbed it too much before the cleaners went in. But I did not want any unwanted bills for the married quarter not being up to scratch. The house we had been given was lovely and cosy. Jack was happy with it too because someone had built a bar in the small cellar room, we never used it as a that and only stored things on it, but we loved it.

Anne came to visit and stayed a couple of weeks as she was now living at a friend's house and sleeping on her floor after the ten-year relationship with farmer boy was over. She had lost her home, her car and most of her furniture and possessions. She was in a very dark place and it was a heart-breaking time for her. I wanted to try and get her a nanny job but did not know how to go about it as there were UK based civilians (UKBCs) working amongst the army community, but she would need a live-in position which was not a possibility.

The other option was to find her a husband in the Regiment and believe me…we did look! But there were no suitable candidates, and it was not meant to be.

Whilst I was at work one day, a little spitfire of a woman came into the Mess to cut the guys' hairs. She would use the little cupboard space in the office of the boss man who ran the Mess. Her name was Shelley. She was loud, and funny, and spoke her mind freely…I liked her from the minute I got over the shock of her small frame that encased her huge personality! Her presence could be felt at the other end of the building, as she was such a force of natural fun and monumental energy. She was a great person to be around and made such an impression that even when she left the building you were stood in her jet wash! The year was 2001 and we became good friends although we did not live in each other's pockets, she was a friend for life that little dynamite pocket rocket.

Jack left on a tour of Kosovo. This was to be a very emotionally challenging time because he would only be able to call home when they were given the Satellite phone, which was not regularly or a planned event. Faye and I went for weeks at a time with no word from him; it was awful. I lost weight with worry that he was okay. He came back on R and R on Boxing Day, so we at least got to have a Christmas with him, and then he was gone again. In the last weeks of this tour with little contact, I had to wait an extra week while everyone else's husbands returned. Because Jack was on rear party, and on the last flight back, so the frustration of seeing the lads arrive back on camp while I was at work grew within me daily. The day he arrived back could not come quick enough and I did nothing but cry for the whole week while I waited for my husband to return. I resented that he was on the last flight and detested the army life more than I ever had before. Of course, someone had to be on the rear party flight, but I was not happy about it.

All these feelings disappeared the moment I set eyes on him, but I will never forget the despair I felt before he arrived back; my heart ached. It would not have been so bad if I had not worked on camp and had seen the returning guys on the coaches.

You may think to yourself well what is so bad it was only a week! But it was torture knowing that the other families were enjoying their men being back already and I psychologically tortured myself. It had been a difficult tour because we had hardly spoken the whole time he was out there, so, for that reason, I found it a very overwhelming and emotionally charged long, six months.

You may also be thinking, *Why did she not just leave?* And my answer would be that having recently tried and found it to be futile because I had nowhere to go, none of my family members had room to house me and my girls it was a hopeless venture. And because I remained hopeful that when the army days were over, that I would magically have a husband who wanted to be more proactive in the marriage and normal life.

I guess I hoped that things would be totally different, and that he would be happy once he had served his duty for his Queen and country, and that Faye and I would be enough for him.

Shortly after Jack's return, we drove over to camp to collect any mail and for him to quickly say hello to a couple of colleagues. He came out of the building and I watched him walk back over to the car with an angst look on his face. Instead of getting into the driver's seat, he opened my passenger door and crouched down. I thought to myself, *Oh God this cannot be anything good!* He said, "I've just been offered a posting back to UK which carries with it a promotion, but I won't say yes unless you agree." They would like an answer as soon as possible though, like now.

There was not much time to mull it over, but in the end, we decided we would take the posting to Harrogate even though financially we had only just back got on our feet.

Chapter 8

UK for Two Years Again

I thought that accepting the posting would give us a little respite from Jack going away. A two-year break which would also mean that I could see my brother and Anne. Although I had tried to stay in contact with Denise, it was difficult as we moved around so much. Letters get lost in the post or reached a destination where the person you are writing to has moved away, which was the case with Denise. I was gutted but hoped one day we would find each other again somehow.

In 2004, we arrived at our married quarter with our removal lorry to follow in two days. We slept on the floor with our sleeping bags and pillows that we had brought with us because knew the beds were on the Autobahn behind us, but until the lorry arrived would have to improvise.

We had far too much furniture for the little house in Yorkshire that had been allocated to us, and as it was marched into by someone from the welfare office; there was no argument to be had. We moved in here or we had no other place to go to. We had been travelling up and could not make it on time from Dover to do the march in ourselves. It was shockingly small! We had to dispose of some of our furniture to fit into it comfortably. This was one of the drawbacks of buying furniture in Germany and then moving back to the UK, it was never guaranteed to all fit into an English army quarter. I found it a costly way of doing things although there was an allowance given for such moves.

Walking Lara was great as there was a field directly opposite the house, and plenty of good dog walking places around the area. It felt like a proper countryside location and it was a similar feeling of open space that the previous house in Yorkshire had. Jack threw himself into his work and training the youngsters and seemed to thoroughly enjoy it, as it was the same sort of challenging job he had in Hampshire. I secretly was dreading it for that reason.

There was one recruit in particular whose name was to pop up frequently and he had become some sort of a protégé for Jack. One day, he came home with pictures of a rescue helicopter on a hillside because the young lad had a nasty accident with a bone protruding through his knee that warranted the air ambulance to be deployed. Jack admired the bravery and courage that the young lad had displayed and took him under his wing. If only Jack had displayed such pride in his daughter.

I had cleaning job after cleaning job, and I got so sick and tired of it, it drove me to despair. The money I earnt was shit! I drifted from one housekeeping job in hotels to another, and it drove me crazy that I failed to settle anywhere. I went to work with an independent small cleaning company that went to different houses and locations daily. But the fuel consumption was costing me more than the wages. After complaining so much to the two bosses they finally gave me a house to go to that was four times a week and less petrol to think about.

It was while I was doing this job that I decided that I would take advantage of being in the UK and booked myself on a Nail Technician course in the evenings. It was twice a week on Tuesday and Thursday evenings, and I also enrolled on the non-vocational flower-arranging course just for the experience. But I was focused on the NVQ that the Nail course brought about. I was driven by the motivation of wanting something that I could progress with. I loved the nail course and really enjoyed the nail art, so I thought that I had finally found something I wanted to do, and I was good at! And after ten months of three hours each evening, I obtained an NVQ level 2 in Nail Technology with certificates to prove I had successfully passed, it was a proud moment when they were handed to me in the A4 sized envelope.

Faye found it hard to make friends wherever we moved to, she was usually the slightly smaller little girl who was a different child at home with her fantastically witty personality. But she found it difficult to bond with a friend for long enough to bring out her cheeky side, the side that we saw. Another school that failed to reprimand yet another bully saw to it that Faye was unhappy. She had retreated into herself.

The bully this time was a young boy the same age as Faye and in most of her lessons. It was an everyday occurrence that I collect her from school, and before she had put her bum in the passenger seat, she would say "he was relentless today".

I approached the headmistress one afternoon to be met with protests of "oh! Kyle would not do that! He is not capable of being a bully…he is one of our top pupils."

I cannot abide bullies of any description.

I also detest people who refuse to even investigate claims that someone is being a bully, even more so than the bully themselves! If a mother came to me and told me that Faye had been bullying or been nasty to their child, I would want to know everything that had happened, and Faye would be my first port of call.

The boy in question even appeared on the little green patch outside our house one day after school and proceeded to kick a football at our fence repeatedly with his friend watching on. In anger, I turned the hose on and sprayed the little bastard who eventually did leave! I hoped that they would return home sodden and to explain to his parents why he was soaked through! I wondered how he knew where we lived? And I considered it as an early warning sign of stalking! He lived nowhere near our house and had absolutely no reason to be near our street let alone the house. But despite my protests to the school, nothing was ever done to stop or reprimand him. Faye later found out that he was in prison for some offence or another, so much for the star pupil!

Little shit more like!

Darren was drifting through life and was extremely distraught when his Decree Absolute came through. I did what I could to talk to him on a regular basis and there were many nights of my brother in tears on the phone because he did not know how to go on without Maggie. He eventually got a friend to drive him up and drop him off on her way to stay with her parents; they lived a bit further up the motorway. I had convinced him that he needed a break and the support of his family and that I would very much like it if he came up to stay with us, I saw it as an opportunity to assess the extent of his grief. It was clearly visible as soon as he arrived; he was gaunt and looked unwell. I made up a bed in the spare room for him and told him that he could stay for long as he wanted to, which was only a week. Darren could only be in the company of Jack for a limited amount of time before he felt that he was in the way.

I did silly things with him like take him over to the local park with Faye on her bike and he would walk over with Jack's bike. When we got there, he would climb on and start peddling under my guidance of when and if he had to turn left or right. I cycled alongside on mine and it was good fun for him, but bloody nerve wracking for me because he sped off and took the initiative that I could shout loud enough if he were in line with a tree! He did all right for a blind man with only five percent vision in his left eye. It was his body and mind that craved an adrenaline rush!

With my guiding him over the fields and Faye just behind him, he had fun riding a bike again! He cast his troubles aside for the time that we were out, and it was just like when I lived at Hayley's when he and I used to get on the buses and go out somewhere for the day. For a short time, I saw evidence that he could get through this tough time. He did not think that he was strong, but we were brought up under tough conditions and I liked to think that we both could weather most storms.

He had laughed and we just acted like we were kids again when his sight was slightly better. But of course, it meant that he could not speed off at the pace he really wanted to. He still enjoyed himself, and then we got home I made him a big chunky cheese and tomato sandwich which he polished off in no time at all! I was delighted to see that his appetite had returned, and he said, "My word, woman! That sandwich was bloody handsome! Go on then, I could go another of those." We sat on the chairs in the back garden and chatted about a plan for his future so that he had goal posts to aim for. I told him that he did need to allow himself the time to heal. He did not want to be on his own, and I understood that. But at the same time, I had hoped that he would not dive into a relationship straight away and would allow time for himself. Jumping from woman to woman would only result in more heartbreak for him. But as the saying goes "you can lead the horse to the trough, but you cannot make it drink the water", and I knew that he was stubborn and did exactly what he wanted. I could feed him all the advice and opinions that he asked for, but he made his own decisions and rarely listened to me anyway. That runs in the family, Faye says, "Why do you ask for my opinion because you go and do the opposite anyway!"

I also took him up a lane and let him try and drive my Fiat as he had claimed that he knew how to drive!

He may have been able to in theory, but in practice, it was different. He was an avid Top Gear fan, and I am sure that he had convinced himself that he could drive because he listened to the guys on there.

Stalled…and stalled, and eventually he gave up bless him and reluctantly admitted defeat.

I could only draw on the experience of Dad leaving to understand what Darren was going through and how he felt, but now…I totally understand fully what he went through, and everyone deals with the pain of divorce differently.

Jack was extremely immersed in his work, and I was extremely fed up with waiting on his return home late most days. I threw myself into another course that was Beauty Specialist and done totally by correspondence. I enjoyed the knowledge that I now had an NVQ level 2 in Nail Technology and a Diploma in beauty specialist, although I only planned to do the nails as soon as I returned to Germany.

One of Darren's fellow blind friends and close confidante had found him a job in Northampton, so his preparations were under way to get the flock out of his old life and start afresh. I was extremely pleased to hear this fantastic news and I was so proud of him for sticking with his job applications! We were taught to be fighters and persevere…never give up! Darren was moving from Kent and out of the house that he had shared with poison-compact Maggie. I considered that if he were no longer in the same space that he had shared with her, then the memories would fade and so would the pain she had caused him. She was now dating a sighted man who was ten years her junior. Both had nasty sides and their words were spiteful and unnecessary. I now wanted to ensure that she never had anything to do with me or my family again. They were not going to affect my daily life and eventually Darren would see how much nastiness she was capable of. She stopped at nothing to get what she wanted, and no amount of begging or reasoning would make a difference. She was willing to trample on anyone to get what she wanted and cared little of anyone else's feelings other than her own, she was selfish and arrogant, and the boyfriend was just as bad, clearly a match made in heaven. Darren was better off without that shit. I just could not tell him things like that yet because he was fragile, but he was standing his ground and holding his own!

He had moved into a rented accommodation that was damp and cold! In my mind, it was not fit for purpose and needed bulldozing! But he did not hang around there long and found a new place quickly. He was so over the moon at having secured employment because he had been looking for so long, it was exceedingly difficult as a partially sighted man to gain employment, which drove him nuts, as all he wanted to do was work and earn a wage. His frustration over the years with regards to having to fight to gain work was heart breaking and soul destroying, and I felt guilty for complaining about my lack of skills and having to work at crap cleaning jobs. But at least I could work!

I drove down from Yorkshire with Faye and Lara in tow to help him unpack in his second rented property and keep up his morale a little. But on arrival, it was apparent that he was gaining some of his old self to a certain degree. Darren was a man's man and was laughing and joking with the lads who were his removal men. I remember him clearly stood on the doorstep of his new rented house cracking jokes with them, nothing dulled his sparkle at this point, he was fighting his way out of a bad situation and embracing his new life, or so I thought.

I attempted to cheer him up and told him that he had made the best decision to move away and get a new life for himself! He was strong, but I did feel his pain and could see in his eyes that he was broken inside. We chatted about the positives that he had achieved recently and that he had been head hunted by his new boss, that was due to his friend Neil telling Mervin that Darren was a top bloke, and that he wanted to work and was a dedicated grafter! Darren was good with I.T and was good with computers because that was what he studied throughout his school years. There is technology to aid the visually impaired and blind, and he learnt every way that there was available, including Braille.

Faye and I helped him settle in and we had fish and chips from the shop which was very conveniently situated across from his house…I cannot imagine why! We could smell it from Darren's house, so it would have been rude not to have treated him to a fish supper!

After a day or two, I had to get home and back to my life, but I knew that Darren was trying his best to fix himself and put himself back together as best as he could, but it was so painful to watch. I told him to take small steps, do not try and walk before you can run! And now, he had his job to focus on so that would help.

Our time in Yorkshire had been eventful what with supporting my younger brother and my shitty job situation. I was not happy with this moving around anymore, and my need for settling down grew with every posting that we were sent on. Anne had found love and was extremely happy in her life which was lovely to see after the turmoil of her last relationship. Wedding bells rang before we moved again. I have to say it was the best wedding I have ever been to, we had such a laugh and Anne glowed for the whole day, my beautiful friend was married.

Once again, I was saying goodbye to my brother…I was breaking inside but I had to go I had no other choice. The drive back over to Germany was so painful as Darren was no longer just a couple of hours down the motorway and it destroyed me when we drove the two cars away from him as he waved us off from his doorstep. I had traded in the Fiat for a Cherry Red Escort. I loved that car, it was very 'me' but unfortunately, that was about to change.

Chapter 9

Germany for the Last Time

The summer of 2004 in Germany was hot! The day our removal truck arrived, it was 39 degrees and awful to work in. I remember the day clearly as Lara locket dog who was now aged 14 was in the garden for as long as she could cope with the heat until it got too much for her and she would retreat to the cool floor in the cellar. She was never any trouble and stayed out of the way while we were unpacking, and the number one priority was always putting the beds put together. After however many nights that we had been without our own beds because they were on the trucks in transit, we wanted to sleep in our beds as soon as we moved in.

As a military family who move around a lot, you learn to buy furniture that is easily assembled and disassembled. The next thing was plumbing in the washing machine. I do not know any woman that can live without her washing machine! Jack had his list of priorities and this was usually his second job to do after the beds.

After settling a little, we ventured out in the main town to stock up with some food as we had nothing except very basic supplies from the main NAAFI, but we refused to do a weekly shop there when we knew that we could get more for our money in the local German shops. We sorted out the landline for calls to UK, and mobile pay as you go phones so I could text my brother. He was so down when we left, and I was very worried about him. The sad and lonely look on his face as I gave him a hug and told him that I loved him indicated that his world had just bottomed out again. He had lost his wife, his home in a place that he had known for many years and now he was losing his only family to a foreign country again! He was always considered the fourth pillar of our family and he made us complete.

I just prayed that with his new job would bring about some companionship and a sense of purpose for him, because he needed it. I had visited his place of work when I had stayed with him for those few days previously. It was a modern building and I had timed my arrival to fit in with his clocking off time so that I could collect him and drive him home. He did not yet have a guide dog and was relying on his walking cane for his guidance to and from work. I had text him from my parked car to announce that Faye and I were outside and that his carriage awaited.

He immediately called me on my phone, and I was instructed to get my butt out of the car, told me that he would meet me at the main door, and that I was to bring his niece with me because he had missed her terribly and that he needed her hugging technique! She would run at him and he would try and judge when to open his arms based on her footsteps and the vibrations on the floor, it did not always turn out well but most of the time, they did succeed. He loved Faye beyond words, and he was proud to be her uncle. He was never going to have children of his own because whilst he was married to poison-compact, he had the snip. He would have been a wonderful father. It was such a shame, but it was also his decision and it was an admirable one because he loved the thought of having his own kids.

On entering the building, he came charging along the corridor as if he had the wind in his sails at a speed of knots that could match the Titanic at full speed ahead! Faye ran at him and a successful delivery of hugs were dispensed freely! They timed it to perfection and Darren's work colleagues cheered them on; it was a moment in time that I will always remember with such admiration for them both, a priceless and treasured memory of my little girl and my beloved brother together etched in my memory bank of Archimedes. Man, that little guy was getting full! But my bank of Archimedes was not full of money. No, it was full of treasured gold that could never be stolen from me or Faye.

Pure gold memories of my brother and the smile on his face, as he embraced his niece.

Shortly after our arrival in Germany, my beloved car had been sold. I was put under pressure because apparently, we could not afford two cars. He had created some fictitious problem with the exhaust and said that it had to go, also Jack hated the car that he had. I wondered if that man was ever going to be capable of keeping anything or anybody for longer than a year or two, it broke me. He claimed that there was something wrong with the exhaust and it was

106

going to cost too much to get it repaired, this was bullshit and I knew it. I had not even been given the time to find a job to be able to get the alleged problem fixed!

He had always come up with a fictional problem for things when it suited him. I resented never being able to keep things that meant anything to me and quite frankly it pissed me off! I had grown up with the mindset of make do and mend, not get rid of and put yourself in more debt just because you suddenly did not like something! The way he was, was really starting to become a problem for me. I had made poor decisions in the past, and I do not claim to have been perfect at making them, but the constant changes without any choice in the matter were seriously upheaving and I hated it. I was always talked at while he gave me reasons that justified whatever action he was about to undertake. But it left me feeling that I had just been manipulated and left with no choice. It was always his way with no room for dispute. There were things that he had done that I had never forgiven him for, and never will.

October came around and Darren had booked himself on a flight to New York! He was so excited because it was on his bucket list and he had tackled the biggest goal first! He was planning his life just like we had talked about and using his time on the planet constructively. I was well chuffed for him although I was anxious about him going alone. His fear knew no limits and he faced whatever came his way. The only fear he struggled with was loneliness.

He told me that he had been chatting with a woman from an online dating site and that they had arranged for her to meet him at the airport to see if they had a connection. She had told him that she lived only an hour away from New York and fed him lots of teasing suggestions that they might end up together. I was greatly concerned about the lengths that my younger sibling was willing to go to find love. But I could say nothing because I did not believe for one minute that the woman would meet him, and that she was leading Darren a merry dance.

I had set up one room in the cellar as a little nail bar so I could start using my NVQ and gain some new friends. I did the nails, while Shelley did the hair styling and we had another friend that did the beauty. We all recommended each other to everyone, it worked out well and we gained clients and the trust of fellow army wives.

Jack settled back into his life as a Sergeant, and Faye started at the local middle school. Life seemed to be going well, and on an even keel, and I kept tabs on Darren to see how he was doing. I also found work as a housekeeper for a local Colonel and the money was good, so we could start living again as the time in Yorkshire was extremely difficult financially.

I enjoyed my job although it was cleaning again, but the lady I worked for was very down to earth and did not carry her husband's rank as was the case sometimes. I could not be doing with all that "do you not know who I am" bullshit. They still poo and pee and create the same problems as everyone else! And thankfully, these women were few and far between.

With some of the higher ranks, it was not deemed appropriate to mix with the lower ranks unless it was a regimental function. There were the ones that did of course make the effort and to hell with the way that they were expected to behave, or who they were supposed to speak to. They spoke to whom they wanted to, and they included everyone and anyone. These became scarce as time went by because no one appreciates being snubbed or that horrible feeling that they are being looked down on. Respect should be maintained on every level, not just expected from the top. Manners cost nothing and smiling back at someone is a courtesy. But there were 'wives of' who would not spare you the time of day and I could not be assed to entertain that shit or be bothered with them either. If I were to bump into any of them today, I would treat them as my equal, and no different to anyone I see or know in person. No one's shit smells of roses! And on civilian street, we are nothing to no one.

Darren asked one evening before his flight to New York, if we could think of anything that we would like him to bring back for us. I had always wanted an official baseball cap with the NY emblem. I had never wanted a fake one, so this was my opportunity to have a genuine article that my lovely brother had purchased from the very place itself. That was my only request, with the subtle suggestion that if he stumbled across a fridge magnet that I would love one of them too. I told him that he could bring Faye whatever took his fancy, and that she would treasure whatever he got for her. I still have my coveted baseball cap!

I was worried about my partially sighted brother jetting off on his own on a long flight, but I also knew he could speak his mind loud enough and was not afraid of asking for assistance. Besides, I knew that wild horses would not stop him doing exactly what he wanted, his courage was admirable and I had such pride in his drive and ambition.

For those of you that remember the London bombings of 7/7, I was always on high alert as to where Darren was. Because the weekend prior to the fatal incident, I knew that he was in London visiting some friends. The day it happened, I called his mobile to receive no answer and I panicked beyond belief! My stomach was in knots, my heart was pounding, and I could quite happily have emptied the contents of my stomach, but I had to know if he was still in London. I managed to find his work number, so I called directly. He answered the phone with his opening speech of "thank you for calling Sight and Sound. You are through to Darren; how may I help you?"

It brings tears to my eyes reliving this memory and knowing that he was safe. Hearing his voice meant that my racing heartbeat would now slow itself, and I could come down from the high wire I had been balancing on. He had no idea what I had been rambling on about incoherently through the tears and sounding like I had someone else's teeth in! He said, "Elise! I am fine, I am sat at my desk listening to you, as you now know, all is good apart from hearing you so upset on the other end of this line. Now, let me get back to work and I will call you tonight but please stop worrying!" And with that, we hung up the phone.

I felt like a fool. But being across the English Channel and a nine-hour drive in total made me a little bit paranoid. I knew that if anything ever happened to him, it would be impossible to get there quickly. I could not just jump in the car and drive up or down the motorway, and this was what bothered me and weighed heavy on my mind all the time.

The week he was in New York went so slowly. I knew he would be fine, but it was only a couple of years after the twin towers atrocity and I would just be happier knowing that my sibling was back in England. I also wished for him to have a fabulous time and to experience all that he could while he was out there, which he did of course! And he brought me my prized baseball cap and gifts for Faye although I cannot recall exactly what. My mind still frets over the thought of him wandering around New York with only a white cane, but he achieved it! And I am sure that he was not the only blind man to ever walk the streets of The Big Apple, but I worried terribly, and I could not stop that from happening. I would not be human if I had not had my concerns.

Darren was with Faye and I for this Christmas, so I missed all the functions in the Sergeants Mess this year (2004) 'silly season' because Jack was away again but I do not recall where, it was just the norm now. With all the Christmas functions in the Sergeants mess, it made the time go so much quicker. I was happy to not go and spend time with my daughter and brother. A new dress was always required, and the wives had to wait for the husband to come home and tell what length or style it had to be. Sometimes cocktail, and sometimes full length. But you had to get it right as the RSM (Regimental Sergeant Major) would fine the soldier of the wife that got the wrong dress code a bottle of Port.

I detest Port, I got very drunk on it once when I was sixteen and it did not agree with me which resulted in numerous visits to pay homage to the porcelain god for a few days it is awful stuff!

But in the Sergeants mess, they toasted to one and all with a glass of Port. I pretended to drink it when we first started going to the functions, but I soon clicked on that I did not have to go near it. Jack would swig my Port, and then, under the table, he would pour some cola in the glass instead!

I had attended a couple of functions in the Sergeants mess in Yorkshire, but it was so much better being back at the Regimental ones because we had known these people for years. The bagpipes and drums played each time, and it was awesome!

The food was always lovely in the mess and the chef's worked their socks off to put on a beautiful, three-course meal, with coffee and cheese and crackers to follow in the main bar area. I enjoyed most of the functions on this posting because shortly after moving back to Germany, I had bumped into Jack's closest friend Josh outside a car insurance place. He told me that his wife and kids were in the car around the corner and that I should go say hello, which I duly did as my car was parked in front of theirs.

I told Jack that I had met Sarah and Josh, and so the family were invited around that weekend for a brew and to get to know each other. We became firm friends for the duration of the time we were in Germany, and along with Anne and Shelley, they became Faye's godparents when she was aged fourteen.

Faye would babysit for Josh and Sarah, and we would all four go together on the transport into camp. At the end of the night and quite a few drinks later, we got on our transport home and went our separate ways until we picked Faye up the following morning.

At this point in time, Faye was becoming increasingly difficult and a little bit unapproachable, but the reason for this was unclear because she would not talk about what was troubling her. We foolishly brushed it off as 'the teenage years'.

She was now at senior school and her temperament had changed completely. She did not want to be around me, and she did not want to be around when Sarah was with me. She just did not want to do anything or go anywhere. Jack and Faye were not getting on either, and it was a difficult time because he was hardly ever home and if she refused to tell me, there was no way she would talk to him. She had always said that he treated her like she was one of his recruits. And that hit hard.

She eventually found a friend that lived in a house that were four rows of houses up, and we used to love hearing her laughter while the two girls were up in her room. Rosie was a complete exhibitionist and loved showing off but did it in such a funny way you could not help but laugh at her! She was blond with blue eyes and slightly taller than Faye, but her character and wit were the things that made her.

I had never heard Faye laugh so heartily and we thought everything was going okay for her at last and that she had possibly made a friend who was good for her. We hoped that she could put the pain, torment and mental scarring of the previous bullying behind her. How wrong we were.

They were good friends for around a year, but Rosie got in with a bad lot and times changed overnight.

Christmas of 2004, Darren had flown over to Dortmund Airport and an excited Faye and I were waiting eagerly for him. Jack was away (now there was a surprise). Darren had managed to get time off over the Christmas period to come see us and have a break.

He walked swiftly through the ticket barrier with an arm linked to the arm of a male guide who helped him through the process of checking-in and customs and had come across on the flight to aid with any assistance that Darren needed, which was usually just an arm and someone to spot his luggage on the conveyor belt, oh and someone to poke fun at in his joking way. They were laughing which indicated that Darren was doing okay if he was not putting on his brave face. He was good at hiding himself away and behaving like he did not have a care in the world in front of other people. But he hid nothing from me, and we were overdue some catch up time to see how he was really doing. I was not playing God, I just wanted to help in any way that I could even if that was to listen when no one else would. The one thing I could not do with my brother was tell him what to do or what I thought unless he had asked for my input and opinion, and even then, I asked, "Do you want me to lie and sugar-coat the bullshit, or do you want the truth?"

That bold as brass confident 5′ 9″ man had lost weight and he looked tired, but smartly dressed and holding his composure. We had just purchased a Vauxhall seven-seater, and it had replaced the two cars including the one that I adored so much. Darren insisted that the stereo was not in tune and played with the buttons to obtain maximum benefit of the sound system. His hearing was acute, so I let him get on with what he felt was a necessary task to help if we wanted the music to sound 'proper pucker'! As he put it. Proud of his insight into this topic, he sat back and listened to make sure that he was happy with the results of his expertise, although Faye was not grateful in the back seat as she could barely hear anything!

We had a lovely chilled out Christmas which I recorded courtesy of Mum and Simon buying us a video camera for Christmas. I recorded Darren helping Faye to open her main present as it was a compact TV and proved to be wrapped too well! I cooked the dinner and relished in my lovely brother being with us, it meant the world to me and I thought it would do him good to see his niece and get away from his life, even if it were for a brief couple of days.

We were sitting on the wooden bench in the back garden while Darren had a cigarette. I had given up the cancer sticks when I was aged thirty and avoided them, so I was trying to sit upwind of his fag smoke! We just sat talking, and Darren eventually dropped his guard and told me how he really felt inside. It was heart-breaking to find out that he was lost. He did not understand or comprehend what he had done to deserve to be in the situation he was in, and he was exceptionally lonely.

I told him that he had done nothing wrong apart from marry someone who had never intended to be in it for the long haul. I pointed out that she had always been flirtatious and that it was bound to happen one day that she would find that bigger, better deal that she was searching for. Except for the flirtatious bit, this all resonated with me and I felt hypocritical because this is how I too felt about Jack, and I was drawing on those feelings. But I said nothing, because this was Darren that we were focusing on and I wanted him to tell me everything. I told him that for me personally, she was a woman with a split personality, a true Gemini and from where me and my opinions stood, that he would be fine if he just gave himself time to recover and heal the hurt. They met at a young age, and that they had grown apart. She wanted to shag everything with a pulse, including women, and he wanted stability. Darren had even overlooked her numerous infidelities. That was not love! That was her treating him like a fucking doormat! And I told him so!

He took all of that on board, but after I had delivered my next opinion, it was a slightly different kettle of fish. I suggested that from a sisterly point of view, I thought that pursuing women in the manner that he had been doing made him look desperate, and that was probably the main reason that these women were scared off! He had mentioned around five women in the last year that he had claimed to have loved after only chatting with them for a short time. And on one occasion, he had met a woman and her child twice! I believed that it would only bring misery into someone else's life when all he talked about was his ex. He absolutely needed to be over Maggie before he sought a new love interest.

I kept trying to reassure him that before he would be able to find someone to love, he would first have to work through getting over Maggie (Poison-compact.) and that it was imperative he allowed himself the time to grieve before pursuing a new love interest. He got annoyed with me and said, "But you are okay! You know that Jack is coming home at some point, your marriage is secure!" If only he knew.

There was nothing that I could say except that I was sorry. I hugged him as he cried because I knew that although I had not sugar-coated it, I had pushed it one sentence too far and I said the things that he perhaps was not ready to hear, or indeed accept. It tore me to pieces to see my brother in the deflated state he was in, there was no consoling him and all I could do was be there. If I ever ask you, "Do you want me to tell the truth…?" Say no!

We spoke over the breakfast table the next morning and he said that if anyone else had said the things that I had the night before, that he would never have spoken to them again. I was just about to state my case before he told me to be quiet and let him finish what he had to say because we would not be seeing each other for a while, and he did not want to board a flight and not have his say.

I listened intently! He said that he was not shocked that I told him what no one else was willing to say. Not even his closest friends had delivered the facts as they saw it in the no frills way that I had. And now that he had slept on it, he knew that what I had said made perfect sense and shed some light on it from a woman's perspective. He was grateful for my brutal honesty and said that he would go home and process it all and plan each day as it came. That was enough for me and I wanted him to take baby steps instead of trying to grab life in big lumps that he could not cope with. He had hit a brick wall, but he would eventually have the strength to climb over it if he took his time.

He reluctantly got his flight back to Gatwick on Boxing Day as he was back in work the day after. Darren said that his new manager was getting a bit above his station and took the new promotion to his head. Which meant that Darren was being worked hard. We said our goodbyes and I told him I would be over in September to pick up the new car as we had decided not to keep the current one and we would upgrade to the new sporty version with the panoramic roof and sports injection button! He could hardly hold his excitement to get in it! Even though he could not drive, he drove through my eyes and the cars we had instead.

Quote;

"Anyone can give up, that is the easiest thing in the world to do. But to hold it together when everyone else would understand if you fell apart, that's true strength."

In June 2005, I had finally set up my nail room and had 30 clients (army wives). I had registered with the German tax authorities and was up and running nicely. I was self-employed for the first time and I loved it. It also meant that I had not invested money in doing the nail technology course and I was not wasting it as Jack had made it abundantly clear he would be pissed off should this happen. I felt the pressure and the thumb screws tighten as he said it. Not everything we all do is successful, and things do not work out for whatever reasons, just because the courses he went on proved to be a step forward in his career, it did not necessarily mean that my little business would the same, but I would give it my all.

His courses were paid for by the army, mine was funded by the credit card so that I could complete it on time! I felt like he begrudged me the opportunity to try and make something of myself and my new NVQ qualification. I was under pressure, but I ignored him and carried on regardless. It did however make me feel that it was considered not good enough or begrudged. I wanted so much to be anything but a cleaner/housekeeper. And despite my gaining this experience, I felt that it would be held against me in that future instead of going with the flow and letting me enjoy it and do my utmost.

In June 2005, I went into hospital for a day or two because I was having severe pains in my stomach that was diagnosed as a cyst on my ovary. It was a simple keyhole surgery, but it was so hot, stuffy and uncomfortable in the hospital that I could not wait to get home to recover there and be with my girls Faye and Lara dog.

Jack was at home to look after Faye which was a massive relief as there was no family that could come and look after her if he had not been. The friends you make in the army become your family, and there were only Sarah and Shelley who I would have asked if he could not have been there for Faye. I was never comfortable leaving Faye with anyone but only because I never wanted to burden them.

While in the hospital, I had an overwhelming gut feeling that I needed to go back to the UK. I put it down to the fact that I was emotional due to my hormones having just been tampered with. But that gut feeling pursued.

When I got home, I got in contact with Darren although we had been texting whilst I was lying in the hospital bed with nothing to do. He would text and describe what had happened on Most Haunted with Yvette hosting it as we both liked the TV series. He joked that he had 'shit himself' at the Clitheroe witches as he obviously was unable to see what was going on but was terrified by the amount of screaming! He assumed that they were being murdered. I was angry and not happy at Jack's resistance in letting me drive back to see my brother using the "we cannot afford it" excuse. I could not shake the feeling that I really needed to get back there and tried to argue the case with Jack, who was having none of it. Money ruled the roost, not me. There were a lot of tearful phone calls from Darren, he was so down again and just did not know how to cope with his life.

I felt completely helpless sat on my hallway stairs in Germany and I kept telling him to hold on and that that we loved him and that although he was living alone; he was not alone! He had us, and he could not give up and throw in the towel. I reminded him of the positives he had achieved such as buying his own little house, and that he now had his long-awaited guide dog named Lex.

He had bought his house in Northampton close to where he worked. He told me that getting life insurance was extremely difficult due to his shenanigans with parachute jumps and ab-sailing down two hundred feet buildings! But he had achieved it, and I was so proud of him and how far he had come since the divorce. I had not spoken to my dad for months again, but as much as I would bother to call him, he never reciprocated. I found it difficult having a one-way relationship, and in the end, I just backed off, not because I could not be bothered but because he couldn't. It has always been the same throughout the years. I never understood how a parent could ignore their children as Darren never heard from him much either, he just never let it agitate him like I did.

As kids, we used to talk about when we found our soulmates that we would marry for life, we did not want our kids to grow up the way that we had, feeling like we there was always something missing and that there was something we had done to bring on the whole situation. We did not want the loneliness or

115

bitterness that we had witnessed after Mum and Dad's divorce. But one of us was divorced already, with the other to follow in the future.

Chapter 10
Elise, Please Sit Down

On 19 August 2005, I rang Darren to ask him what he was doing for Christmas. He reprimanded me and said, "I can set my bloody watch by you! It is the middle of August and you are planning Christmas!"

He had also told me off because it seemed to him that I had ignored him on messenger, that had not been the case at all, and it was only because I was still learning how to use the social media platform and every other part of its different communication techniques. I simply had not seen his message. Darren was always the computer geek and I was still teaching myself all these gadget things and the communication that they empowered. Facebook was quite new, and I had only just discovered it.

On the phone one evening, Darren explained that his new boss was being a bit of a dick and making his life a misery. He said that he had tried to book the time off so that we could stay over at his at Christmas, but his boss was sending him away on work for a month. He also said that he could not have the time off in September when I was due to drive over to the UK and pick up the long awaited new sporty car. I was devastated, because I had waited since the gut instinct back in June, and I was desperate to see my brother and Faye to reconnect with her uncle again, we had not seen him since last Christmas.

I had not been allowed to fly over quickly in June, but it was permitted that I went over to the UK to pick up the new car, always on his terms!

The new boss had even rung Darren while he was on holiday in Cornwall with his friend Gail to inform him of the upcoming dates that he would be away, and that he would be travelling to Hamburg.

On 20 August, Darren was with his friend Mark at a pub in Tonbridge, Kent. He used to live there with Maggie poison-compact, it had been the last time I had said goodbye to her on their doorstep. She had cried more than usual, and I felt at the time that it seemed a bit weird, she had never behaved this way…She clearly knew that she would not be seeing Faye or I again. Her escape plan was already in action. Darren had managed to keep in touch with most of his close friends from his school days because they understood each other's capabilities regarding their sight; he held these pockets of friends all over the country in high regard. It was heart-warming to know that he was acting like a child and mucking about on the swings on that sunny Saturday afternoon and probably had a few beers to chill out a bit and let his hair down.

But I know from speaking to these pockets of friends that Darren was extremely down in the dumps and still grieving the loss of his childhood first love, Maggie was still haunting him.

On Sunday, 21 August 2005, he visited two other friends in Kent. A married couple who formed part of the band he played in before he moved away, the band was aptly named Blind Drunk! Upon receiving a phone call from his close friend Neil in Milton Keynes, Darren was sent abruptly like his hair was on fire to catch the next train up to Neil's house, because he was about to miss the Christening of Neil's daughter!

Darren had made it with little time to spare, but he had to leave the celebrations early due to another of his headaches. Neil informed me that Darren had seemed very disorientated and disordered. He had even forgotten a water bowl for Lex the guide dog, which was most unusual and out of character, because Lex was his lifeline as well as his pet. He loved that dog to bits, and it was his obligation as a Guide Dog owner to take care of him and Darren took pride in doing so. So, this was totally out of character for Darren because he took that obligation very seriously.

With his work commitments, my brother had travelled from Northampton to Glasgow to do a Power point presentation with another work colleague who was the driver. The colleague told me on the phone that during the entire journey, Darren did not get out of the car much as he perhaps should have to stretch his legs, he was feeling a bit rough and although could not pinpoint why he felt this way he had seemed to be in good spirits.

I remember the colleague telling me that Darren was on a treadmill in the hotel while they were staying over, and he had to hit the emergency button. Darren had lain on the floor and blacked out. Through my own investigation after learning of this incident, I discovered that this is one of the symptoms of deep vein thrombosis. Darren had undergone blood tests to try and ascertain the reason why he felt ill all the time, but was still none the wiser, and we never found out any results of these blood tests.

On 24 August, while I was at the Colonels house there was a knock at the door. I answered it as the lady I worked for was out at the local swimming baths. Stood before me were two ladies with Bible pamphlets in their hands. I was asked if I believed in God, to which I replied, "If there was a God, why do bad things happen? And if there is, then why does he allow these things and do nothing to prevent it?" One of the ladies seemed quite taken aback by my bluntness, and although I do not condone anyone for their beliefs, I do not wish it to be forced on me. So, I was quite abrupt for that reason and the fact was that I was supposed to be working not having the bible thrust in my face. I simply did not want that conversation at that precise moment in time, and it was not my intention to appear rude and obnoxious, had they have been on my doorstep in my own time not my bosses, I probably would not have been so forthright.

On 24 August, Darren and his driving companion visited their fellow work colleagues in Newcastle Upon Tyne before their return journey to Northampton. One of the two ladies that I spoke to on the phone was someone that Darren had a romantic interest in, and he had spoken to me about her on numerous occasions, the only difficulty was that she was married to an abusive husband, Darren detested that, and wanted to help her get out of her current misery.

She told me that they had climbed a couple of flights of stairs and Darren stopped midway up, he was breathless. Despite that he smoked sometimes, he was generally very fit and active. He walked to work and had purchased himself a treadmill which he used in his bedroom, his drum kit and guitars took up the spare room, but he was more than capable of working up a sweat on those too!

Darren and his colleague travelled back down to Northampton and he arrived home between 9.30 pm and 10 pm. the colleague told me Darren was 'right as rain' when he left him opening his front door. His love interest in Newcastle told me that they had been on the phone until around 2 am the following morning, and that whilst talking, he got up to go get a coffee but started crying out loud and saying, "Ow! Ow! Ow!" He said that there was a tremendous pain in his leg and although he physically could not feel anything, he could feel a lot of pain in the back of his knee.

26 August 2005. Approximately 10.55 am.

Now the part that I cannot to this day explain, but I just 'felt it'.

119

The lady I worked for was pottering around upstairs and she was sorting out the ironing for me to do, which I had started and had set the ironing board up.

The only way that I can describe this feeling is if you have ever watched Avengers: Age of Ultron. There is a scene where the male twin is shot multiple times and killed by one of the robots. The female twin is not near him, but she feels it, and drops to her knees in pain at the loss of her sibling because she 'feels it'. She then tells the robot Ultron, "That is how it felt," as she rips his metal heart out. I knew that something was wrong.

There was a three-year age gap between my brother and myself, but I felt the moment as he passed. I cannot and do not know why.

I asked Meredith the time, she replied that it was 10.55 am German time; in the UK it was 9.55 am. The exact time that Darren passed, aged just 31 years old. His birthday was 10 July.

I knew nothing of this until I got home. I was making stew and preparing the beef while Faye was watching TV. On answering the house phone, I remember the first words, "Can I please speak to Elise?"

I replied, "Yes, speaking."

Her voice lowered and she said, "Can I please ask you to sit down, Elise." I later regretted having not done just that as she announced her name, and that she was calling from Northampton General Hospital.

I started to panic and asked, "Has he walked in front of a car or something? Is he okay? Please tell me he is okay!"

She proceeded to say, "I'm so sorry to have to tell you that, unfortunately he died."

I could hear my heartbeat in my ears. It was deafening me! My pulse raced and my hands shook as I replayed the words on a loop and at high speed in my head over and over. Although it was only seconds that passed, I felt that I had died a thousand times over.

There was a long pause. I simply could not digest what she had just said. I got defensive as the panic took over. She had been trying to get a response from me, but it was just white noise to me. I could not open my airway to respond. I felt my heart break and split into billions of tiny shards like a planet exploding. This was something that I would never be able to repair and there would be no coming back from it. If anyone had their hand or head on my chest, they would have heard and felt it break.

I had no control as to what came out of my mouth next. I said, "You are fucking joking me, right? But he is fit and healthy, I just do not understand!"

My vision blurred, my mouth dried like the sands of time had been drifting through for years, my head was spinning uncontrollably, and I felt sick. My heart was pounding like an overfilled balloon that was about to burst. I had never experienced this kind of intense pain of mind, body and soul before.

My body gave in. I fell to my knees having lost my grip on the sideboard, my legs were too weak and unable to support me, but I still clutched the phone in my left hand. Darren was gone. He had left me.

Faye had run into the kitchen asking me what is wrong with tears in her beautiful, brown eyes. I was scaring her, but in that split second of hearing those few words, I had completely died inside. Now my daughter looked on helplessly as her normally strong mother collapsed in a heap on the floor.

Chapter 11

Lost

Time seemed to stand still. It was like a scene out of a film where they spin the camera around a person who has just learned an unthinkable tragedy. But now, the person whose world was spinning was mine. I stared out of the kitchen window for an unknown amount of time.

Reality bites. And it had bitten every ounce of my very being and tore it to shreds, leaving me in the meat suit that felt like it had been through a grinder, I was in so much pain.

I had managed to take down the number to call the consultant, but I had no recollection of doing this. I think that my subconscious must have taken over while my spiritual body was crumbling and could not cope with the task of writing down a phone number. After the initial shock had worn off and I was able to talk, I returned her call because I wanted to absorb all that she could tell me. We went through it, piece by piece and at a slow pace. I wanted every detail because maybe then I could process it.

That is how I deal with everything in my life, if it affects me directly then I will dissect it piece by piece and work through the jumbled pieces to fully understand and comprehend. I listened to every detail to make light of the events as they had unfolded and were then referred to me. I stripped it all back and stored it in Archimedes for safekeeping until I was ready to deal with it all. But for now, I wrote down everything that I was told just in case I forgot or had missed something out.

She said that I was brave, but I replied that I felt nothing of the sort, I was terrified! I had composed myself enough to break this down in my head and work through what she had to tell me a little at a time.

Faye was with me in the kitchen, but she sat quietly as she waited for me to be able to give her the facts. She knew that her uncle had passed away, and she was old enough to understand everything but waited for me to finish on the phone. I could not accept it myself let alone explain it to my 12-year-old daughter.

The consultant's name was Fiona, and she explained that Darren had collapsed on his way to work and banged his head on the concrete. A passing motorist had been a witness to this and stopped to assist and called an ambulance. Darren had his new Guide Dog Lex with him, and consequently Lex also went in the ambulance. The paramedics had revived Darren when his heart had stopped and brought him back around. On arrival at the hospital, he was described as 'extremely grey in colour' and 'breathless'. He was complaining of pains in his leg, chest and head. She went on to say that they worked on him for a long time but that he had slipped into unconsciousness. His heart arrested, and he passed away.

My brother passed away on Friday, 26 August 2005, at 9.50 am. The exact same time I asked Meredith the time, in Germany it was 10.50 am, and my asking was not a coincidence. I knew.

How do I explain that I felt him go? I just knew that I did and that feeling will last until my day that I join him.

When the conversation ended with the consultant, I knew that I had to pass on the terrible news to immediate family. I had to write a list in order of priority.

I rang my friend who was on her way over as I was supposed to be manicuring her nails! I told her what had happened, and she insisted on coming anyway because she wanted to make sure I had someone with me and Faye while we waited for Jack.

Oh my God…I had to get a hold of Jack!

She rang the welfare office to try and tell them that I needed Jack home, but the Welfare Officer did not care who she was married to (her husband was a Captain in their Battalion Welfare Office and it was not the same Regiment as us), he said that if he did not hear it from me that he would not pass on the message.

As requested, I rang the Welfare Office myself to inform them that my brother had just passed away this morning, and could he PLEASE inform my husband at the earliest bloody convenience. And that I needed him home as soon as possible. It was Friday afternoon, and I knew that Jack was on a mandatory Regimental run which meant that he would be passing the door of the Welfare Office, a few times as the camp was not that big!

I expected Jack to appear at any time to relieve my friend who stayed with me and Faye even though I was preoccupied making phone calls to people in order of what I considered priority.

I called my dad first, even though we had not spoken for months again, things like that would be put aside, it did not matter right this minute how long it had been or what had been said before. On answering the phone, my dad clearly already knew, and his voice was low and in shock. He said that he had been informed by the person who was stood by Darren's side as he slipped away. It was Darren's boss. He had been the only person that the hospital could reach by phone, and he was there with Darren until the end.

Next, I rang my mum. Darren and Mum had not spoken for eleven years before he passed. He hated the things Mum had said about Maggie in previous years, and he had never forgiven her for our childhood and the way she was with us. He just could not let go and never forgave.

I informed Mum of where Darren was currently located, and I knew she would go straight to the hospital to say her goodbyes and see her son for the last time. I do not care what anyone thinks or says because I know that this broke my mum, how could it not?

Then I called Aunt Karen and Uncle Alex. I also called Anne as she had met Darren on a couple of occasions. This phone call was the one too many, the straw that broke the camel's back. I stood at the front of the house and broke down before she had even answered the phone. I tried so hard to say the words, but my mouth was failing me. After several minutes of inconsolable crying, I managed to say, "Darren has died."

Silence.

She cried with me. I felt my heart break over and over with each phone call I had made. I could not believe that these words were coming out of my mouth and that it was all too real. It was happening to me. My family had lost the youngest member, and it would never be fixed.

Jack finally came through the door after the phone call to Anne had finished. My lovely friend Laura who had stayed made a silent exit and left us in a heap in the kitchen. Jack said nothing, our eyes met, and I could see the pain in his face. He did not need to say anything, I wanted to not talk. I just wanted the day to end and that I would wake up from the nightmare I was having.

The day ended mostly in silence, and the shock gripped our very souls. I remember drinking tea as advised by another friend that turned up to help and support in any way that she could, but I just wanted to be alone.

I wanted to vomit.

I wanted to go to sleep and not wake up.

The tea that was plied down my neck came back up as I had not eaten anything all day, and it was clearly an overload of something that was not meant to be put in on an empty stomach. Pain was all I felt. My head was pounding with a piercing migraine. I had flashing lights and ringing in my ears that was my constantly racing heart. My shoulders ached as if I had a concrete pillar resting on them.

I had experienced heartache before, Paddy, Whiskey, Dad leaving, Nan and Granddad passing way, but this heartache was exceeding the pain by a thousand times. It pierced right through the heart and soul of everything that defined me. The only reason I slept was through sheer exhaustion, and from all the crying and the stabbing pain in my chest.

I called Meredith the next morning to say that I would not be in work, I had no idea how long for and told her the reason why, she replied, "Oh you are joking?" My brother's death was not something that I would be joking about. This had happened! It was real and it would take time to recover.

I ended up going back to work on the following Tuesday. Meredith called and suggested that doing everyday normal things would benefit me in the long run. What she probably meant was that she wanted her house cleaned and I should carry on as normal.

On Saturday, 27 August, Jack and I set off for Northampton. We had dropped Faye and Lara off at a friend's and stopped at the NAAFI to pick up fuel coupons for the drive over. I sat and waited in the car unaware that a friend I had known since we first got married was watching the tears flowing out of my broken body. I was completely smashed to pieces, I felt like my whole being was as fragile as rice paper and if anyone touched me or talked to me, I would disintegrate. I was encased in the middle of it, unable to care about anything other than getting to England and seeing my brother for myself. I had to see Darren for my own closure. I had to know it was really him and not some case of mistaken identity.

Jack and I hardly spoke on the long drive. In Holland, there are advertisement boards every few hundred yards, and on each one was the same picture of doctors and nurses holding defibrillators in their hands. The song by Coldplay *Fix You* came on the radio and was instantly switched off by Jack. He wanted to avoid the mental picture that came with the billboards that were already screaming at me, "YOUR BROTHER IS DEAD! But this is how we tried to fix him."

Passing through the Dartford tunnel was a painful reminder of the time I helped Darren move back down to Kent from Loughborough College. We had driven over the crossing with U2 *With or Without You* blasting out of the little car speakers. I had my lovely cherry red Escort at the time. It was my favourite car. I had always liked every shape of Escort that ever came out since I was fourteen years old and I swore that one day I would have one, no matter how long it took to get one! Every time he was in my car, he would play with the sound system and say that I my speakers were not equal at the back, and he did this in every single car! I just let him get on with it, but we always had a total laugh and I really wished we lived in the same town. I worshipped him and his humour and positivity; in every bad situation, he would still crack jokes.

It was six hours drive on the Germany to Calais side, and then we drove through the night up to Northampton where I had arranged to meet Darren's boss Mervin who was at his side when he slipped away. He had signed for the possessions that my brother had on him at the time. His wallet, his keys and his mobile phone. Plus, there was a walking cane. I still have these, all except for his mobile. I do not recall whom I had to give that to, but I think it was my dad.

Mervin met us in a layby on the outskirts of Northampton at around 2 am, bless him I felt awful, but he said that he did not mind, and we had no other way of getting the keys unless we waited until the following morning. But he was more than willing to show us where Darren had bought his little house five months earlier.

It was an awful feeling as we pulled up outside the little red brick house. I so desperately wanted to feel close to Darren in any way that I could until I could accept that he had really gone, and he was no longer with us.

I do not think any of us wanted to enter, but Mervin passed me the envelope that contained Darren's possessions. I turned the key, opened the door and envisaged Darren closing it the previous morning. As we entered one by one slowly, we took note of how silent it was. As I entered the little kitchen to my left, it was like Darren was still there! He had fed Lex, washed the bowls and placed them on the dish drainer. He had eaten coco puffs for breakfast before setting off to work. He left the empty box on the side ready to take out to his recycling bin on his return no doubt.

Mervin stayed with us for a couple of hours, as I wanted to know everything that he knew. He was the last person to see my brother alive, and every little detail mattered to me. I asked whether Darren suffered. Mervin said that it just looked like he was sleeping, then he arrested, and slipped into a coma, but eventually he passed away. I could see that he was broken by this event, and again I felt bad for asking him for his account of what he knew at the end, because he was clearly upset with my brother's loss too. He was an absolute gem of a man for the part that he had played in helping me come to terms with it, and I will be forever in his debt.

Early the next morning (we had been up all night), Mervin drove us to the spot where Darren had collapsed, it was less than two hundred yards from where he worked, but he never made it. It was a wide path, and quite an open area with the main road next to a grassy area alongside a long hedgerow. Quite a pretty place, and it would have been an enjoyable walk to work when the sun was shining. But I imagine on winter mornings, it would have been quite exposed to the cold winds. Darren enjoyed his walks to work as it made him feel that he was doing his bit to keep fit.

When we got back to Darren's house, I text my friend who was looking after Faye and Lara dog to make sure everything was okay. Even though it was a Saturday, I called the hospital to arrange to see my brother before things were moved along to find out the cause of death. I could not bear the thought of seeing him after he had been explored, it was arranged that Jack and I could see him on Tuesday morning at 11 am.

We set about organising as much as we could over the weekend, and as difficult as it proved to be, we had to find information for bills that may need paying and start putting Darren's affairs in order, if they were not already. We had to drive back to Germany on Tuesday. I missed Faye, and I hated that she could not be there but selfishly, I wanted her to remember Darren exactly how he was at Christmas. That way, he would always be helping her to open her TV. Not see her Uncle the way that we were about to see him for the last time.

We felt like we were totally invading his privacy, but I could not leave everything for my dad to sort out. He was just as broken as I was. I went through some paperwork and found something that absolutely crushed me. It was Darren's typed out last will and testament, along with some memoires that he had typed out over a few months with breaks in between. He had typed out how he felt every so often, I guess it had been an attempt to clear his head and sort out his thoughts.

Chapter 12

Breathe. Just Remember to Breathe

Heartbroken. I could not begin to describe how I was feeling. I knew that I would never recover fully. I had lost my best friend. The wind beneath my wings was gone. The wind in my sails was no longer blowing. I had no idea how on earth I could carry on without him. I wanted the moon and stars to stop shining, as I could no longer look up at them with appreciation. I wanted to die with him so that I did not have to endure this eternal relentless pain. It was overwhelming, and it consumed every cell and my thoughts turned to how I could end it just to be with him. The main thing that stopped me was my daughter, I could not do that to her! Darren would have never forgiven me. It brings tears to my eyes writing this as it is twelve years and a few days (September 2017, I have come away on holiday to Mallorca to write this part of my book) since he passed. (Also edited January 2021, it will be sixteen years this year. I still cried like it was yesterday) But the pain of his loss never leaves, and the heart still aches when I think about him. I talk and think about him every day to this day. He lives through me and I will honour him on his imaginary pedestal until the day I go to meet him.

I collect every feather that floats in front of me just to say "I know that was you and thank you I miss and love you too".

Darren's last wishes, or I should really call it what it is, it was a suicide note, and he wanted to die. This was written before he obtained his guide dog Lex, the previous Guide Dog Russell was retired and Darren had to wait a considerable time for Lex, which also hampered his ability to get out and about as much as he wanted to. Lex gave him freedom, albeit for a short time.

This document was the one thing I found that showed me just how unhappy he had been.

It reads in his own words:

Dear Reader,

I think I am pretty much of sound mind as I write this. It is not the first one I have written, and I have thought so many times about what I would write when the time came. I am filled with so much despair and really cannot see any other course of action under the circumstances.

The story is a long one and not particularly pleasant. I hate my life and have done for the last three years or so. I cannot see things improving, although everyone keeps telling me that it will. I have just had a short relationship. The first since my marriage break up, and that showed me I could be happy. But as usual the bubble has burst and so now, I have nothing.

No one is to blame for this, my confidence in myself and my belief in human nature is at rock bottom, and I will just be scared to look for happiness in the future, and that is what I want the most.

I would like the following people informed in order of priority:

*1. Beth on 017******** I would like to think that Beth would have Russell (the guide dog) for me and make sure he is okay. He is really my only concern.*

*2. My sister Elise on 017*** ****** I would like her to have everything in my house which does not have to be sold to clear my debts. I want her to know I am sorry for quitting, but I really do not know what else to do. I love her, Jack and Faye dearly and I hope this does not hit them too hard.*

*3. My dad on 020***********

*4. Suzanne on 013******** I really thought we could have some sort of future together and that I might have been able to make her and Sophie happy, it certainly would have given me a purpose and I was happy for the short time that I knew them. I do not understand why she made the decision she did, but I have no control over it.*

*5. My solicitor Jeremy on ******** he will no doubt inform my ex-wife.*

*6. Claire and Damon on ********

*7. Jessica on ********

*8. Mark on ********

9. Anyone else in my personal planner that needs to know.

So that is it really, everything is in order. I need to figure out how to make sure Russell is not left on his own for too long. I am calmer now and thinking straight and I am not even sure if I will go through it this, but at least this is written ready in case I do. I do not wish for my ex-wife Maggie to have anything from the house at all.

That is all, thanks for your help.
Darren.

Finding this absolutely destroyed my will to live.

Rewriting this word for word, as he wrote it has just destroyed me again, and always will. The knowledge of how deeply low he felt is prevalent in me, but I use this knowledge now to stay strong. Because he would be furious with me for following his path of despair. I genuinely believe that sometimes you should be careful what you wish for. Darren did not commit suicide. Something took his life. Something that no one in the family could have prepared themselves for. It was a hereditary, tragic accident that happened to coincide with the fact that he no longer wanted to be on the planet because he was feeling so alone. He had described to me on many occasions that "you know that Jack is coming home at some point". Jack may have been coming home, but Jack never really came home, his mind was always somewhere else, whether it be his work or on his laptop, but I never discussed this with Darren as it would have been futile.

I had tried to reassure him that before he could meet someone else, he must recover fully from the breakup and divorce. I justified that I was alone a lot of the time due to Jack always being away with his army commitments. But Darren was right, it was a different set of circumstances, and yes, I did know that my husband would be home eventually. That did not mean that I was happy though I kept it to myself.

Jack and I stayed at Darren's house and even slept in his bed as it was that option or the couch, of which there was only one because Darren's living room could only accommodate a three-seater. I had found a porn magazine beside the bed and got rid of it before anyone found it. My dad would be clearing the house and I did not want him seeing it, so I disposed it off. But I did have a fleeting thought, and silently imagined myself talking to Darren and saying, "But what did you use? A bloody magnifying glass with your good eye? One eyed Willy with five percent vision in your good eye!"

Darren only had five percent vision in his left eye at the time of his passing, so I just use the humour that he and I shared about his being blind. Even though it had always bothered me more than him! He just got on with it and accepted it. But to this day, I remember the way we turned the situation around and I let him crack the jokes about his lack of sight, so that I did not offend him, he could insult himself all he wanted! But I was damned if I was going to chance it for fear of retribution! He was venomous if you crossed him and absolutely did not suffer fools gladly, he would shoot anyone down if he thought he was right. I will be honest he could be hard work at times, but you always knew where you stood with him. Bullshit was intolerable in his vocabulary and he simply would not accept it as a part of his life. I respected him for that but in recent years I am aware that we are similar in personality, I am just a little bit more tactful until I have had enough. Now I am just as outspoken. I was not put on this planet to fit into anyone else's world and I do not expect anyone to fit into mine.

On the Tuesday morning, we drove to the hospital. I was completely numb but knew that I had to see Darren before I let him go. For me, it was not an option to never see him again, I had to have closure. My dad said, "I don't know how you could have done it." But I am not my dad, and I had to, or I would not have lived with myself. Jack also wanted to say goodbye, although he had the option of not going in the Chapel of Rest if he chose not to.

We were instructed to go to the A and E department, where we were then advised to take a seat and that someone would be along as soon as possible. This was something that I did not want my daughter seeing. I felt terrible about not allowing her to be there, but I was not coping. And it was taking every ounce of my strength I had left to stay on my feet. I should have given her the option to go with us, but I did not want her to be witness to the way I would react. Selfish of me, but I cannot change it now, it is too late. I made my decision and I had stuck to it for good reason. There was also the other side of it, that the cost to travel over would have increased because we would have had to take Lara dog too, and Jack was always going on about money as it was! I did not want that bullshit to deal with, so he is just as much to blame for her not being able to go as I am. I focused on what was about to happen, but I could feel the bile rising in my stomach. This became apparent on my face and the comment that was spoken to me next absolutely blew me away, and not in a good way!

We were sitting in the packed waiting room for what seemed like an eternity. I did not actually care what anyone would think if I burst into tears as they had no idea what I was going through, or indeed, what I was about to do. I know that I appear to be selfish and possessive of my brother in my description, but I know that no one loved him like I did, and he was 'my' brother. People were staring around the room, but not specifically at me and Jack.

Tears filled my eyes. I had no control over my tear ducts, they were leaking and there was nothing that I could do about it. Under the circumstances, I think

132

anyone would understand. Instead of putting his arms around me and consoling me in a way that a loving husband should, Jack firmly blurted out at me, "DO NOT CRY!" I tried to force back the tears, but it was too late because my heart and stomach were having an emergency meeting in my throat at this point, to stop crying was virtually impossible.

I stared at the wall. I tried so hard to compose myself and think of something bland. But the urge to let the tears flow was overwhelmingly intense, and even the reinforcements on the wall of the dam that I had built around myself were crumbling, I was breaking. The water was waiting in the wings for the moment to release. Again, Jack said, "This is not the place to cry. Do not cry." The look on his face meant that if I let it go, he would be embarrassed and mortified. I lost count of how many times he had repeated it because I had zoned out and I was no longer in the room. I was a person who sat silently working through the seconds of the ticking clock on the wall, it ticked so loud for the longest time that it may as well have been right next to my eardrum. I wanted to shout at Jack and tell him to leave me the fuck alone! I could not help that my heart was broken, and I no longer cared what he thought. But I remained as calm as I could by repeating Anne's words that I had used since the phone call to deliver the news, she said, "Remember to breathe."

It had slapped me like a wet fish around my face! In that split second of his first dictation, and the statements that followed as he was trying to stop what should flow naturally. Jack and I would never be the same people, let alone as a couple. I would never forgive this lack of understanding and selfish inconsideration. Please do not judge me for feeling this way about him, as I know the man like no other can ever do. I hated the fact he thought that he could control me at a time like this when I needed him to understand the most. I had also felt that there was an element of resentment because I loved my brother unconditionally, blood is thicker than water in this scenario, and Jack was the water in this situation. Eventually, it would come to pass, that water had started to trickle away gradually, whereas my blood would always remain even in death. I would have died if it meant saving my brother. That caused a slight wedge between Jack and me, but it was never discussed. Just like most things between us, it was always brushed under the carpet. It was not his military mindset, but the man that he is. He does not like the truth said out loud. I like to say everything and get the whole sentence out to solve the issue, but he always stopped me mid flow saying, "Okay! I got it!" I always felt over the years that this would become like a time bomb inside me. I store things unsaid, and it eventually explodes. After a certain amount of time, it festers. It is like poison running through your veins. Hence, the reason for writing this book and the planned follow-on book, I need to release the poison to cleanse myself. Until then, the poison in the pot drains away slowly, in the form of words. And I WILL have my say.

We were finally called by a man in white cotton trousers and top. I hastily got up and walked towards him as he guided us out of the main door, which thankfully, was the nearest as I could not even speak at this point. I had to walk and let some of the bucket spill out, just enough to clear the airway so that I could breathe and ask the questions I needed to ask.

We walked around the back of the hospital for about five minutes to the Mortuary. I thought I was prepared mentally enough to cope with this, I just hoped my knees would hold me upright. We were advised of certain things before entering (all these things that were said escape me, because I focused on my breathing). Jack and I walked through the door to where my brother lay.

His hands were crossed on his chest, and he looked like he was asleep. He looked thinner than the last time I had seen him; he was gaunt. I presumed he had not been eating before he passed and was trying to lose weight. He was always trying to maintain a healthy weight. We both had lifelong struggles with our weight; mine seem so trivial now.

We sat for a while. I gently brushed my hand over Darren's face just to know that I had for the last time seen him and said goodbye. He was ice cold for obvious reasons as it had been three days since his passing.

This is extremely difficult to write as you can imagine and it is a pinnacle time of my life where everything changed, and not always for the better.

I know that I was not there to support Faye or Jack, but I could only breathe for myself. We were all in a state of shock, and the acceptance part of grieving was a millennium away as far as I was concerned. I had to just get through each second of every minute. My heart was broken into an unrepairable galaxy of stars that would never shine at full capacity again.

I did what I had to do for my own closure, told him that I loved him and left the room. Jack remained, and at last, I was able to release the tears without being told not to. I was not alone as the people in the Chapel were there, a man and a woman, but I was not ashamed of my tears falling I am sure it's a daily occurrence for them and quite the normal thing. And I no longer cared. I needed to shed them, as the dam could no longer hold back the torrent. I sat with my head in my lap and released.

Jack sat with Darren for a further few minutes on his own, making his peace, I guess. Darren had always tolerated Jack and always said if we were to ever split up, it that it would be because of the arguments over money. But that was not the case, as I will get to when the time comes in the story. Darren had also tolerated the way Jack controlled me in his discreet way that was not always evident. But I knew how he felt, he had just never said anything to Jack because he could not be bothered with the fallout that would ensue.

We left the hospital in silence, nothing needed to be discussed at this point, we both just wanted to be silent. Thoughts turned to where do we start? What do we have to do now? How will we arrange a funeral from Germany? I knew that I was in no way ready to think about it, and probably not in a fit state mentally to do this. I was the one who kept Darren in touch with the family and bothered with calling to make sure he was all right. I wanted him to live with us after his divorce, but he refused and wanted his own house and independence, which I accepted but I was gravely concerned about the things he was thinking and talking about. Like the fact he did not want to be alive without Maggie, and that he did not know how to carry on and start again. He mentioned topping himself, and then grasped the fact that he had upset me by even joking about such an act, and so he turned it on its head, made another wise crack and said, "I would probably fuck that up too!"

My dad arrived at Darren's house with the lady friend of one of Delores's sons. I had never met her before, but she presumed to tell me that my dad was a broken man. Well, she would probably know as she got to see him a lot more than I did. Over the years, the ravine between my dad and his two biological kids grew monumentally. Any attempt to build a bridge has been shaken or set fire to by the troll underneath it. Said troll had cut her foot and was not able to make the journey to my brother's house which I can say I was pleased about. Making pleasantries and trying to pacify a childish mind were not on my list of high priorities and had any of her verbal drivel exited her mouth, I just would not have held back. Her bullshit was the last thing that was needed at this present time. I would not have been responsible for my reaction and I would not have cared if all the years of frustration came out in one sentence, because this was one specific occasion that was not about her.

Dad remained at the house for less than a couple of hours, he had literally come to pick up the keys so that he could sort out the house clearance and hand it back to the mortgage company. He knew that we had to go back to Germany as our life was there, and Faye and Lara were being looked after by a friend, but he also knew we would do what we could as far as being so far away would allow.

Jack called a popular menswear shop that Darren had an account with. They were exceptionally helpful and understanding and wiped the bill clean as it was not an exceptionally big amount owed. We were grateful for their kindness though.

I felt like I was ransacking Darren's house for loot, but I was doing as per his instructions. We still owned the car that my brother had sat in and I felt he was loading himself in to come to Germany with us. I also knew that whatever I did not take with me, Dad would have to sell or give to charity, and my brother's possessions meant more to me than a charity shop. I still have his acoustic guitar and a hand drawn picture along with other items I will never let go out of my sight.

Darren had been to Cornwall recently with a friend and I knew that he had brought Faye a teddy, and a keyring for me so I made it a mission to find these items. I found them in a box in his bedroom, I had to make sure that Faye got the last present that her uncle had purchased for her.

I also found his wedding ring and put it on my necklace for safekeeping. I would decide what to do with it later. His laptop was in the living room and we decided we would take that as on his list of wishes he suggested that everything went to me. I gave little away, but I did give Neil a silver bracelet as something to remember Darren by. He hurriedly arranged for the photographer who took the photos at the Christening to mount the best ones of Darren as a gift for me. We dropped by on our way back down the M1 to pick up the beautiful silver frame and verse that Neil had written in honour of his friend. The photos of Darren were taken four days before he passed. He was smiling, and he looked so handsome. It broke me when I saw them.

Dad and I agreed that we both felt terrible, we felt like we were dissecting his life and it tortured both of us. But at the same time, we were following his wishes.

Jack and I set off back to Germany, and Dad left with the keys to Darren's house and the knowledge of what was to follow. We parted company with such heavy hearts, and a feeling of utter despair and complete loss.

The loss of a precious life, a life of the one person that kept our father daughter relationship gelled together, who knows what would happen now. At this time of departing, it was not important, but I knew that the ravine would deepen.

For the next three weeks, we had to wait for the call from the Coroner with the official cause of death. It felt as if I could hear every tick of the clock for the entire three weeks. Knowing that my beloved brother was being explored to find out the cause of death was like a stab in my brain every time I thought about it. It was pure torture, but obviously it had to be done or we would never know the cause. I eventually could wait no longer and made the call, and called, and called! I finally got a very direct and forthright answer from a very frosty man on the other end of the phone like I had pissed on his lawn! Quite rude and not as helpful as I was thinking he could have been, in fact I will say that he was bloody rude! Someone reminded me afterwards. "He was only doing his job and they detach themselves."

"Yes, but not with that level of bad manners!"

It was a Pulmonary Embolism. A blood clot blocked his lungs. There was nothing that could have been done because it was already too late once he had reached the hospital. I called the consultant who had initially informed me of Darren's passing, and she said that was what they had presumed it more than likely was. I wanted to yell at her and ask why they had done nothing if that was what they had thought at the time. But yelling at anyone would not bring my brother back.

My dad arranged Darren's funeral, it was booked for early September in Northampton and the Crematorium's Church was packed! Guests were spilling out of the doors at both ends. Darren thought he had no one in the world. He thought he was alone, but all of them were extremely shocked that he had passed so suddenly, and devastated cries echoed around the walls. His untimely passing rocked everyone's boat. No one could believe that he had been taken so young; it was such a tragic loss on every level.

Darren's boss insisted on funding the food for the celebration of Darren's life at a lovely pub when the funeral was over. I could only help from Germany as much as the distance would allow. I could by contacting the list of names in

Darren's mobile that I had brought with me. Most of those I spoke to had accepted the invitation.

I had requested Anne to attend because I felt that Jack and I would need a close friend, she had adored Darren and expressed a wish to pay her last respects. We picked up Mum after driving from Luton airport and changing our clothes at her house. We had been up since 3 am and Josh (Jack's friend) had taken us to the airport on the Germany side. I had not allowed Faye to go purely because I did not want her to see me in the emotionally broken state that I was trying to shield her from. Money was tight too from the journey previously, and this was pointed out by Jack. Not letting her attend is a decision she resents but I felt that I was doing the right thing at the time. Now of course I should have let her say goodbye, but I desperately wanted her to remember the man that used to throw her over his shoulder and act like a child himself when they were together.

Friends of Darren's approached me while we were outside waiting for my brother to arrive on his final car journey. I had never met most of them, but I had spoken to some after calling with the invitation that nobody ever expects or wants to receive.

Comments of how alike we were; "oh my word, there is no mistaking you are his sister" being the most common one. I found solace in this observation; it meant that I could look in the mirror and still see him.

Darren's friends got up and read beautiful eulogies. I recall the words "miss me but let me go" and "I will be waiting in the next room".

I remember a lady wailing uncontrollably, she was a lady that Darren had been seeing and had grown fond of. But he said that although he really liked her, he was not capable of fighting the demons that she was harbouring as well as the ones he was battling daily. He may well have found love, but now speaking from my own experience, it must be the right time. If the pieces do not all match in the beginning, then there is not much room for compromise. That comes later when you discover for yourself that there is no perfect person, there is only an element of compromise to find the right person…if you ever find them at all. He had been severely hurt and damaged and he wanted the next relationship to be the right fit.

We had visited a theme park in Germany a few weeks before our world bottomed out. Faye had chosen a soft toy that resembled one of the white tigers in the park and this was to be a gift from Faye for Darren on our planned trip in September to pick up the sporty new car. He was a soppy sod when it came to his niece. I asked the people at the Crematorium if that little teddy could go with him on behalf of Faye when the curtains closed. It had been placed on top of Darren's coffin as I had requested, like a little guardian that would travel with him to their onwards destination. I have never felt the immense pain of that type of closure before.

As the curtain closed around the coffin, the pain engulfed my heart and soul! My body weight suddenly felt like concrete was setting from my legs upwards. The words "he is gone" rang in my ears. "He is gone, and you will never see him again."

I sobbed uncontrollably without any shame into Jack's shoulder. I could not see or hear anyone or anything; I just felt the pain in my chest. My heart was heavy like a boulder the size of Arizona, it made me feel like I had no control over my body, and that Jack could have picked me up, to carried me outside and I would not have noticed. I just wanted this moment to be the one time that I was permitted to cry and grieve and let it happen without being told not to cry because this was not the time or the place. In these next few moments, I wanted to just let the tears flow freely for a lost brother who should never have been taken so young. I was lost, and that was where I wanted to be.

The pain in my chest was too much to bear, I think I lost my balance, but Anne and Jack were holding me up. Mum was the other side of Anne and was more concerned about me than anyone else bless her even though she was hurting too!

Darren had fallen out with Mum eleven years previously in an argument over Maggie. She had always reminded Mum of Delores and it had caused such bad feeling, because Darren defended his woman fiercely and would have nothing said against her. Even though it came to pass that Mum was proved correct in that Maggie cheated several times, and openly confessed that she liked the men and flirting was just the way she was. But Mum and Darren never spoke again, and I cannot imagine how she felt losing her only son and not having spoken for so long.

The funeral was tough and by far the worst day of my adult life. But it was a beautiful service and a packed audience wishing to say goodbye and pay respects. Darren was played out with *Against all Odds*, it was a song that took me a few years to be able to listen to because it was a reminder of the last time that I said goodbye to my brother.

The funeral reconnected me with my cousin Mark who I had not seen or heard from for fifteen years. I was chatting to him and gave him my number with a promise that if he failed to stay in touch with me that I would never forgive him, hence we are still in touch to this day and although we have never lived in each other's pockets it is good to know he is there and would drop everything if I was in town and suggested meeting up.

The funeral also brought about the reunion of my dad and Delores in the same air space as my entire family! It was clear that she did not want to be there and was uncomfortable with the whole situation, as you would expect. I mean my mother and the wicked woman that stole my dad away! I tried to speak to everyone and touch base with as many of Darren's friends and colleagues as possible to thank them all for coming and being supportive. My dad was not up to mingling, and by this stage, I felt that he had done enough. He also had further emotional trauma to face with the handover of Darren's house, because the Building Society (a national company which coincidentally no longer exists) were being a total hindrance and not helping under the circumstances.

Some of my family were a little disappointed that my dad failed to make any effort to speak, but there were two reasons for this as I tried to justify that 1. It was not the time or the place to rekindle old friendships and 2. He was with Delores…enough said. Dad was a broken man.

I was blown away by the lovely comments that were being spoken about my brother, fond memories and tales of times that they laughed with him, and of his stubbornness! It was such a warming experience to hear that people respected him even though sometimes he could be a prickly pear! But you always knew where you stood with him. I think that the people that really knew him also knew when it was best to leave him be if he was in a mood. But if you wanted an honest opinion, he was your man! And if he was your friend, he was a friend for life with no holds barred.

Mervin presented me with a memory book that displayed a photo of Darren on the front with a bottle of wine placed directly in front of him. It was full of the emails and cards from the company's clients who had learned of his death. They all sent condolences to Darren's family, stating that it was a tragic loss of such a wonderful man, and that they would miss his joviality and bubbly character on the other end of the phone.

He was not a man that you could ever forget in a hurry. There are those of us who will never get over him and would not want to, therefore will never forget and celebrate his life to this day.

Chapter 13

The Brick Wall

On arrival back in Germany, Jack and I drove straight to pick our girls up. We had a massive argument over money in the car because I wanted to give my friend some Euros towards the feeding of Lara dog and our daughter. We sat in the car around the corner from my friend's house and tried to calm ourselves down so that she would not see we had argued. Jack stayed in the car.

I could not calm that quickly and it was clear on my face that I was upset about something other than my Brother's funeral. She questioned me a little, but I was unable to share because I was not actually sure what had just happened. I was finding Jack very unsupportive in his comprehension of the pain I was in. He had lost grandparents that we were both really close to and no offence, but they had all lived full lives and died at old ages. I know others have lost people, but all I was asking was that I be allowed to deal with my grief in my way, and not be advised by anyone on how they thought I should be dealing with it. It was my experience to cope with, in my own time and I could not predict how long it would take me to pull myself together. And quite frankly, I did not want to, just yet!

I could not be responsible for how Jack felt; they were his feelings not mine and he had to sort himself out! For me right now, it took everything I had just to breathe. And in this case make sure that Faye and our Lara were cared for and that Faye did not suffer as a result of my grief. If Jack were in the house, I needed him to kind of be there for his daughter for once so that I could let my mind run free with what I had to process. I was not asking for much, you know just the normal things a parent should be doing for their only child.

The day after the funeral and the previous argument in the car, it all came to a head. Darren had always called Jack Mister Atmospheric and now, there had been an unnecessary atmosphere in the house that had been building like a pressure cooker. We were unpacking our funeral outfits in the bedroom and the conversation escalated from heated to spiteful, I was not in the mood for bullshit and today was not the day to piss me off! He spat the words at me; "you are not there for me".

I was totally shocked! I had no words! I felt numb to my core already without all this carry on. I knew that he could be childish and selfish but bloody hell!

How I was supposed to be there for him when he was a fully grown adult is beyond me, I had trouble peeling myself out of bed in the morning and wanted to die to be with Darren to take the pain away! But I stuck with it. The only person I could be there for was Faye because she was old enough to understand the full impact this event would have on us because she was already witnessing it. She was old enough to understand that it would take a long time for the family unit to recover, and she only came to me when we were alone, when Jack was at work.

Unbeknownst to us, Faye was going through her own personal living hell at school and being consistently bullied by one extremely nasty piece of work. And as it transpired, a group of kids. The severity of this bullying became clear a few years later. She did not feel that she could burden me with her problems, and I had shut myself off from everything. I just could not deal with everyday life things as well as I would normally be able to, surely anyone can understand this. I just needed enough time to work through the process although I aimed to be as strong as I could be at the relevant times.

In temper, Jack had kicked the bottom of the bed leg and put a black scuffmark on it from his boot! His next party trick was to pull down the biggest army bag that he owned and start throwing his clothes in it. I refused to sit back and take this today, so I shouted back at his repetitive statement about moving into camp that I had heard a million times. "So pack your fucking bag, and if you threaten me with moving into camp again, I will pack it for you!"

After every heated argument in nearly every location we had lived, I heard it so many times and today was not the day to be threatening me. It was always his resolution to the end, and I was sick of hearing "right, fuck it. I am moving into camp!" It had been said once too often, and despite living in Germany, I would make sure that Faye and I would be okay no matter what. *Bollocks to him*, I thought to myself, what a selfish thing to do and I would never forgive him. But I no longer wanted to live under the threat of him packing his bags.

He went away for two weeks after this outburst as the Regiment went training for the upcoming operational tour to Iraq. It was a monumental relief not to have to deal with him in the house, I could think a little clearer and deal with things in my own way without the added pressure of whether I was saying or doing something wrong in his eyes, because I really did not give a shit right now.

While Jack was away, I drove over to the UK with Sarah for company to pick up the new car. I also made a long detour to a service station further up north from Eastbourne where I had collected the car, to meet Anne who had, at my request, picked up Darren's ashes and brought him to meet me in the car park so that I could take him back to Germany, I wanted him with me. I strapped his Urn which was enclosed in a cardboard box into the back seat and drove back with him in the new car.

Darren would get to ride in my car after all, and he would have been extremely proud.

Shelley and her husband were staying at my house with Faye and Lara to look after my girls while I was gone for the two days and bless her, she had cooked me a casserole for when I arrived back. It was lovely and well needed after I had dropped Sarah back at her house; she had been a complete diamond on the journey to and from UK knowing what my mental state was like. I was doing okay, but it did not take much for the floodgates to open. She is still a good friend and like Shelley, she was always there when needed. I had a good support network of friends and they were my family. Shelley, Sarah and Anne were Faye's godparents, and they all came through for us.

I felt I could not let go of the tears when Jack was around, I tried not to let my eyes leak in front of Faye but sometimes it could not be helped as it becomes too exhausting to remain strong. I believe if you need to cry you should let the emotion out instead of bottling it. But I did bottle it more than I was aware. Jack had a way of knowing I had been crying even if it was hours before or in the shower trying to disguise my grief that was flowing out at every opportunity. So, I tried harder to save all the emotions knowing that he was deploying to Iraq soon when I would have a different set of emotions to deal with…fear.

Before he deployed, he suggested that he would be much happier if sought some counselling. I was nose diving quickly and not coping with daily life, everything was an effort to achieve and the worst one was getting out of bed. Depression was setting in, but I had never experienced it before and did not know how bad it was getting. All I knew was that I was in severe emotional pain, and my heart ached every second of every day to the point that I did not want to wake up in the mornings and was disappointed when I did for months after the funeral.

I went to the medical centre and broke down in floods of tears before doctor had even opened his mouth. He was extremely patient with me and as I could not bring myself to say the words through the uncontrollable tears, he handed me a pen and notepad. "I recently lost my brother, DVT" was all I could write.

"You need to see a CPN." It was not a request or a question, he had told me that was what I needed. In reply, I nodded. He started typing and I managed to compose myself enough to say that my husband was leaving for the tour in Iraq in the next few days too and it was at his request that I see someone so that he would know I was not going to do anything stupid.

My first appointment was booked, and my community psychiatric nurse was called Naomi. She was a single woman who had also suffered with blood clots and ended up in the Frauen and Kinder clinic for treatment of them, so she understood what it was about.

One of the first questions she asked me in the first sitting of counselling was whether I had considered joining my brother. It was easy for me to answer that because the truth was that I had, more than once. I was in so much heartache and pain at some stages that I just could not see a way out of the trees. I used to walk Lara through the woods by the house with Laura and we discovered a bench by the river with the names of two children aged only three and five, along with their mother's name and, age I cannot remember but she was young.

The story was (as it was told to me) that she lost control of the car on the range road just up the embankment from the river, it was a dark night and the roads were wet. The car landed on its roof in the flow of the river, all three were killed. It was something I had considered, although I finally woke myself up and smelt the coffee, and it became abundantly clear that I needed help when I found myself driving at speed towards the biggest tree that I could find on the same bend that the lady had lost control. I scared myself at the notion that I did it without even considering my daughter. It was a moment of complete and utter despair. I just did not know how I was going to go on without my brother.

My dog-walking friend Laura was a complete rock; she would drive over from the other side of town and come over with her dog Haggis to tell me I needed to get out of the house. I was working but cleaning someone's married quarter is the same job as cleaning your own, you can do without even thinking and therefore I could allow myself to try and process the bubbles of thoughts in my head that kept popping and flooding my daily life.

On one of our walks and before we even got to the end of my short road, she told me that my skin looked grey and pale. And that she hated seeing me so broken. I knew that my eyes were puffy and had dark rings around them; she suggested that I had hit that brick wall. That brick wall of pain after a loved one dies. I cared not of how I looked, I would deal with my appearance when I had learnt to control my emotions, but until then, I could not stop the pain in my chest that sat with me every minute of every day.

I went to work one day, and Meredith said I should go with her out by the shed for a cigarette to calm myself down and stop crying. I had not smoked for ten years but I thought under the circumstances I could be forgiven. During the conversation, I said that I had no idea how to cope with the loss. Meredith's reply was "oh come on, you have got to snap out of it". It had been two weeks and she had never lost anyone.

Anyone who truly knows me would know what my reaction would be to that comment, but on this occasion, all I can say is that I was horrified, and it was a comment I could never forgive. I left her employment shortly after to go and work for another Colonel.

I lost interest in everything after the loss of my younger brother. I just wanted my world to swallow me whole and for the pain to go away. I stopped doing nails but left my room intact. I just did not allow myself the time to think about dismantling it in case I ever wanted to start it up again. Jack moaned that I had wasted thousands on getting qualified and not using the skill. I needed time to grieve and recover and that was a simple fact he seemed to overlook.

Darren owned a laptop which I had taken with me from his house on the weekend of his passing. That laptop was then apparently the property of Jack according to Jack! He said that it was not working and put it into a shop on the main road for repair to see if they could sort out whatever was wrong with it. But to my horror and disgust, two weeks later, he walked in the house with a brand new one claiming that "it was broken beyond repair, so I traded it in for a new one". It was not his property to trade in! I felt that he had manipulated the situation and took advantage that I probably would not even notice that it had gone. I did not give him permission to take it out of the house let alone swap it for one that only he would be using! NOT HAPPY!

I felt betrayed and totally mortified that he could be so insensitive, to my knowledge the original laptop worked when Darren was using it just before he died! Again, this was Jack using a situation and twisting it for his own advantage. The laptop was not his to do anything with, Darren had left everything in his house to me, I had that written in black and white and just because I was married to a selfish bastard, it did not automatically give him the right to 'trade in' anything! And again, this was something else to add to my list of things I would never forgive Jack Bastard for!

All the housekeeping work I had done was for future reference when we eventually moved back to the UK. Housekeeping jobs in hotels are ten to a penny and if you are good at the job, it helps! The next lady I went to work for was lovely and she gave me time and space to grieve without judgement as I still did my work. I only fell apart in my own time and whilst sat in with my counsellor who was helping tremendously. I stayed a long time with the second Colonel's wife and only changed jobs to go and work full time as a driver for the welfare office. It was good money and I thought it would be a nice change from cleaning. The job involved picking up the army wives that could not drive or needed transport to the airport so that they could leave their cars at home and not pay parking fees.

It was exhausting yet rewarding, there were some long drives to and from airports that were three hours each way, so a six hour round trip. And if you got stuck in traffic, oh my word it was a long day! I went to pick up an Officer's wife and kids at 4 am once but as it was the middle of the night, I could not hammer down the door when there was no answer, and no lights came on. I could not call the office because no one was in yet! If I woke up the German civilians with my persistent knocking on the door, there would be hell to pay!

I went home and gave up after about half an hour of knocking. It transpired that she had obtained a lift by other means and neglected to inform the welfare office. I was furious and refused to go there again and she got a dressing down from the welfare clerk who run the joint, she had been there years and zero tolerance was what she took from anyone. She had also got me the job.

I met an incredibly good friend that also started working at the same time as me, in the form of a young lady called Natalie. She was a gentle spoken woman but wow when she fired up it was fierce! She drove the big military trucks and for her size she was inspirational! I admire her strength of character to this day. I adore her and we remain friends beyond working in the welfare office. I am godmother to her gorgeous son, it is an honour, although due to my life recently taking a turn for the worse (or better whichever you look at it), I have been crap at staying in touch I am ashamed to say.

Although I still had all my nail equipment and accessories, I never really went back to doing it properly. I could not give up the money I was earning doing the housekeeping jobs and face the moans and groans that we had little money.

Faye and I carried on with life, and somehow got through the operational tour that was Iraq in 2006. Jack had left with the knowledge that I was being counselled and believing that I was strong enough to cope with this tour. My friend Shelley and so many others such as Sarah were a constant staple, we were together during this tour while our husbands were out in the sandy place, we all supported each other no matter what. The Garrison was empty except for the minority of guys who were on rear party to run the camps and keep things ticking over. There were less English cars on the roads, and the main NAAFI was quieter except for the kids running around with no fathers to tell them off, not that the mothers did not reprimand but you know what it is like kids listen more to a booming voice.

There was a common feeling when the soldiers deployed on these operational tours in massive numbers. It was as if the pilot light was lit, but the boiler was not fired up and working to its full potential. It felt like your life was on standby, and that you were waiting for the fires to be stoked and the wheels to start turning the same way that they did when the Garrison was at full capacity. I guess one could relate to this weird feeling during out third lock down 2021! Our life has been put on hold to stem the flow of the Coronavirus pandemic, and we are all waiting for our lives to return to some sort of normality (if that is ever going to be possible again).

The end goal was the day the coaches started returning with the husband's bums on the seats. They obviously did not all return at the same time, they arrived in dribs and drabs. It was never a scene of celebration like the Americans perform where they are all out with marching bands, banners and parties of celebration.

Our lot just arrived back silently, with the waiting wives and children on the main Regimental or Battalion square, but we were all focused on the days they arrived back safely. And we prayed that the number of returning men would be the same as the numbers that left.

Like for everyone else, Iraq 2006 was the worst six months of my life. It was an extremely terrifying time for all of us and the wives lived by the seat of their pants, and on raw nerves! Just as much as the soldiers doing the job out there! The news reported something happening nearly every single day, a bomb going off killing or injuring soldiers, an IED (improvised explosive device) exploding, or someone being shot. It was relentless! And, although the other tours out there were just as bad this one...it affected me because this was Jack's first tour, and it was so soon after losing Darren. I would not cope with losing him too. Even if he was capable of being a controlling, selfish dick sometimes, that did not mean that I wanted to lose him as well, especially not under those circumstances.

During these types of tours, you find yourself hearing what is on the news and radio a lot clearer. You take more notice of what is happening because it may or may not affect you directly. You inadvertently become obsessed and more acute to the news in general and your ears become sponge like just in case! And I am afraid that a little bit of paranoia had immersed my rational way of thinking. Because I was terrified! I detested feeling this way, but it was beyond my control, and the only reason that I slept was because these emotions wore me out.

I had a complete and utter meltdown in the main NAAFI after hearing an announcement on the radio that someone had been shot in Iraq. I wanted to fall to my knees, but my adrenaline kicked in and I hurriedly told Sarah that we were going to drive to camp which was five minutes away. She quickly finished paying and we left. I grabbed the first person I came across which, luckily for me was the current RSM; he told me he was unable to give a name, but that it was neither my husband nor Sarah's Josh. In fact, it was no one in our Regiment. Our thoughts drifted to the family of whoever it was that had been killed.

Relief swept over me, but this was still early in the tour and there were months still left to get through. I tried to pull myself together and not fall to pieces every time something happened. I watched the news 24/7. I could not help it. If I was in the house, the TV was on and so was the news. Faye never really sat with me in the living room but if she decided to, we would put on a film and lose ourselves in something different for a while.

My friend Laura, who was with me straight after my news of Darren, was a frequent visitor. Having learnt that she could knit after one of our lengthy chats whilst walking the dogs, I decided that I wanted to learn the basic knitting that she could do. I learnt quickly and it was good to have something to focus on other than sit staring at the TV watching for any impending doom. I also learned that I was not alone in seeing my counsellor; there were a couple of other wives

149

that were not coping. The length of time apart took its toll during any deployment, but this tour struck fear into the hearts of even the strongest. I was shocked to learn that my lovely friend Shelley was seeing a counsellor too.

One day, the day that the fateful news had broken a soldier from another Regiment had been killed, and the wife had been informed, we learned that she lived on the same army quarter estate as me. They had young children, and everyone's heart stopped beating for that wife. Even though it was impossible to know absolutely everyone on the Garrison, we were all experiencing the same fear and dread of that knock on the door to tell us that our husband would not be returning.

Six whole months, every minute of every day, that terrified fear that we buried in the back of our minds because it always happens to someone else, it never happens to you, right?

Chapter 14

The Close Call

I arrived home one afternoon to a ringing house phone; it was Shelley asking for a ride home because her car had broken down at Ikea in Bielefeld. I told her I was on my way and I would be there as quickly as possible, a friend in need and all that!

I arrived to find a red-faced, angry little fire starter that was my friend, and our mutual friend Kim who was doing her level best to calm Shelley's jets and diffuse the situation as much as she physically could. I knew that the journey home would mean the air would be blue! It would be in her humorous way because when Shelley had a bee in her bonnet, it could get extremely vocal! You just had to let her get her anger out and offer any help if you could get a word in, which was not worth the attempt until she came up for air, but it was for this very reason why she was loved so much, because of her fire and spark.

Whilst I drove and Kim sat in the back seat, we were chatting about the tour, and the guys, and trying to reassure Shelley that the car would get towed and all would be well! An impossible task because she was on one and justifiably so. Shelley's spitfire fuel would run out eventually, and then she would laugh about the whole thing, but Kim and I distracted her until that occurred. Kim asked if I had spoken to Jack, and she told me about how she had seen her husband on the news because there had been an incident!

She said, "I thought you would know about it because Gray is with Jack!" They were in the same troop at the time and worked together.

If something happens while the guys are away, the communication systems are cut to stop the rumours and any false information getting out and scaring people needlessly. This news set my panic button in motion, but Kim assured me that they were okay because this had happened a day or two previously. All I could do was wait to hear it from Jack…but my heart was in my stomach until the moment I heard from him.

It was May. The regiment had only just deployed so this 'incident' happened a couple of weeks after they got there. I finally got the call to tell me what I needed to hear. I did not want any fine details; I just wanted to hear his voice.

He said, "I have something to tell you, but I am hoping no one has told you before I had the chance, I am okay and I cannot go into detail, but I will tell you that I am okay." The knot that had been wrapped around my intestines unravelled slightly and allowed me to breathe properly!

I said that I already knew, but that I also understood why he could not tell me before. He was due back on R and R soon so I presumed that I would hear all about it if he wanted to talk about it. The news reported on incidents and bombs going off daily. My addiction to the news was like an obsession that overtook my daily life, and although I am not religious and never go to church, I prayed! And I prayed hard! I prayed to Darren to watch over Jack and bring him back safely. Losing my husband so soon after my brother would just be too much. I fell apart in floods of tears quite frequently and it must have seemed to my friends that I thought I had it worse than everyone else, but this could not be further from the truth. I was struggling in my own way to deal with it, that was all.

We all lived on our nerves and literally got through each day going about our usual business of taking the kids to school and working, but it was torture, and by far, the worst experience of my life. The two most important things in my world pulled me through this difficult time. Faye and Lara dog. Faye and I would keep our selves busy by going into the city centre with Sarah and the kids for something to eat, and most Sundays, she would cook a chicken roast so that she knew her kids had eaten a good meal at least once a week. Sarah is an amazing cook! It was on one of these days out that I told Sarah that I would one day write a book, she reminded me whilst we talked on the phone, and we can remember exactly where we sat in a specific restaurant in the Sud-ring!

Shelley would host parties such as candles or a naughty underwear shindig! With our host being so open about sex, these parties were the highlight of the months that the guys were away! She was just an amazing little woman who was nicknamed the pocket rocket because she was short and so hilarious! With a contagious laugh, and her zest for life and having fun, she made our time together as wives and good friends more bearable, it was a tonic to be around her. On one of these occasions, Shelley talked me into buying my first vibrator! Now that was money well spent! I am sorry in advance to my family members and my bosses who may read this, but we are all adults.

Even though I was more mortified that people knew what I had bought, I still went ahead. I knew that Jack would not be best pleased either, but I did not care. I received the parcel shortly after the party. It was as if the company knew that our men were away and maybe they thought that there were a lot of horny women roaming the camp! I hasten to add that those Rabbit things became a necessity when your husband is away for months on end! You learn to become good at DIY in more ways than one with a little help from a two-pronged attack! The men use their hands, so why should we not have some silicone help?

For medical reasons, and long-term pain in my abdomen which had been caused by repetitive cysts on my ovaries, I was booked in to have a hysterectomy. The date coincided with Jack returning home on R and R so that he could look after Faye. As I was being wheeled down to theatre after the pre-med tablet in the Frauen and Kinder clinic, I cried for my mum for the first time ever. A male porter was pushing the bed that I was laying on, and there was a lovely German Nun right next to me holding my hand. She wiped away my tears, and she told me in her soft, gentle voice that it will be it will all be okay. I always recall her beautiful face and her kind words at a time when I felt at my most vulnerable. She was a mature lady, with a small frame. Her eyes had glistened as she spoke those five words of reassurance to me over and over. I felt blessed that I was being accompanied by a wonderful heavenly lady who had the smile of an angel. She did not let go of my hand until the sleeping potion had taken a hold of me and my eyes closed. She was the last thing I remembered, but what a lovely way to fall asleep.

When I came to and was back in the room, I was comforted by the knowledge that the lovely Nun had been with me when I was terrified, because I knew that there would be a long recovery period afterwards. But I also knew that having this operation would be the best way to move forward from the constant pain that I had endured for so long. It also meant that I would be able to plan my tummy tuck in the future!

The operation was massive! They had to open my sunroof again because they could not go through the tunnel for whatever reasons. I caught an infection in the wound shortly after, and it leaked one night after I gently pulled my tummy back a little so that Jack could have a look because it was itchy and red raw! He started shouting at me that I was bleeding to death because all this blood was pouring out on the right-hand side.

Having asked the advice of a nurse at the medical centre on camp whether I could have a bath because I felt so unclean, I wanted to submerge myself and relieve the pressure of my healing tummy just temporarily, and she had said that it should be fine, just do not stay in the bath for too long. But of course, the wound was nowhere near healed and the water had seeped in and caused an infection. I recall the itch inside the wound was like a hell fire had been lit under my skin! It was the same itch after my caesarean section with Faye.

I wanted to subconsciously take a fork and scratch as it was so fierce, I just wanted it to stop. Another trip to the medical centre at around 11 pm secured some strong antibiotics after I refused penicillin due to being severely allergic. The nurse had run her fingers along the scar a few times from left to right to push out the water that was still festering in there, and to say that feeling was heaven is an understatement! It was a scratch I could not perform myself because of the angle, and the fact that I would have to use a mirror to be able to see it!

After that little scenario, we were having a brew in our back garden shortly before Jack and Josh (Sarah's husband) were due to go back to Iraq. Josh had arrived a week after Jack as he was home for three weeks instead of two to support me after the operation and look after his daughter, Jack made it abundantly clear that all he wanted to do now, was get back out there to be with his men. He had twelve men under his command at the time, and he felt that his place was with them fighting the bad men in a sandy country.

He resented being in Germany when his duty was out with his men.

Sarah and I listened as Jack and Josh were tactful in their conversation as to the things that went on in said sandy place. But the conversation turned to the 'incident'. Jack began by using our mobile phones to demonstrate where the two army land rovers were positioned when the improvised explosive device went off. It had been a device planted under the bridge, the wires concealed and the triggerman lay in wait in the distance for the unsuspecting military personnel in their land rovers.

I would really like to tell the full version as we were told it. But unfortunately, I have been silenced and therefore, not permitted to tell the stories exactly as I was told because I was not there. They are not mine to tell. The less said the better. Besides which, this book is from my perspective and no one else's.

Disclaimer: A formal statement saying that I am not legally responsible for these stories, such as the information given in a book or on the internet, or I have no direct involvement in it.

I have, however, been informed by other military colleagues of similar accounts that resemble the same mode of operation, so this was not a unique occurrence. There were many thousands like it! This section was revised and cut short by me to protect myself against legal action being initiated, I am sure you will understand. The only reason that I have included this little section is to enlighten you, as the reader, why the fear factor was so justified. If I were able to tell the full version, it would add weight to the reason why I was so terrified. Imagine if you will, being told of the events that unfolded, and then that person returned to the same place with the likely hood that it could happen again and that they may not be so lucky.

While Jack and Josh were talking, it became crystal clear to me that I had nearly lost my husband, and the worst of it was that he and Josh were returning in a couple of days to that place. I felt my heart crack and then shatter into a million pieces at the thought that the longest stretch was yet to come. After he returned, he would not be home until November which was four and a half months away. It would be four months of fear and worry. All we could do was put it to the back of our minds and pray that the Regiment returned as a whole and that no numbers were missing.

It was hell on earth for the whole duration of that tour and I have never experienced fear like it, nor wish to again. It was like pins and needles engulfed my whole body; it was a weird sensation that was present twenty-four hours a day. I had a heaviness in my ears as if I had cotton wool in them, and I was constantly poised for bad news. I often wondered if it be much different if my brother had not passed away, because he was no longer there to tell me that I needed to toughen up and ride this storm out. I was so fearful of losing Jack and I wished he had not described the details of that one incident because it had made it one hundred times worse! All I did day in, and day out, was picture that horror scene that nightmares are made of. There were also the photographs from the Iraqi news that came to light of the vehicles on fire. This did not help one little bit I can tell you!

It was said that every time they drove out of the compound, they did not know what would happen, or if they would all return after their patrols. They could not think of their families and focused solely on the job at hand, which I was totally understanding of and I would not have wanted it any other way. I recall one photograph of Jack leant up against some storage containers fast asleep. He had literally fallen asleep where he had sat down, upright with his head against the container and his hat askew! He looked so cute! There had been lots of photographs on his previous tours but this one had been the one that showed his true character. He worked until he dropped. His career came first. It was such a shame that his family never received that level of commitment.

The months passed slowly and there were lots of tears. I decided that Faye and I would drive back to the UK to stay with Dad and Delores, and I arranged for my friend Laura to have Lara dog for a couple of days. Laura later told me that Lara paced her house constantly while she stayed there. My scar and tummy were, in my opinion, healed enough and I would pick up any remaining possessions of my brother's that Dad had kept at his house for safekeeping. He simply did not have the room to store the last remaining items that he had been unable to sell.

I drove the six hours on the Europe side and Faye, and I boarded the Calais to Dover ferry. I had been prescribed stronger anti-depressants. Naomi believed that they would be beneficial to me. But they were having an adverse effect and were not agreeing with me at all. Once we drove off the ferry ramp at Dover, I managed to get us an hour into England. But I was so exhausted, and I felt that I could not physically drive any further than necessary, so I pulled into a budget hotel car park and got us a room.

I discarded the tablets that were making me nauseous and went cold turkey! I felt better for making that decision and never looked back, and I never wanted to take them again unless it was under extreme circumstances. I felt that they only served to cloud my judgement and make my head fuzzy. It was worse than being drunk and I detested the lack of control over my own thoughts and actions. Those tablets were left in the waste bin and as Faye and I left, I did not give them a second thought, I was done and I told Naomi so.

I called Dad to tell him that I could not drive any further and that the tablets had made my head spin due to the extensive drive over and exhaustion had set in. I am also not a massive fan of the ferry journey over and if I had eaten before boarding, I would have been guaranteed to vomit, so I declined any food and just stuck to drinking tea.

Delores saw her own ass because we would not be there early evening to go for the Chinese meal that she had booked a table for. I could not help it! I felt that driving any further than I already had on that day would have put mine and Faye's lives at risk, and no bloody Chinese meal is worth that.

Delores was a nightmare from the minute we arrived! As if Faye and I were not going through enough! Delores started picking holes in my weight, Faye's hair, and lectured my daughter on how bad shop bought hair dye is for her hair. She spent hours going on about it! Dog with a broken record bone!

To say I was pissed off was an understatement. It was good enough of them to put us up so I kept quiet and did not say anything, but I did wonder if we would last the week. On one of the evenings, Dad and I stayed up talking after Delores and Faye had gone to bed. I told Dad what had happened from my side of it back in 1990 in Tunisia. Of how I had never forgotten that I had been left by myself in a foreign country due to her pettiness with regards my comment about the weather being taken out of context. At first, Dad refused to accept that it was my stepbrother who had told Delores that I made the comment, but eventually he believed me and could see that I had no reason to lie about it! He said that was mortified, and that he would never forgive her either.

I told Dad that I probably would not stay for the whole week as planned because Faye and I were not coping with her constant sniping and belittling. He said with a frown on his face. "Do not leave, please do not leave! I see so little of you both!" I took that to mean that he genuinely did not want to see us go on account of not knowing when he would see us again.

But it was a challenging time not to just pack our bags and get in the car. We used Dad's as our base while we went off to see other family members like Karen and Alex who lived within driving distance to spend some time with them; it was good to catch up with my family members.

In the middle of the week, we were watching the news in the evening, it was news footage of the disruption in Iraq and I heard the news reporter clearly say the name of our Regiment!

Someone had been killed and it was the latest breaking news. Panic flooded my senses, I sat bolt upright on the edge of Dad's couch and tears fell immediately with the onslaught of the shaking hands. Then followed the knot in my stomach, followed by the pain in my chest. My eyes failed me, I could not see straight, and my hearing was intensely acute to tune in and focus on what was being reported on the TV. I questioned my dad to make sure he had heard the same, but he was unsure because he was reading the paper and not paying much attention until I jumped up in terror. I had heard correct! It had been the name of our Regiment! There was no mistaking the abbreviated letters that rang through my ears. Then she said the full title of the Regiment concerned! It was coming to the end of the operational tour and it was sod's law that the attacks became more frequent and hostile. The troops were exhausted from the length of time out there, and they were ready to hand over to the next lot who were deploying out to relieve them. The bad guys knew when these handovers took place and took full advantage!

I got straight on the phone to my trusted friend Shelley who knew nothing other than the same that I had just seen on the news. She told me she would find out what she could because she was over in Germany, and I was not. Dad had never witnessed what he saw that night. Losing my brother broke both of us and the damage could never be repaired. Losing my husband would have tipped me over the edge. Dad told me to follow him downstairs. "Stop watching the bloody news for five minutes and come and have a stiff drink with your old man!" It was not a request. It was an order.

Dad's remedy came in the form of Whiskey, which is not something I would ever have considered but he swears by it and he forced me to take a swig! Typical Irishman!

I will never touch the stuff again, but that night, I needed something to take the edge off and my dad's remedy worked. It was not long before I was heading back up to the lounge (it is a townhouse) to see if there had been any development. I sat cradling the tumbler of Whiskey in both hands on my lap like a distraught child that could not stop fidgeting. I text Shelley who knew nothing either because the communications had been cut and everyone in Germany was waiting with a nervous anxiety too! Our world stopped temporarily as we waited for any kind of news to filter through.

It eventually was announced with a sincere apology from the same news reporter, that she had got the name of the Regiment wrong! For the sake of one letter, it had set in unnecessary panic amongst our wives. So, for example, say that the Regiments have three of four abbreviated letters, she had said one of them wrong, an easy slip of the tongue because these abbreviations sounded so similar that anyone who was in a hurry to report could make the same error. If I could disclose them, they would sound similar! One bloody word, one letter, one simple mistake equated to sheer terror. It would have been better if the full title had been used as opposed to the abbreviation, then there would have been no mistaking which one it was, but I am sure that she would have understood the consequences of such a monumental mistake.

Shelley and I swapped texts to share what had just been said on the TV and Dad and I settled a bit, he calmed me more by threatening to ply more Whiskey down my neck! He was bewildered by it all and said that he had never had any comprehension or idea of what an army wife would be going through until he witnessed it for himself first-hand. I told him that there was no way anyone could know unless they had experienced it themselves.

During this time of staying at Dad and Delores's, Faye and I had really had enough of her constant digging at the both of us. For me, it was about my weight, and that I should not be eating the things that I was. To be frank, it was really none of her bloody business what I ate, whom I saw or what I drank. But she seemed to think that while I was in her house, she could say exactly what she saw fit whether it hurt mine or Faye's feelings or not. Truth is she just wanted us to leave, I mean a father's love for his daughter, and flesh and blood grandchild was unconditional, but it was something that quite clearly bothered her because she had driven her own son's away with her petty arguments and now, she was doing the same with me. She wanted my dad to herself. Simple!

I left my dad's with a heavy heart, but I could not wait to get away from her which is what she wanted. I felt bad for my dad because he was literally her slave and had made his bed years ago. Over the years, she had sapped the life out of him and dragged his backbone along with it too! He would never leave now, as he believed that he would never find love again, and that he loved her to bits despite her being a bitch. There was no hope for him, he was beyond talking to and he would continue running up and down the stairs for her, bringing her bloody Vodka and whatever else she demanded. I wanted to tell her to get off her fat ass and get her own drinks! Lazy cow! No love lost and I do not ever want to see her again. I hate the way she treats my dad, but I said nothing except offered for him to come and live with me. He refused.

At this point in time and unbeknown to me or Jack, or anyone for that matter, things were awful for Faye at school. She never told anyone until a few years later when we were safely out of Germany and back living in the UK.

From the time we had arrived back in Germany in 2004, and right up until the time we left in 2009, our daughter was severely bullied. By one main girl initially, but there were a group of them in the end and they all got involved at some point whether they were just bystanders or throwing punches. She was beaten, intimidated, harassed and mentally tortured every single day. They had to travel to school on the same coach put on by the military.

The main perpetrator was a girl who I have chosen to call Shithead. (Her real name begins with N, and she will know who she is!) She was the cruellest and most barbaric one of all of them, the others were only her admiring followers, she simply led by fear and intimidation, CLASSY! They were most likely scared of what she would do to them if they did not rise to her vicious demands! She clearly ruled by fear and used her great weight to back herself up and follow it through. Her ugliness was on the outside as well as inside. There were lots of others; my daughter still has a list. She approached the school tutors for help and told them what was happening, to no avail. She saw a counsellor who was appointed by the school for a short time, but I know that she clammed up and refused to talk about what was happening to her for fear of reprisal. I still to this day feel responsible for not knowing the severity, or indeed, even that it was going on with as many as ten people tormenting her everyday life. She never showed any bruises, because Shithead always beat Faye on her body, not where it would be visible. Faye was very elusive and would hide herself away and became withdrawn and angry.

There were lots of other bullies, one of which was the son of a couple in the Regiment. I disliked the mother and stayed away from her as much as possible because I found her to be rude and arrogant. I never took to her and preferred to have nothing to do with her. She thought that I was jealous of them both at one point. I found this hysterical because her husband was only placed in the RSM seat because no one else was available. Jack had refused it on account of wanting to finish his time back in the UK so that Faye could go to college. No one wanted her husband, and he was eventually removed before the standard two years so that someone more capable of doing the job could take over. She carried his rank more than he did! Jealousy did not come into it. I did not give a shit about her, but I gave a shit about what her son was doing to my daughter! Even the older son stepped in on one occasion to avert an inevitable beating by the Shithead when he told Faye to walk a different way home after he had seen the girl and his brother walking their way! And there was the rude arrogant one believing that her precious youngest was perfect in every way. While all the time he was part of the group who called themselves 'The Superiors', I can think of other things to call them other than superior! But…I have created fictitious names to keep them away from my daughter. They did enough damage to her in her school years.

I have named these people as I see in their characters. I will not allow anyone to edit my book because this group will eventually own the responsibility of their actions. I see their smug faces on social media, and I feel sorry for their parents who I am sure are proud of their off springs. Me personally, I would be devastated if I ever found out that my child had inflicted such cruelty on another. Just because they could! I went to the school on one occasion and our Welfare Officer met me there to see if we could come to some sort of understanding with the Head teacher. It proved to be futile and only made things worse for Faye. The school system failed to uphold her confidentiality, and there was little to no duty of care. It appeared that whatever tactic was used to stop these bullies getting away with what they were putting other pupils through, the school simply failed to acknowledge any wrongdoing.

A girl I have named Cow-bag (Her real name begins with R.) had been Faye's best friend. But it stopped the minute she got in with Shithead. The main girl was, in my opinion not particularly attractive, and had a face only a mother could love. Of course, I am going to say that my daughter is beautiful, and I say that because she truly is, inside and out. I can only imagine that Shithead felt threatened by the fact that Faye was prettier. One day in the grounds of the school at break time, Shithead dared Cow-bag five Euros to punch Faye in the face, which she duly did. They tormented Faye getting on and off the school bus. They would pull her bag off her and throw all the contents on the ground. Faye told me once of the time that Shithead punched and kicked her on the ground while the others just watched and cheered her on. Finding all this out years later was totally heart-breaking. And my only justification for not being there for her was, I simply did not know! She hid it and refused to tell me anything was wrong when I asked her.

I was not even there for myself. I was still grieving the loss of Darren, and terrified of losing my husband who was still in Iraq. I was broken myself, and I just did not see what she was going through. I will take that guilt to my grave. But at the time, I was not running with all my cylinders working. I was running on fumes and it took every ounce of strength that I had to get through each day.

I once was turning out Faye's coat pockets to put it through the washing machine and found a note from her that was addressed to me, the main sentence that stuck in my head was "you think you have it hard? I wish you were me, then you would see that my life is shit, I hate you."

Chapter 15

Faye's Entry. Her Tortured Days

As a mother, this chapter is especially difficult to write but write it I must! I copied from the notes Faye has given me, and I will put it down in her words so that it is true to how she felt.

I offer no apology for the way that I have written about these people, because in my humble opinion, there is absolutely no excuse for being a bully. Unfortunately, there are many tactics that the bullies use to subdue their chosen targets. The verbal, physical and emotional abuse that went undetected and unpunished in Faye's case was unforgivable.

But there are millions who suffer in silence.

I have called the main bullies by names that I felt were befitting to their bad selfish personalities.

Number one bully =Shithead. Her name begins with N. If I ever set eyes on her, I would not be responsible for my actions or what exited my mouth.

Number two bully = Cow-bag. Her name begins with R.

Number three bully = Bog-Witch Her name begins with C. Because this girl was the one who smelt, had greasy hair and was built like a brick shit house with a face attached that could win first prize in a F-ugly competition!

The son of Lucifer is number four = Dick head. The name begins with D! Go figure! Enough said.

And lastly, Horror-bag. Her name begins with M.

There were plenty of others, but these were the main ones who saw fit to do whatever damage they felt like at the time.

Karma never loses an address, and they will get theirs.

Faye's account.

When we moved from Yorkshire, Dad and I played marbles for hours while the removal men loaded our furniture onto the truck. Dad let me win of course and it felt nice that he wanted to play. Dad was not around much, or if he was, I did not remember it; I know he thought of me.

We moved from Yorkshire back to Germany and I do not use the words lightly when I say "it was the worst experience of my life". Living there and experiencing the torture that I endured was not in any way shape or form my parent's fault. I know that the series of events could have been managed had I have said something initially, but I did not. And I suffered as a result, so I have no one to blame but myself.

The house in Germany was small but big enough for what we needed, and the back garden seemed to go on for miles! On our arrival, I started at middle school, and because I knew no one I kept a low profile in my usual way and tried to hide away as much as possible. I just went about doing my own things and did the best that I could to hide.

Our Science teacher was called Mister Bracken, his breath always smelled as bad as his attitude! He made no secret that he did not like kids of our age and made no attempt whatsoever to disguise that fact. During one of the lessons one day, he paused and said, "Okay, let us pick on someone who looks like they do not know anything." And then he chose me! He then proceeded to laugh at me in front of the whole class who joined in with him. This left me feeling humiliated and demoralised. I cried out of embarrassment, and then found myself the talk of the school after the other kids spread the word.

I cried a lot during my time at school, because I felt that I was being humiliated with no comeback or defence. Mum brought me some shoes that I had really liked. I was persistent in asking for them until she eventually got them for me. They were big and clumpy and although I really liked them, my first day of wearing them did not go too well after I became aware that they were too big for my skinny feet and ankles. I was walking towards my friend called Jean; she has stuck by me through thick and thin throughout my school days. But before I knew it or had time to react, the colossal girl called Bog-witch was in my face! Something had been said, and apparently, it had originated from me!

She pointed her finger in my face with such force. This was then followed by her face right up in mine while she screamed and shouted her obscenities. I was covered in enough spittle to drown a cat! I had no recollection of what I had allegedly said or done to provoke this attack, but through all her high pitched screaming the only words that were coherent were "slagging me off, you tramp".

I know for certain that I did not say anything of the sort because I would have remembered having said such a thing about someone who, up until now, that I had never met. I am not quite sure even to this day if I was in the room when I allegedly said the offensive comment. I think that she was frustrated by the end of the screaming and shouting because she huffed and took the piss out of the way that I walked as she waddled away.

She was the first proper bully I encountered at my new school, but only the first of many and it was not the last time I had to endure her horrid face in mine. She had a friend who I will call Michelle; Mum and Dad were friends with her parents, so I had to be civil with her. When it was just me and Michelle, she was lovely but when she was with the Bog-witch she was a total shit! I would go as far as to say Bog-Witch was a meathead!

I was tiny compared to Bog-Witch; she towered over me to the point of intimidation. She struck fear into the very heart of me when I saw the pile of skin and bone hurling towards me. She called me all the names under the sun. We were in class once and she proceeded to make fun of my hair with a couple of the others that were sat on the same table. I felt ugly, scruffy and embarrassed. During her mocking and taunting, and amidst the laughter, she told me that I would never amount to anything and that I was just a speck on this planet that no one gives a shit about. She added insult to injury by saying that my parents were embarrassed by me. I remember asking Mum words to that effect and she got quite angry and asked where that statement had come from, but I evaded tell her and said that I was just wondering.

Once in P.E., Bog-Witch came waddling into the changing rooms and pushed me out of the way, as I was changing my top. It was always smelly in there because of sweaty bodies and dirty clothes, but this was another reason for abuse being hurled out of her foul mouth. She would stand grimacing and saying, "You absolutely stink! You need to go home and give yourself a boiling hot bath and get rid of that scum in your hair." I was mortified and wanted to hide, but instead of rising to it, I just grabbed my T-shirt, got changed and went into the hall where the teacher was asking us to do stupid exercises that were in my opinion, inappropriate for kids.

I always used to think that the Bog-Witches eyebrows looked like slugs trying to escape from her face! If I were ever to write a letter to her, it would say something like this: You ruined school for me. You insisted on making my life as miserable as possible, and yet you are still allowed to live a happy life. I always hoped that you would be smashed in the face with something solid and bus shaped. When you were hit in the face with a cricket ball and it burst your eye socket, I hoped you would come out of hospital just so that I could do it again myself. Harsh as it may seem, you are the scum of the earth. Bullies like you should be put away in a dark room filled with rats. That is the least that you deserve. You made my life a misery, and I hope that the little boy you now have never has to endure what you put me through.

You humiliated me to the point that I did not want to live. And when you were confronted about it many times at school, your reply was that I asked for it! What the fuck did I ever do to you? You always told me how ugly and scruffy you thought I was, but did you ever look long and hard in the mirror? You are certainly no oil painting, you never will be, and neither will I, but I am not ugly on the inside. You made me feel so ugly and petty that I had no defence. You are the very image of a bully, a fuck ugly girl and for that reason, you take it out on everyone else.

Why was I the centre of your universe? Why could you not have bullied someone else? Oh, sorry I forgot…you did! Why did you listen to the rumours that I had said something when I had said nothing at all? Do you honestly think that I would continue to allegedly say things knowing that you would smash my face in at any given moment?

I am not blaming you for your actions, as you are quite clearly a fucked-up woman. To be honest, I expected to see you in the papers a few years down the line, because you had taken it too far and were heading to prison. I still await that day if it ever comes, but I shall not hold my breath because people like you think that they can do and say whatever they like and get away with it. You hung around with people that filled your head with shite and took it out on the little people.

I will never forgive you, but I will forget you. You were the one that started the bullying rumours and the petty insults, and I just want you to know that you are a terrible person. I would not wish anyone to go through what you repeatedly inflicted on me. You are a cold-hearted bitch.

Also, since leaving your pettiness behind, I have picked myself up, brushed myself off, and grown a pair! Should our paths ever cross, which I highly doubt, please do not delude yourself into thinking that you can insult me because I would not stand there and take it from you now. I sincerely hope I can dance on the grave of one of my tormenters that stole my childhood from me. I would take great pleasure in doing so.

The Bog-Witch started hanging around with a girl Mum has named Daffy. She was also nothing but trouble for anyone that got involved with her. Daffy always reminded me of a duck the way she would walk around pouting and sticking her chest out. She had a toilet mouth and anything that came out of it was lies and shit. I was friends with her for a short period of time before she became a bitch, and she shit on me rather than be my friend. She got me into trouble with the Royal Military Police after she broke a beer bottle and walked around scratching any car that she passed! Thirty cars in total around our housing estate were scratched. I remember sitting with the police absolutely shitting myself! I had no idea what was going on, but I knew that I would be in trouble with Daffy if I grassed her up! Mum and Dad reassured me that I was doing the right thing. Once the police had left our house, Mum forbade me to hang around with Daffy anymore. Daffy knew that I grassed on her and never let me forget it!

She may have been glamorous on the outside, but she had a shocking personality. She was so up her own backside and such a bitch with a cackle for a laugh that went straight through you and grated on your teeth! It was no wonder she did not have many boyfriends but who was I to talk! I never classed any of the lads I went out with as boyfriends, because they were all the same and most had been dared to go out with me. Daffy had been around the block more times than I cared to mention, and in all honesty, I was glad to be away from her. I would not give her the time of day if I ever saw her again. All she ever did was dream up something that I had allegedly said or done, and happily spread it around until the appropriate person received news of it. She would just hang around with the Bog-Witch and company, while they all went about taunting and verbally tormenting the smaller kids who were younger than themselves. To make themselves feel important, I guess.

Most of the time I spent in School in Germany was a fucking nightmare. Incorrect and idol gossip went around by the hour, and I was not the only one that they picked on. There were other boys and girls but when you are on the receiving end it feels like you are the only one.

When I started Senior School, it took a long time for me to settle down, four and a half years to be exact. I had initially made a friend in Cow-bag, and while we were friends, she made me laugh like I had never laughed before! We had lots of sleepovers and silly giggles as all teenage girls do. She made me laugh so much that my sides ached. She pretended to speak with a Scottish accent in front of her mum and dad because they were Scottish, but she did not have an accent, not really. She always had to do chores before being allowed out and I sometimes helped her, but if it were only a quick chore, I would wait outside. It was always Faye and Cow-Bag. I had expected it to end at some point, which it inevitably did, and she went over to the dark side along with the others, I did however enjoy it while it lasted.

Cow-Bag and I would meet up after lessons and walk to our next ones together; if she were not in the same lessons, I felt a bit lost. I could live without her, but I felt anxious being in a room full of people that I did not know, or who could be my potential future bullies. It got to a point where we were not meeting as frequently in school as she was off finding new friends, she was moving on. I never stopped her doing her own thing as I had no right to dictate that, but I did feel that she was leaving me behind. But as her best friend, I understood that no one can have just one friend, and that we all needed to find our feet, but that did not mean that I wanted my head trodden on with those feet once they had walked away. We still hung out at home a fair bit, having sleepovers, staying up late listening to shit music and browsing the internet until God knows what time. Her mum and dad went out frequently on the piss and left us to babysit. This also dwindled; I think I had accepted that I was losing my best friend after year eight. Everything changed in year eight, and it was as if my peer group was thinking with their genitals rather than their heads.

Everyone was competing to have the hottest/fittest girl in the school and be the best they could be, or the best looking. I used to look at them sometimes and think to myself, *You are a dick, you are a dick, you are an even bigger dick! You are gay and no one knows it yet!* I was becoming judge mental and I did not like it, I felt bad, but the guilty feeling never lasted long. I found the more I just kept my thoughts to myself the better I could cope. But then, they tormented me for that too when they noticed that I was the one sat with the boys and then I was called weird!

Going back to year eight, I do not remember much of it as I have managed to block it out for my own self-preservation. But I recall that I was calm, and I did not have too much to worry about because no one knew each other, so the bullying was not that bad. Midway through year eight, Cow-Bag was secretly envious of some girl on another garrison. Apparently, this girl had everything going for her. Then, to my horror, I learned that this other girl was moving to the same garrison as us!

I was aware that Cow-Bag was already talking to her in advance of her announcement that she had no intention of remaining friends with me. At this stage, I had no idea why, but I left her to her own devices. Cow-Bag turned into a monster in year eight. She became bubbly, but reserved at the same time, and did not speak to me at all. I became a loner, as one would expect. I no longer had my well-known sidekick with me, so I spent my time alone. Again.

My experience at this school is long-winded and emotional. I have buried most of it but there are a lot of painful memories that I think should be expressed. A few letters need to be written and emotions to be eliminated along with past experiences that need to put to rest. Once this whole thing is written and done, I want the whole world to know that bullies are everywhere, but you do not have to suffer in silence, and that you are not alone!

Year nine was when my school experience started properly because I was already developed and I had stopped growing while everyone else seemed to carry on, it made me feel quite strange and isolated. I would wander around with these giants who towered above me! I constantly wondered who was going to bop me on the head next or push me down the corridor or snatch my bag and throw my things around the hallway. There was not a single day that I was not looking over my shoulder and expecting the worst to happen.

I was walking to German class one day and there was this boy called (D) for Dick head. He was the class clown, and to be fair, he was funny when he wanted to be, but he was also associated with the 'popular people'. Therefore, that made him a knob in my eyes. He barged past me on his way up the stairs and offered no apology for this deliberate action, the stairway was packed with kids and my belongings were all over the stairs where he had thrown it. The knob stood at the top of the stairs cackling while I picked my stuff up. I could feel my face turning red with anger and embarrassment, but what could I do? It felt like nothing, other than retrieve my things while people trampled all over them with puzzled looks on their faces. But no one offered to help me each time it happened, as it happened so frequently. I tried to pick it up quickly and get to my German lesson, but I was evidently late which resulted in my face being bellowed at by the angry beer bellied Mister Dunn. Although he was a dick, I did like him. He told some funny jokes…but some were bloody awful too! I sat right at the back of the room and liked my seat because it meant that I could keep my head down and not draw attention to myself. We were not allowed to choose our seats, but I liked where Mister Dunn had placed me.

Mister Dunn was inappropriately funny, but he was one of my favourite teachers in that shitty Military School. He had the attitude of "I will teach you the basics and you can learn the rest in college", which suited me fine! Most lessons were spent with ten-minute tests on words, and then the rest was telling jokes, and doing other stuff like homework you had forgotten for another class! I was moved from the back of the class in year ten and I hated where I was relocated as it was right at the front with all the 'popular people'! But I was seated on the edge of the row, so I leant on the wall staring into space most of the time. I do not think many people noticed but Mister Dunn would clap loudly at nine o'clock to ensure everyone was awake. It used to scare the crap out of me, but I felt like I had stepped out of a freezing cold shower and back into the room. I was sat in front of a lad called Mike who always reminded me of Sid the Sloth, and he took pleasure in mimicking that character. He had an extremely deep voice which made everything he said funny in my eyes, I never fancied him, but I did find him humorous.

In English class, the teacher was a frail woman with a stern personality, she was terrifying when she wanted to be, but it was always said amongst the kids that if you poked her that she would just snap, as there was nothing to her fragile frame. I had English with all the 'popular people'. I was no smarter than any of them, but I had to sit next to a girl I literally detested! Most of this lesson was spent with orders being barked out to "shut up, sit down, get off that window ledge, or write the answers from the board". I hated year-nine English class and everyone in it so much so, that I once pleaded with the head of year to "please move me to another class". In the vain hope that I may make a friend or two, but it was met with a laugh and a gesture to go away.

We were tasked with roleplaying news presenters, and we had to deliver our given topic of research in front of the class. I cannot remember what I chose as my topic, but I made sure it was so boring that I failed to attract anyone's attention. Which did not go down very well. I had to redo it all again because the teacher could not hear me on the recorder. I failed to see how she could when she was recording from the back of the classroom!

I remember being terrified of everyone's reaction. But they were far too interested in whose menstrual period they matched with, or what colour underwear they were wearing. So, I just went ahead with reading it out regardless. I was never interested in which makeup was the best, or whose hairstyle was pleasing to the eye. I wore what I wanted and focused on comfort. That was until people started making comments on how my shoes, hair, nails, makeup, jumper and bag looked.

I was already seeing a counsellor who had been appointed at the school. One day, I walked into the last remaining fifteen minutes of a lesson to be met with blank stares from the kids in the room. They were classed as 'kids' in my eyes. They were not people, just immature kids. As I sat down there was a boy called Dean who Mumbled, "She is back from the loony bin!" I later found out that he knew where I had been because someone had watched me walk into the room.

The whole class fell silent and as it was a small room, everyone heard his comment, followed by the insistent cackles of everyone else. A girl called (M) Horror-bag was usually the one to start something at my expense, so it surprised me that this weed had started this taunting just to make himself look cool. He could never understand the detrimental effect this would have on me, but he did it to win Horror-bag's approval. Fifteen minutes felt like an hour and that was not the only comment. For fifteen minutes straight, I was shouted at, laughed at, bellowed at and poked, I was pushed and nudged consistently for the whole duration of the agonising time left in that lesson. Such things being said were:

"So, when are you popping your clogs then? Soon I hope!"

"She's in the loony bin because she's ugly and she knows it."

"Look at the hair on her! Give it a brush, girl!"

"I heard she is in there because she is emotionally unable to get a boyfriend, no wonder though, have you seen her?"

"Why did she even bother coming in today? She does not listen to anything. She will be working in McDonalds by the time she gets out of here."

I did look at the spineless teacher who was sat just a few rows in front of me. She failed to even look up to see what was going on. She did not even move, she just carried on marking someone's book with a lot of bright red crosses. I left there feeling fragile and stupid, I just wanted to go home. On the way out of the classroom, I was forcedly pushed into the table next to me; it was with such force that I had a bruise on my leg for days afterwards. My hair was pulled, and someone tried to kick my foot so that I fell over, but I was in too much pain to care.

Math in year nine was my best subject, although when I was growing up, it was never my strong point. I really excelled at it in year nine and above. I understood the questions before the teacher had finished asking, and I was always the first to finish the questions. I quickly moved up the math sets although I failed to reach the top set, but we cannot be perfect at everything; it is the taking part and doing your best that matters. I was just below because I never understood fractions and percentages.

I went on holiday one year, but I had written down the equation that had been set for homework before we left. On my return, I handed in the homework book and off I went. Only to be called back in a few minutes later with the teachers bellowing voice telling me that I "could not be assed, and obviously did not want to learn anything". Everyone was now leaving the room and I remember feeling like a child with this big man shouting in my face and everyone staring at me!

Yet again, I was subjected to humiliation, only this time it was by an adult who should have pulled me to one side. But thought that he would embarrass me in front of the whole class instead, legend! Obviously, I told my mum, but I did not mention that he was in my face; she would have lost the plot! She did however call the school, because as we were entering his next lesson, he stopped me and said, "I have received a phone call from your mother, which I will address in class."

Fuck! was my first thought! Not only had he shouted at me unnecessarily, but now, I would have to sit with humiliation written all over my face while he publicly apologised to me. I cared not for his apology, but I did care about the comments that followed. "Ahh, go running to Mummy, did we, Faye? Mummy's not here now, Faye! Nobody cares about your little life, Faye, you are a no body!"

The teacher sat down whilst letting the kids abuse me. I did not feel that I could get up and walk out, I had nowhere to go and I would have had to go back in the end. There was no point. Apart from all that bollocks, I did like the Maths lesson. I wondered if I could ever have been an Architect with all the knowledge. Obviously not! I had now had it drummed into me that I would be a no body, no matter how much Mum and Dad said I would always amount to something brilliant I had my reservations after this treatment in the classroom, it totally knocked my confidence and self-esteem.

I appreciated Mum calling the school though, because that teacher was an asshole in the first degree!

I sat in the Math class once when a new girl arrived; she had a long name which I took no time to remember because she did not look like she would be staying. She was only there a month, but for that whole month, she was tormented as much as I had been. I wanted to befriend her, but I just could not bring myself to initiate a dialogue. I did not think it was worth putting me or her through the hassle. To my shame, I left her to be tormented by the 'popular people' and it took the pressure off me because they had a new target, even if it was for a brief period.

I managed to get a whole month of relative peace. I did feel bad for her though, she was Asian and extremely pretty! But as soon as they saw her headdress, she was doomed, and she did not even have to say a word for the abuse to start. They were ruthless! She had things thrown at her from across the room such as pencils, rulers and a compass at one point! She sat crying for the whole lesson. When she left the room, the boys had strategically place spit balls of paper in her headdress; they were complete bastards!

P.E classes were a nightmare. I had thoughts of just forgetting my kit and pretending I did not know I had forgotten it. Anything to get out of the lesson because the number one bully was in attendance! I was sick of having to bend over and do silly stretches while someone I loathed got a good look at my ass, which would result in future derogatory comments. It always was the case that because I was the small one, I got pushed around, kicked, slapped or the wind knocked out of me by some brute that had seen fit to have a go. I was waiting for the ball to come near me in a game of Rounders once and unfortunately, the Bog-Witch was near me! She was blissfully unaware of the ball that was hurtling at speed towards her because she was so busy burying me six foot under with her laser death stare and she failed to catch it! Dozy bitch! She was looking so entertained at the fact I was shitting myself while watching this whale running towards me! She took me off my feet as she barged past!

We were miles away from the teacher, so he missed all the action taking place at the other end of the pitch. I rolled over and tried to catch my breath on the freezing grass, as she walked around me kicking my shoulder on her way past. I tried to move back in an unsuccessful attempt to get away from her, but she put her massive foot on my tummy and applied all her weight behind it. I was in agony for the next few days and still did not understand why she hated me so much, but at least she enjoyed herself.

Her final act of humiliation was to kick my shins repeatedly before walking away laughing and spitting on the ground like a complete tramp. Grot bag! I was in such a bad mood that day because the physical education teacher sensed that something was amiss, and was frowning at the foot mark on my T-shirt before asking, "Did something happen?"

Sarcastically, I replied, "No, everything is just peachy!"

We walked back into the changing room, and I remember what happened next so clearly it feels like yesterday. Horror-bag was hanging around with a nasty piece of work who I will call Skank. I was getting changed and I only had my jumper to put on over my T-shirt when there was suddenly an almighty commotion going on in the corridor, and it was getting closer! This commotion was a girl being dragged by her hair by HB and Skank! They dragged her to an open toilet cubicle and commenced banging her head off the rim of the toilet! Everyone in the changing room stopped and looked on in absolute horror as this was taking place, the urge to intervene was immense...but what could I do? We all knew that anyone brave enough to step in and help the girl would suffer the same fate. This went on for fifteen minutes while they banged her head against the toilet rim and flushed her head down the toilet, she was clearly traumatised and struggling to comprehend what was going on or why.

The poor girl slumped against the toilet when they finally released her, both were quite clearly impressed by their work and the floor was covered with her blood and toilet water. As onlookers, we thought they had finally ceased the attack when they both stepped backwards. But they both then started hurling abuse at the defenceless, weak and bloodied girl. They called her a waste of oxygen, a tramp and a good for nothing, ending their sentence with "that is what happens when anyone slags off the Superiors, and that goes for any of you little shits! Do not mess with us or we will put you in hospital or go down trying."

(Mum adds...WOW! I bet their parents did not know about their activities. I bet that would cause a shit storm in a teacup! If I were ever asked for the names of these girls and I believed that the person who was asking was the parent of one, or both, of these girls, I would tell them with no hesitation.)

Skank then bent down over the girl who was now unconscious and pulled her knickers and trousers off. HB lifted her up and they pulled her T-shirt off. She was not as developed as some of the other girls and was now completely naked. After that, people finished getting dressed as quickly as possible so that they could leave. I waited along with a few other girls for the 'superiors' to leave. When we were alone with no bullies in the room, one of the quieter girls walked over to the victim who was lying naked on the floor and began assembling her clothes. We found her bag and started to dress her. I could do nothing to out of shock and terror for fear they returned! I watched as the others helped her, but I had been rooted to the spot unable to interact and thinking to myself, *This is the school I am in, and this is what they are capable of.* They will have shared this story of a good beating with all who were willing to listen, and they will have laughed about this poor girl's incident like the cold-hearted bitches that they are. The others will wish they had been there to witness it and give encouragement to their peers egging them on.

While the girl was being dressed, another went to find a teacher who, immediately on entry of the room, gasped and ran straight back out to call an ambulance. The girl came to in the process of being dressed and let out a howling cry! Understandably, she was in considerable pain and totally distraught and humiliated. Others left to go get help, and along with two other girls, we tried to console her as much as possible considering the circumstance. She could not open her eyes because they were both blackened. Her nose was broken. There were numerous splits on her lips and a burst cheekbone. The bullies had done a serious job of rearranging her face, we could not even tell who she was, it was only when we looked at the name on her schoolbooks that we found out who she was.

Needless to mention that it went around the whole school, but the girl who I will call Sarah did not speak at all for the whole time she was there. The head teacher at the time wanted a full investigation as to who had committed the assault, why they had done it and why had no one stepped in to help. But the girl made it perfectly clear that she did not want to say who it was and the whole thing just fizzled out and was labelled as 'another girls' playground fight'.

I will never forget that day, I will never forget until the day I die. There was a pool of blood where she had lain and it had stained the grout on the floor tiles, it was a constant reminder of the ruthless attack that was so unnecessary. It was a constant reminder of what that hellhole of a school and its attendees were capable of.

During my time at school, I once had my hair cut short in the same style that one of the Spice girls was sporting at the time; it meant that my hair could not be pulled in the same way I had witnessed happen to Sarah in the toilet. I left the hairdresser's house who was Mum's close friend, and my future godmother, Shelley. As I walked out her front door, one of the superiors was walking towards me. I saw Dickhead D coming around the corner long before he saw me! But as soon as he clapped eyes on me, he burst into dramatic fits of laughter, as did his friend Jordan. I immediately regretted my decision to have it cut so short but there was nothing that I could do about it now. With my hair that had been chopped off in my hand, I went into my house where Mum and Dad said it looked lovely. It was a huge difference! But I knew that eventually it would grow out.

By the time I got to school the next week, the whole year knew of my new haircut which resulted in lots of name calling. The first one being that I was a lesbian and that this was my way of 'coming out' which totally incorrect but it made no difference no matter how many times I said it was not true.

I walked into the P.E changing rooms and (N) Shithead ringleader, shouted across the room, "Cover up, girls, the lesbo is in the room!" I turned to face the wall and waited for everyone to finish getting changed, which only added to the overall sense of "she's a lesbian". As I walked into the lesson, there were a big group of people who looked me up and down individually, right at the fore front was the big old sausage unit that was the Shithead. Even her legs looked like sausages that had been squeezed into her skin.

I felt so embarrassed by the way I looked and my hair, it made no difference how much makeup I wore or how I styled my hair, they always found the slightest thing to comment on which then escalated into "what are you looking at, bitch". It was relentless and they never let up.

(N) Shithead seemed to hate every bone in my body and the skin around it throughout senior school. At every opportunity, she would punch, kick, push and nudge. If I were sat down, she would slap me around the back of the head followed by a "silly little shit" comment. Sometimes she would follow me down corridors and push me up against the wall or go behind me and trip me up and then stand laughing about it. She really was a pathetic excuse for a human being with nothing better to do than make someone else's life a misery. She had a stare that knocked the wind out of me and froze me to my very core. She also had a short fuse with everyone and the sense of humour of a shark! Coupled with her loudmouth and willingness to show how tough she thought she was, it made for a very overwhelming experience. At one point, I thought I would lose control of my bodily functions and basic control.

On one occasion, she pushed me to the floor and kicked me in the stomach which meant I accidentally let out a little bit of pee, luckily my coat hid the fact as I rolled over to get up, but she managed to get in a kick up my backside which jolted me forward. My main concern that day was that I would potentially smell of pee after the little leak, so I pretended to have a massive migraine and got sent to the nurse who cured everything with Polo mints while she surfed the internet.

In summary, my school years were the worst of my life! All because of the group of people who got away with it. I reported some things to teachers who I thought I could trust in senior school, but nothing was ever taken seriously, and when I challenged the school a couple of years back, they had conveniently lost any documentation on anything, even my records from seeing the school counsellor.

I hope that there is some karma in the world that has all my tormenters on its list.

I hope they get what is coming to them all these years later now I am an adult, and I can see that bullies pick on people because of their own shortfalls. The greater extent of bullying, the greater their own insecurities. They know they are ugly on the inside, even if the face is pretty, it makes no odds if you are an animal on the inside.

Chapter 16

A Mother's Heartbreak

Writing the last chapter was just as difficult as writing the death of my brother. I wrote as much as I could a little at a time. The traumatic time that my daughter went through in her entire last years at school at the hands of other military children absolutely broke me. But I re-wrote it in her words, I felt I owed her. I wrote this chapter to expose how these bullies behaved. I wanted to let people know how awful it was for Faye and all the other kids who were tortured by the group called The Superiors. There is no forgiveness for their actions or the level of consistent cruelty that they inflicted on the ones that they considered 'Little Shits'. There is no pride in being a bully, they may be adults now and the years have passed. But the memory will remain forever, and they will forever be bad.

Faye is strong enough, but I would not want her attacked any more than they have already done previously. These kids got away with assault, and nothing short of blue bloody murder! As for the school in question, they were a joke! Nothing was ever done, and no apology was ever offered. It simply 'went away'.

Faye informed me recently that she did contact the two main girls to voice her opinion and give them the opportunity to say sorry. The (C) Bog-Witch said that Faye was 'deluded'! She then involved her mother and launched yet another verbal attack on Faye.

The other one (N) Shithead with the sense of humour of a shark did the same, both refused to see the error of their ways or show any remorse. Instead, they chose to enforce their hatred towards Faye and reinforce the fact that they are simply put…cold-hearted, ugly bitches inside and out.

I hope their parents are proud, but then I am guessing that their parents have no idea of their bullying capabilities, unless they are the same way inclined.

In addition to what was happening to Faye at school, this year of 2008, turned out to be the year that we as a family had dreaded. Lara dog was now eighteen years old. And after a visit to the vets in town, they had discovered that the dark mass in her liver was cancer. We were to lose our girl after twelve years of the best life we could give her. She had been adopted in 1995 from The National Canine Defence League in Darlington, and she had travelled everywhere with us unconditionally. She had never been ill, aside from the mild stroke in 2006 that she had fully recovered from.

Anyone who has loved and lost a pet will know that this day was extremely painful, and it had come around too quickly. Jack took her to be put to sleep, while Faye and I broke our hearts in the house. Jack said that she had licked his hand as if she knew that it was the end and that her suffering was over. She was no longer in pain, and we arranged to have her ashes brought to us by courier a couple of weeks later. Faye and I still cry for Lara, she was such a special girl, and everyone loved her. It is a difficult subject to write as you can imagine so I hope that you can forgive me for not dwelling on this subject for too long because she is still very missed to this day. My last memory was of her walking out of the front door. As Jack led her out to his car, her tail was wagging. We had said our goodbyes all morning and gave her lots of hugs and kisses. The tears now streaming down my face at the memory, I miss her, as does Faye. Like all the other memories and history, Jack has probably wiped the memory that we even had a beautiful dog, but Faye and I think of her often to this day and I still have her ashes sat next to my brother. They are waiting for the day that I find my forever home, where I shall plant two trees and scatter them both. But until that time, they will remain with me. My other four dogs will be scattered in the same place when their time comes too.

A few days later, I had gone into a clinic to have my long-awaited tummy tuck. My apron of skin that was causing me so much discomfort was being removed privately, not paid for by the army. Some women had cosmetic surgery such as breast reduction or enlargements through the army system, but my reason for wanting a tummy tuck was not seen as a viable case as I was not suffering from depression because of it. I just wanted it done because it was so heavy, and I was having to constantly put rolled up tissue under it to stop the sweat from making it sore. I had always hated my overhung tummy and I had waited fifteen years for the opportunity to get it sorted so that I could move on from it.

I had loosely planned it so that after the hysterectomy in 2006, I could then get the spare skin removed and start working on my stomach when the time was right, and it was completely healed. I was only in overnight and in the morning,

Jack came to pick me up. I could walk fine, and I had on a big Velcro waistband to support the weight while it healed. Obviously, I could not get it wet at all! So, I spent the next few days sitting on the edge of the bath and washing everything I needed to that way. It was called improvisation!

My friend, Laura, was administering the thrombosis injections because I could not bring myself to stick a needle into my own ass! I do draw the line on my pain threshold, and this was not something I could do to myself, one because I could not see my ass, and two, because the fluid that is injected causes a very unpleasant stinging!

Laura also took me to my appointments at the clinic which was half an hour away and I was not allowed to drive, which I did adhere to for fear of tearing open my new scar. The wound became a little infected on the right-hand side again like last time, and to my horror, I had a hole! I called the surgeon at the clinic and he told me to go up and collect some antiseptic cream from him but not to use anything else! After my previous experience and the scar getting so badly infected, I avoided getting water anywhere near my tummy. I devised a plan that would prove fruitful and helped dry it all out. It involved clamping fans onto my bed, so I sat on the bed for a lot of my time with the fan pointing straight at the scar and literally watched it heal so much quicker than if I had just left it! It was the only time in my life that I have obeyed a doctor's advice and sat and recovered without doing much. It damn near killed me!

Like a lot of people, I do not make a good patient. I like to be up doing stuff and being active, especially now at the time of writing this book, I go to the gym and have four dogs to walk and take care of (but that is another book). I waste no time at all. Every minute is carefully used productively and resourcefully.

As the time went on in Germany, it was becoming more and more apparent to me that Jack preferred being at work or in the gym. Little to no patience was displayed for Faye and me and before we lost Lara, he was never around much to walk her despite being the person who wanted her in the first place. I was becoming aware after receiving our photo from mess do's that we looked more like friends as opposed to husband and wife who were supposed to be in love. Our body language spoke volumes to me; this was not a 'forever marriage'.

I take responsibility for half of this, because for my part, it stemmed from the A and E department while we were waiting to view my brother. I could not recover from the insensitivity and lack of 'for better or worse' part of our vows, because that was me at my worst, and he broke his promise to be there for me.

Just like I had broken my vow 'Forsaking all others'. People who had known us for years would never have guessed how I felt because I became particularly good at hiding my true feelings. A lesson I learnt at an early age when I learnt to store my bubbles of memories in my Archimedes shell, where they would always remain until I had the time and inclination to deal with them. This book is dealing with all of them one by one! Popping each bubble and discarding it as it is written in black and white. I can now discard the things that have plagued me for years until it was the right time, and I had what I considered enough life experience to write it all down. And perhaps now Archimedes can retire!

We waited in 2009 for news of where we were to be posted back to the UK for Jack's remaining last two years. His twenty-two years were nearly over, and the months were flying by at an alarming rate of knots! I started to feel anxious about leaving Germany and there was absolutely nothing I could do about it. We had to go as Jack had refused to take the promotion of Regimental Sergeant Major in favour of getting Faye back to the UK so that she could go to college.

He came home one day and delivered the news that we could not have the posting we would have liked above all others because the other person who had applied for it had stated that if he did not get it, that his wife was going to leave him! It was a place in Cambridgeshire which would have been nearer to where we were originally from, but no…we were to be posted much further up north!

Our boxes were mainly packed in preparation and the house looked like a big removal was about to happen, but we always started packing the little things a couple of months before we were due to move because we never knew a definite date until quite close to us leaving. I always started with silly ornaments and things that we knew we were not going to use and could live without.

The problem was, there was sometimes that one little thing that would slip into a box of 'not needed' and then actually it was! So, the commencement of rummaging would go on until the item needed was located, always in the last bloody box!

The married quarter that we were vacating was a substantial size, and I would miss it greatly. It had served us well and allowed us to spread our furniture out a bit more and have room to move about comfortably. It had been my favourite house in the army life so far, and it held my last treasured memory of my lovely brother's final visit at Christmas 2004. A memory that now sits in my head with only the vision of him tucking into his turkey dinner, and demanding that we have cranberry sauce, cheeky bugger!

Just before we moved, it was announced that Patrick Swayze had lost his fight with cancer. I was devastated and I had read his autobiography. In his last few pages, he had told of how he planned to write another book, so it was a total blow to have lost such a powerful character. Michael Jackson overshadowed the death of Patrick though because his was surrounded by the controversy and scandal of how he had died.

It was August 2009. We were moving again and the famous last words that came out of my mouth were "we will go and buy our first house and finally I may have a husband that comes home every night. I have only waited twenty years for it." (I meant the bricks and mortar. I knew that Jack would never change and believed that if anything, it would probably get worse.)

There would be no more Sergeants Mess functions with the Regiment. No more, big functions for the families on camp, or Saint Patrick's weekends, and no more collecting our mail from the Post Bunk. We were leaving friends and everything about the Regiment behind us. We were on our own heading back to the UK on our last two-year posting. Jack was not interested in becoming an Officer and commissioning into the upper ranks, he wanted to go back to England as the RSM of a territorial army camp for his last two years, and then walk away with his lump sum of gratuity money and his army pension. His pension was secure, but this would prove to be a tool that he could and would use against me in the future!

For Faye, the move back to the UK was a massive relief because her tormentors could no longer touch her. Her ordeal was over, but the severity of it would be hidden for years to come.

Before we departed for the UK, my lovely best friend in the whole world had found me on social media! Denise and I chatted on the phone for hours, the last twelve years of separation melted away like we had never been apart! So much had happened and we just picked up where we left off. I was so pleased to have my first ever-best friend for life back! It was never the same without her; she had always been the one person that could tell straight away if there was something was wrong before we even spoke! We just connected from the moment we met, and I never felt like I could not say anything and everything to her, and most of the time, she would be thinking the same thing.

She was back and I was so grateful, it also became evident in future years that I would need her more than ever and she came through, every single time.

I had also made a friend at the eleventh hour. Literally, a month before we left Germany, Jack had invited a gym buddy and his wife Amanda (Ajay, who is still one of my closest friends) around for a brew one afternoon. Faye set about making her shortbread biscuits as she loved being able to bake them, bless her! It was so lovely seeing her bring them into the living room with a beaming proud smile on her face at her achievement and having baked them from scratch all by herself. It goes without saying that I love my daughter, and this is a very treasured memory because she was at last able to genuinely smile, and I had missed that smile so much.

Jack's friend (Whom I call Ruddy, because he was bloody horrible!) was someone that I had spoken to in passing but never spent any length of time with. His wife Ajay was lovely, and we hit it off in an instant and did not stop chatting so much we found it hard to believe that we had not met before! But that was sometimes how the cookie crumbled. I was also busy cleaning the married quarter so that it was spotless when we left. Consequently, I had backed off from my other friends to make it that little bit easier to say goodbye when the day came for us to leave.

I spent a lot of time with Ajay and we agreed that we would stay in touch even though they were going to be posted to Cyprus shortly after we left. And stay in touch we did, she bought two of my butterfly creations and I sent them out to Cyprus to her to auction for the stray dogs that she was heavily involved in rescuing.

By the time we left Germany, I was ready to go and I wished for a quiet life. It was all that I wanted after the turmoil of the last five years and to have a respite from pain and drama.

I would miss the noise of the tanks rolling off the trains as they headed back to the camps via the range roads, and I would miss the sound of the ranges. I would miss the close friends I had made, and the German shops. But we were getting out of the army system in a couple of years and it would all be a distant memory where no one would remember us anyway, only those that really knew us all the years we had been around would think of us and vice versa.

Chapter 17
Hello Private Renting

We said our goodbyes to the people that we needed to, anyone of relevance that needed to stay in our lives would do so but most people we knew would fall away, perhaps not straight away but eventually the lack of communication would weed out those who were in our lives for keeps. Social media was the most obvious way to stay in touch.

We drove away from the house we had lived in for five years and did not look back because it was the last time that we would see it. It was a strange feeling knowing that I had my brother and Lara's ashes in my car. But I refused to pack them onto the truck that transported our furniture; they were too important to me and I cherished them both too much to not have them travel in style across Europe and into the UK. Plus, all our worldly possessions were going into storage whilst we looked for our next suitable house because where we were going there were no army quarters!

This made things a bit more complicated and we faced the prospect of living out of a hotel room until our next accommodation was found. We were assigned a liaison officer who had faxed us the choice of three properties for consideration, and as we now had no pets, we could have any one of them.

We had brought our last tax-free cars. The plan was to run them with as little cost as possible and once Jack had his gratuity money they would be paid off, and that meant that we could look at buying a house and focus on that. I was so proud of my lovely sporty Corsa with the body kit and low-profile wheels, it was a bit boy racer in style, but I absolutely adored it and joked that I loved my car more than my husband. But the question is, was I joking?

The answer is no I was not joking. Jack had become a selfish bastard and I did not know what I was going to do or if I would ever do anything, but I knew one thing for definite, he was not going to change because he had already got worse. So, I knew that everything about driving back to England and finding our hotel on the other side would be stressful. It always was.

The minute we hit Dover, it was not an option to stop to rest, Jack wanted to get up to the Midlands as soon as possible. So, we drove through the night. Exhausted and needing the toilet, I text him to say that I could not go any further, and that I needed a break and to get coffee. He hated spending money at service stations and I always felt bad that Faye and I were being needy, but in this case, we had driven six hours on the Europe side and then an hour on the ferry where rest was impossible with seasickness kicking in! And now, we were making a journey that would take roughly four hours.

I hated travelling with him, it was always a rush to do everything and eating quickly became the normal routine that Faye and I had got used to. We were never able to finish what we ate without feeling like the plate was literally snatched away before we took our last bite before we were heading out of the door! He could never just take life at a normal pace and it was as if there was always somewhere to be, or something that he had to do. It was very frustrating, and we had learned to live with it, but I often wondered if it was like this for other couples. (Now I know that it is, and for some couples it is worse!)

Why he was always in a rush, I will never know, but Faye and I detested it.

We arrived at the hotel which was to be our home for the next few days until we had been allocated a house. We had been sent the three different houses to look at by the army liaison officer for the North West area. He was extremely helpful and patient with me because I wanted to try and pick the right house that had enough room for all our stuff that would be arriving on the truck!

It was stressful to say the least as every house we viewed was totally inappropriate and small! One of our favourites (on paper) in the beginning was a sixteenth-century pump house that had supposedly been renovated, but even looking at it from the outside was a little traumatic because it was small with a couple of broken windows, and spiders were happily dangling from the thatched roof every few inches! There was just no way we would be able to fit all our furniture in it either, just no way! Hindsight is a wonderful thing, and had we accepted it we would potentially have had a better quality of life than the house I chose. It was a drastic error of judgement on my part and I hold my hands up to that fact. The cottage was detached and was snugly surrounded by high established hedges, it was a private little drive too.

We next viewed an end terrace townhouse with four bedrooms and a very strange layout on the ground floor. The kitchen was at the front of the house overlooking the small and restricted parking area, which was housed by a wall on the main road with a small courtyard. There were enough spaces for two cars per house, but it was a tight squeeze! The back room on the ground floor was again, small! And led into an unheated conservatory that was the length of the house so we decided that the dining table and any excess furniture could live out there, but we made the small room our lounge instead of using the room on the first floor. That was to be our bedroom and the top two rooms were to be Faye's so that she could have one as her chill out room. I made the other middle room the clothes room as there was a massive wardrobe in it on the back wall.

I only chose this house because I thought it would be beneficial to have the room to spread out and not be cramped, as it is one of my pet hates. But in making this decision, I had no idea that it would be to the detriment of the family, I could not have predicted what was to unfold in the early days of our residing there.

One evening, we were watching TV when clearly an argument had erupted between the adjoining neighbours. It sounded like they were in the same room as us as it was so loud! They were a younger couple with two children, the youngest of which was a baby. The sound of crashing became apparent that she had either fallen or been pushed down the stairs, with him shouting obscenities of what he thought of her and her appearance and that she was a slapper. This was an event that was to occur frequently and as much as two or three times a week. It was only a matter of time before they started on us.

We kept ourselves to ourselves and went about securing jobs and trying to live with this explosive behaviour when she obviously was not prepared to do anything about it, and we did not want to be involved for fear that the drama would spill over to us. But spill over it did.

I must admit that my resolve to listen to it any longer was waning and I dreaded the inevitable onslaught of abuse when they started on us. She would stand at her kitchen sink looking out of the window at us when Faye and I were arriving home with a look of utter hatred for the both of us. It was very undermining; she seemed to make it her purpose in life to make us feel uncomfortable. He was called Mark and I will call her bad egg, just because she was just horrible for no reason.

It happened every time we drove into the courtyard and seemed like she was waiting for us most of the time; she clearly knew the times we would be home from work. We had lived there just short of ten months and Jack had been away on exercise with the recruits for a week when the shit hit the fan, and we were stood directly in front of it! Faye and I had been made to feel like prisoners in our own home.

He entered the door to find the two of us in the back living room with the TV on, but the sound was turned down low for fear that was the reason they were so pissed off at us. We had crept around the house making as little noise as possible, but the death stares continued no matter what we did. The next day and without my knowledge, Jack had put an A4 piece of paper in the back windscreen of his car for them to read. I cannot remember what was written on it, but it was basically goading them to start something. I heard shouting out in the front courtyard and went to the front door which was open, Jack was out there, and the mouthy bad egg was shouting obscenities at him until I appeared to which she then shouted at me, "Oh here she is, the fucking Oompa Loompa!" Eluding, to the fact that I was overweight and round. Her Manchester accent was strong, and her foul mouth made her sound like a typical person that just loves a good argument and show down in the street. I would rather be fat than look the way that she did! Make-up smudged all over her eyes where she had been crying, her hair resembled an abandoned bird's nest and her abusive mouth capable of spilling poisonous bile.

The bloke Mark was watching from over the pub wall along with his mates who were obviously waiting for Jack to start something and get a fistfight going. But Jack was talking in his low voice that he used when he does not want anyone but the person on the receiving end to hear what he was saying, he was saying something to her that seemed like he was trying to diffuse the situation although I could not hear him. I said that I was calling the police which was met by further abuse from the mouthy bad egg in the courtyard. Her mother who was also present was trying to calm her down too, but the reason there was no talking to her was evident by the giant size red wine glass in her hand. It was not even twelve o'clock midday yet, classy until the last!

Heaven knows where her kids were, or who was looking after them while Mark was gawping from afar and she was in the courtyard in her drunken shit state launching a cheap, verbal attack on us! She looked rough. Her mother was with her telling her to calm down, but it failed to work.

On the opposite side of the road was the local pub which we had only ever been in for lunch once or twice and it was okay in small doses, but once the

Friday feeling hit the small town, the music and partying started and unfortunately, we lived right opposite it. I would have liked to go one night but Jack was not up for going clubbing, I mean, who would want to go out with a fat wife like me? I felt stuck in a rut and old before my time. I was 39 I did not feel my age, but married life certainly made me feel restricted. Quite happy to sit in the house drinking his fucking tea and ignoring me while he played his stupid games on his laptop.

While bad egg's verbal attack persisted in the courtyard, Jack kept telling me to go inside the house. In the end, I gave in and stood in the kitchen so that if all of Mark's friends decided to cross the road, I could call the police. But as it happened the threat dyed down and Jack came in the house having decided to let it go, whatever it was. I told him that I really could not take any more of living like this and it was not fair on Faye. I could not believe he had stirred up trouble with her but as it turned out it was to have a positive impact.

Jack went into work the next day and got the ball rolling that we would be moved on welfare grounds. A lady called Angela came around to see us on Wednesday after the courtyard incident had happened, and we described to her that we could not take living like prisoners in our own home. She made it clear after our description of what had been going on in the last few months that, as there were young children in the house, she would have to report the domestic abuse that was happening so frequently to social services.

Within two weeks of seeking help from the welfare team on Jack's camp, our removal truck was parked outside on the main road and we were moving to a small bungalow in a different town. The family was not told of the social services being brought in until after we had left the area and out of the way. Her reaction would not be one that we wanted to witness but they had brought this on themselves after the months of abuse we had endured, God only knew how she would react otherwise!

Bad egg commented while we were helping load our things on the truck that it was "about time you lot fucked off".

I was so glad we were leaving. After all we had been through in the last few years, all I wanted was a bloody quiet life, but it had been completely the opposite. I had been to the doctors who had prescribed antidepressants, my second time having been given them after the loss of Darren. I had thought that I was doing all right up until we moved into this current place and I hoped to be able to stop taking the tablets. I did not really cope with being on them because they made me feel like I could not control my spaghetti head and they clouded my judgement. I like to have a clear head and see things in black and white, but these tablets were giving me grey areas that meant my brain was spinning in my skull at the slightest bit of stress. I did not like any of it and started weaning myself off them.

Faye and I stayed at our jobs as room attendants in Macclesfield, but it was such a long drive from the bungalow that it affected on us financially, and tiredness was paramount all the time. We never got weekends off unless we fought to get at least one of the weekend days off. There was once I lost my temper because I could not remember the last time that I had cooked a Sunday roast or went shopping on a Saturday! Faye was exhausted too, as she was learning to drive and working to pay for the remainder of the lessons she needed until she passed. While we were still in the previous address and just after moving back to the UK, Jack and I had bought her first ten lessons, as we wanted her to be independent. Jack used to get annoyed that one of us would have to drive her to work even on our days off, but at the end of the day, she was doing her best and it was not something that could be rushed. I used to get annoyed and frustrated with the situation and took it out on Faye much to my shame, but I just wish he would bloody give things time and not expect everything to happen yesterday! He pissed me off on more than one occasion and I used to go and sit in a layby and call Denise to talk to her, as I knew she would listen and give impartial advice.

I found Jack extremely obnoxious, arrogant and damn right rude at times and he was not patient at all with Faye and me. I felt like he was using the fact that I was on the antidepressants to make me feel like I was losing my mind and that "there was something wrong with me!" He had said it on more than one occasion. I now know that this term has a name, it is called Gas Lighting. It is basically manipulation of someone to make them doubt their own memory, perception and sanity.

Gaslighting is abusive, it is a form of emotional abuse whether done consciously or subconsciously. It is a form of control that distorts the victim's perspective and leaves them questioning their reality, making them feel like they further need to depend on their abuser. This carried on for a few years, but I was not aware that it was happening and that there was a name for it until recently when I heard it on the radio. (It is February 2021 when I am rewriting this, and I found out the term used for this kind of abuse in the summer of 2018!)

My last summer working in the hotel was probably the hottest ever! It was absolutely stifling in the middle corridor where I was in and out of the rooms changing the beds and cleaning. There were people poking their heads out of their rooms and looking up and down the corridor. I immediately became aware of what they were investigating as I pushed open the door in the middle section of the corridor to let some air blow through from the fire escape once I had opened it at the far end.

As I walked up the corridor, the screams and groaning got louder! I tried so hard not to laugh, as it was abundantly clear that the residents in that end room were having an extremely good time! Anyone who has ever booked a hotel room for some unadulterated fun will understand, but this went to a whole new level of fun!

Well, I can honestly say that I did eventually burst out laughing when there was a crash from inside. I was standing outside the room to open the fire escape door, and I did it loudly to make them aware that the sound travelled!

The couple carried on as if there were no one else in the world that could hear them and bearing in mind that this was around 9.30 am, they certainly had some acrobatic bedroom skills going on. I found it hysterical, but I carried on with my work at the other end of the corridor. I was getting sheets off my trolley a bit later when I saw them exit the room. They walked casually up the corridor with flustered and red faces. I stood and waited for them to pass with a cheeky grin that I could not hide. As she walked past me, she walked like she had a run in with Red Rum! She smiled at me shyly and before my brain engaged with my mouth, I said, "I hope you two enjoyed yourselves? Have a good day!"

They carried on without looking back but I thought it was funny, and I was a little jealous that Jack and I never had as much fun like that! Not even in the early days had we had rigorous sex like that, so I started thinking that I had missed out on something there!

Unfortunately, as it was on my corridor the room that they had vacated was mine to clean. Oh, the joy! As I turned the key and opened the door, my chin must have hit the floor! The scene was one of total carnage and destruction. I genuinely did not know where to start! The beds had been split down the middle, they had zippers so that we could split them into single beds if needed, but the zips had been ripped down the length of the bed! So, the zip was totally knackered! The sheets were on the floor in a pile, they had obviously removed them while performing their trampoline acts across the bed.

The lamps were in the corner, obviously put out of the way so that the swinging around the room would not knock them flying, so I was grateful for that premeditated action. The bathroom looked like they had been swimming and brought Nemo and company for good measure! You get the picture…it was just trashed! I had never seen a room left in this way before, it was also the reason I decided that it was time to look for a job closer to home. I had to report the broken zip and the other damage, but I cleaned the room and left as that was my last one for the day.

In 2011, I registered with an agency that was advertising for a housekeeper vacancy. I physically did not want to be cleaning shitty hotel rooms anymore, and Faye was going to college in September of this year because she had missed the opportunity to go on our arrival from Germany in 2009 on account of Jack's boss keeping him longer than he should have. We lost child benefit because Faye was not able to go straight to college because of this delay in Germany.

Faye worked for the year with me, which was hard going for her, but it gave her an insight of the difficulties of the working world if you have no qualifications to fall back on. Fortunately, she had the qualifications to be able to go to college.

I was so proud of her and relieved that she could chill out and make friends, she could just be herself act her age and not become embroiled in adulthood before her time. But I think that reality and working in the hotels had already hit home, bless her. While she was at college, I am pleased to say that she did eventually pass her driving and theory test, and she got a little run around to get her started. She had made a friend in the form of a young man who she nicknamed Beardy, and they did nothing but laugh together. She had finally told us of how bad things had been in her school in Germany, with Shithead being the main bully. I was devastated at what this girl had done to my daughter, but I did not know what I could do about it now that we were so far away, and who would believe it when there was no evidence after the fact?

So, I vowed that one day, I would find a way. A way to make the girl famous, and here we are, you are reading while I am writing about the little bitch.

The agency I had registered came through for me and I left the hotel to start work in a private residence for a family who lived only fifteen minutes away as opposed to the hour I had been driving, it was great! All three of us lived and worked a bit closer to home.

The family were nice, and they had three school age kids. I was there for just under a year before I became unhappy with being moaned at for doing things that were wrong. I could be working for more money with a footballer that had been advertised on the agency website. I approached my agency lady and she put me forward for it and she tried to coach me on what I should be saying and how I should be behaving, but I was having none of it! I was always going to be myself and it was not like I was a rude type of person. My nan taught me to be respectful and that is how it is.

In 2011, I had arranged with a friend whose nails that I did, for her newly Ordained Brother to bless our wedding rings. It was our twenty-year anniversary, and her brother was more than willing to help. We even kept the little bottle of holy water that he had used. Looking back at the pictures now, I know that I was fat, and that bad egg's opinion was justified, but still hurtful. I also see now looking back, although the photos are in a distant memory tucked right at the back of my brain, in the smallest bubble in the furthest corner, that the body language of Jack and I told a thousand stories. Neither of us was really 'in love'. I think that we loved each other, but even after twenty years of marriage, our body language was not what a loving couple should be. There was no gazing lovingly or looking into one another's eyes. We were broken, and no amount of ring blessing that was going to fix that. We were detached, but we were not yet completely aware of that fact. We just carried on our lives and I think we did it out of habit more than any other reason. We did not know anything else.

I think I had been broken once too often and suppressed by this man for too long, and the cracks were showing even though I could not see them at the time. I remained hopeful that once Jack's time was up in the army that he would settle into a normal job and come home every night. But I knew that he would never settle for that and he would never be happy with that scenario. He was too career driven and wanted everything his own way all the time, and it was still the case that I fell in line and still was not able to be myself…I resented that. Oh, he would joke that I wore the trousers, but there was not much that I did without asking for permission first. I even took to keeping receipts after I had been to a shop so that I could answer when he asked, "How much did you get rid of?" He made me feel inadequate in respect of that I never earnt much.

For our anniversary, we had pre-booked a holiday to Crete and arranged that Faye could stay at home under the close watchful eyes of the next-door neighbour and our friend who was in her '70s. She lived in a little bungalow across the other side of the close which was literally the end of the road, you couldn't drive any further our rented bungalow was adjacent to an alley.

Faye was old enough to be on her own for a week and I spoke to her by text and Anne was texting and calling her as was Denise too. We met a couple who I stay in contact with even now, they live in Wales and did not turn their backs on me when the impending marriage doom happened a couple of years later.

While walking back to where we were sitting by the pool one day, I was talking to the couple who were in the room next to us. Without realising, I was not far over enough to avoid the kids smaller pool at the end of the big one, so I fell straight in because I was not looking where I was going! The splash made everyone stare as I was the only one that seemed to have braved the freezing water albeit involuntarily!

No one laughed except me. Jack calmly got up and sauntered over at a slow pace as if he knew I was okay but wanting to make himself look like the dutiful caring husband, he came over and offered a hand to help me out of the kid's pool. But he made it abundantly clear that I should seek some help and get some counselling as there was "clearly, something wrong with me".

The truth of it was, that he made me feel on edge! To the point where I started believing that my brain was not functioning to full capacity; he had me convinced that my spaghetti head was present all the time not just some of it. I was constantly pre-empting what I was going to do in advance and assessing whether I could do it without accidents happening or being accused of there being something wrong with me. Because apparently, I was not capable of doing anything without dropping, breaking or falling over something. This is what happens when someone makes you feel like an idiot even if they do it without saying the words. Even a look can tell you what they think of you, and this was something he was extremely good at, along with looks that could be of death stare level that chill you to the bone! Because it was a look that you would only really give to a sworn enemy or someone that you think is a complete idiot without any justification, but Faye and I were on the receiving end of these looks frequently.

While we still lived in the bungalow, we had to extend the tenancy a further eight months while our house was being built. We had chosen a four-bedroom town house off plan, so it was just an empty shell when we first viewed it, no windows and scaffolding still up around it. It was an exciting time to know that everything that would eventually be inside once it was complete would be unspoiled, and that it was only us that had lived there!

We used Jack's gratuity money to pay off the cars that we had purchased before leaving Germany and set about buying the last little things we needed for our brand-new house. Over the years, I had always collected the things that I planned to keep for our own long-awaited house so that all the colours would go together, and I would not be spending money on replacing things just for the sake of it. I was given a budget to work with and so I set about designing our house top to bottom. Neutral colours and red accessories in the kitchen and some union Jack soft furnishings in the living room to add a bit of brightness. Not to everyone's taste but this was to ours at the time, it was kind of patriotic. I binned it all at the end though! And will never have it again because of the memories that it would dredge up. No thank you, I can live without them too!

Faye's room was to be neutral with a vintage style double bed and accessories that in my opinion were beautiful for a young lady. She would add her own colours with the various crafts that she enjoys. I spent a small fortune on a heart shaped mirror which I wanted her to know symbolised that she was loved and cherished despite what ever happened in our lives, or the outcome of whether her father and I made it past our twenty-fifth year point which I was very much in doubt of! One would ask why did I continue with the charade if I knew it was not going to last? And my answer would be that I did love him. But, after writing this book, I know now that it was not the 'in love' type. And of course, I wanted it to work, but in truth, I knew that I was never going to have the man that I had married, because that man had changed completely. Now, he was a cold-hearted person that came home when it suited him claiming that it was not worth him driving home from camp during the week because of traffic.

I had delusions that one day, this man would become the father to Faye that he should have been from the start. And that he would want to be the husband I dreamed of. A husband who wanted to come home and be with his family, and a man who could be loving and romantic. Delusional fantasies.

What I was receiving were the signs of infidelity. We had been here before and I had ignored it. But the signs were there to read again, and this time he was nothing short of a nasty bastard.

Deep down, I knew the signs of detachment were there. He had never appreciated the woman he was married to, he claimed to love me but love does not hurt if it is real. Love is capable of compromise and does not want or need to control every situation and pretend that it was for the good.

The laptop was the first sign, he would disappear into his little battle games and not want to talk or sit at the dinner table for any longer than he had to, that was when he did put in appearance at home. But I always made sure that dinner was either on the go or was dished up and waiting for him. Things proceeded to grow worse over the coming months.

I had a call one day from my agency lady after my enquiry for the footballer job that she had tried to groom me for. I had an interview!

During the call, she was unsure which of the footballers it was. I did not care, as I have never been a football follower apart from two football games that I had attended at age fourteen with Karl. West Bromwich Albion and Queens Park Rangers had lost against my home team. I was deemed a good luck charm by the detested boyfriend Karl because our home team had won on both the occasions I had attended!

I went for the interview suited and booted. I left my car on the road outside and walked up the driveway of the address that I had been given. The gates were open so I presumed that they would be inside and expecting me. Or at least I hoped so!

I was exceedingly nervous because I knew that there would be a lot of hurdles to get through to get this job and be able to convince these people that I was trustworthy. As I went to knock on the door, it gently glided open by the hands of a fit black young man with a beaming smile and pearly, white teeth. He laughed as I stared at him and then said, "Come on in!" I had absolutely no idea who he was. I just do not follow football.

I followed him into the living room, and on entering, I saw that there were four men scattered on various couches. One of them was staring at me with his laser eyes that penetrated my soul! A suspicious man who quite clearly was unable to hide that fact. It was unnerving to say the least, but I refused to look at him until he spoke directly to me instead of at me or about me, I found him rude and arrogant. As he started talking, he asked me all the general questions about where I had been, and where I had lived and told me that the work experience on my CV was good. He was the liaison man for the black man who was the footballer, and my agency lady had warned me that he was an abrasive and forthright man. Which was fine, but I was not going to be spoken down to like I did not have two brain cells to rub together and I would not tolerate his rudeness.

I did, however, feel that he was scrutinising everything I said. I knew that this was a VIP that I was being interviewed for, but that VIP was in the same room and seemed very chilled out. In the end, I got sick of being spoken to like I was a second-class citizen. I addressed the footballer himself, and whilst looking directly at him, I said, "I can get your house cleaned up, it will take a couple of weeks to get into a routine, but I can sort your house out. And I am trustworthy, as I have signed the Official Government Secrets act on more than one occasion in the army life, and if they can trust me, then I am sure that you could learn to!"

He replied, "You do not even know my name, do you?"

I replied, "No, I do not, but this is an interview for a housekeeping job, and I am not into football so there is no fear of me getting all starry eyed and gooey! I am here for the job and nothing more." And I will sign whatever confidentiality clause that you require me to.

I remained calm and stayed in my professional composure, talking directly to the man who would be hiring me was my chosen path, if they thought that I was being obnoxious then I fully expected not to get the job.

Two days later, the phone call came from the Agency to say that I had got it! But they obviously wanted me to be self-employed, and to sign the Confidentiality Clause, neither of which I had any problem with. I gave my notice with the little family and started the next week with the footballer. My first three weeks working there were about finding my feet and getting myself into a routine. I worked so hard to get the place up to a standard that I was used to, and my fingers were sore from scrubbing with crème cleaner and scourers. I am going to fast forward a little because basically I was working with these guys for about a year and I totally respected all of them, all except the girlfriend. I had asked her who was to be my point of contact, as I was not supposed to bother the footballer with trivial questions, but I had to ask questions with regards to their house and I needed to know who to go to. She took it upon herself that she could call me 'The Cleaner' which I forcefully corrected her on my title being bloody housekeeper!

I did not want to be around her and preferred working when she was not there. I will not elaborate any further but the hours I was working were thrown into question. She did not seem to believe that I was working what I was charging them for, and that pissed me off because my honesty was being thrown under suspicion. I was where I was meant to be, but her approach and the way she

196

spoke to me was the reason I left. I was devastated because working for him was awesome and I really missed them after I left. I just could not tolerate her any longer. She was only fucking eye candy anyway with not much between the ears to speak of.

She spoke to me like I was beneath her, and quite frankly, it got my back up. Jack drafted a letter of resignation and I went to the HQ where I handed it in with the keys. It was not a decision I made lightly because I really like working for him, he was funny and bothered to speak to me like I was a human being. He told me once that his family were just a normal family and grew up in a normal street. I was gutted to leave. I was having so much drama at home that I had no patience to stay. I had to try and save my marriage, but in leaving this job, I probably made it worse.

Chapter 18

The House That Jack Built

On the day to pick up the keys for our new house which I had watched taking shape, Jack subsequently took away my excitement monumentally by exclaiming, "I shall be watching your face as we walk in the door!" No pressure! I had driven regularly to see it being built and I was so excited until he had said that.

He said this because I had dreamed of an older building with some character, and the opportunity to do things and put our own stamp on it. I still have that dream and maybe one day it may come true. I hope so. It is more of a goal that I have set myself, but I would like to buy a plot of land with a big oak tree so that the staircase can be built around that tree and I can design my own house and live like a Hobbit lol!

The phrase "pissed on my fireworks" sprang to mind after he said it! Because despite that it was not a cottage in the country, I had accepted a long time ago that it never was going to be. He wanted a house that needed nothing doing to it and only the responsibility of paying the mortgage. Plus, we needed the government backed scheme to get on the property ladder.

Jack was never good with taking on anything that to anyone else would be considered a normal responsibility, this was the biggest purchase of our lives, and one that I hoped to one day have paid off and pass the bricks and mortar on to Faye. Our ages went against us and we could only get the mortgage over twenty years instead of twenty-five, therefore, increasing the price every month.

When I was asked by the sales representative before the kitchen was put in, to go and "choose my colours". I had to ask what she meant, because I had never owned a house and only lived in army quarters and so for a split second, I thought she had meant curtains!

We arrived at the sales office and we were greeted by the lady we had come to know as Debbie. She had cats and as we got on well, we always talked about her feline pals every time I saw her because we had no animals since losing Lara, who was missed more than we showed. We walked around to our new house where two housekeepers were literally backing out of the door with air fresheners and a hoover in hands. It felt like a hand over or a march out, as we knew it by!

It was shoes off, as I had opted for cream carpets in the hallway. (We had no pets so why not?) I wanted it to be as light and airy as possible after living in army accommodation because they could be a bit depressing at times with the restrictions of the carpets already being there when you marched in. As this was our house, Jack kind of let me get on with it and just provided some cash if needed, although I never did anything without consulting him first as per the norm. After Debbie had shown us around our finished house, we stood at the Juliette balcony in our living room and just stared out of the window. We opened it and stood for a few minutes to take in the view of the back garden which was of course basic, we could design it our way.

The building development was ongoing as ours was at the first part of the estate, but we did not mind as we were now in our town house and we watched all the other houses being built behind and to the side. It was great, and we were proud that we had finally done it. Until we became aware two weeks later that the adjoining neighbours were not quiet at all, in fact, EVERYTHING about them was noisy! This was to be a contributing factor in the marriage breakup as I was home more than Jack who stayed in camp (he claimed) and it was me that had to listen to doors constantly being slammed and the thumps of the heavy set two young boys up and down the stairs. I tried my best and made the effort to get on with the Nigerian parents, but they just did not listen to my pleas of being a little more considerate.

The mother would be in the kitchen at the back of the house shouting at the boys who were sat in the same room, they were sat at the same dining room table as her! It was just constant loud noise and ground-shaking thumps that we could feel vibrate through our entire house. One of my final comments to a friend when we were departing Germany was "we are off to seek our quiet life after everything we have just been through". Unfortunately, this could not have been further from the truth and the decibels grew week by week. In fact, after we left Germany, things had grown progressively worse and I felt so lonely even in Jack's company.

It affected my relationship with Faye and although kids do things wrong, I felt that fault was being found for the slightest trivial thing, and it bothered me that she was apparently to blame because she (allegedly) had an attitude problem all the time. The only respite I had before I quit the footballer was that I enjoyed my job, I had the freedom to get the place up to my standard and the money was good. This was the only time in our married life that I heard the words "I am happy and content, I have no money worries". Everything came down to money!

Jack always controlled the bank and made sure the bills were paid, but that did not mean that I was not capable of doing it as I had done it during our entire married life in the army too. He may have been the main breadwinner, but it was me who was living in the married quarters bringing up our little girl and caring for the dog and working, albeit part time. The main reason I started writing this book was because I kept hearing from people, "Bloody hell, what those poor soldiers go through." And yes, they are correct that it has been an awful time for the lads in the recent years with all the operational tours and the after affects it has had on them after they return.

But the wives and girlfriends go through hell too, the lack of communication and fear of whether her man was coming back alive or in a box. And when they return, they do not always come back as the same person that left. Adjustments and compromise had to be made, along with acceptance that you had to learn to be in each other's space again. For me personally, as the tours began to wind down, I grew anxious because it would take time to assess how much was left of the man that went away. They changed dramatically, with issues that sometimes went unaddressed, and these issues led to all sorts of mental torture, not just for the men, but for the families. It was like a domino effect.

There were/are accidents that happen that no one hears about, the accidents while training with live rounds and deaths that happen whilst not on operational tour. It is not the case that deaths and accidents only happen as a result of being away fighting for Queen and country, but also everyday incidents that are not spoken about. That is life and we do move on. But for someone to obtain counselling and help, they need to first admit that they are not coping with their mental state of health. They need to first acknowledge it, and want to fight the depression, or the Post Traumatic Stress Disorder. This is something that a lot of military people (as well as civilian sufferers) struggle with. Some do not even consider that they could be a sufferer (wives included), and therefore, it goes undetected. They have been trained as tough fighting machines. So, to admit defeat off the physical battlefield and fight that bad little chimp on their shoulder, is probably the hardest battle of all.

Whilst we now had our beautiful brand-new house and apparently no money worries, there was a major worry in the back of my head. How long would it be before this bubble burst?

The feeling that I had was overwhelming, to the point that I could not put my finger on what it would be, but that something was going to go dramatically wrong with a monumental impact. I pushed it to the back of my head and tried to enjoy the house and putting things in their place to make it ours, and I just hoped that the bubble would stay afloat and not burst, for now!

In 2013, we went on a family holiday to Mallorca, Faye had found herself a boyfriend who, on first impressions seemed 'okay', and I was willing to give him the benefit of the doubt, but I was on my guard because after all the years of meeting so many people from different cultures and moving around, it can make you a good judge of character. Okay, I will be completely honest I thought he was a twat with an attitude problem! And body odour that rattled my teeth! But Faye liked him for whatever reason, so in the beginning I shut my mouth and let her get on with it. They say that subconsciously we look for father figures, so heaven help us on this occasion!

As a parent, we have a certain obligation to let our kids make their own mistakes, up to a certain degree. We all did things as kids ourselves, right? But I had an overwhelmingly bad gut feeling on this occasion with regards to this lad. Something was not sitting right, and I took to calling him Alex the asshole…because that was exactly what he turned out to be! I did not find out the whole truth from Faye until a couple of years later. And! My gut instinct proved one hundred percent correct!

On this family holiday, it was just the three of us, and I admit I did chip away at Faye to the point that I was probably unfair. But in the end, I was justified in thinking that he was a wrong one, my suspicion proved correct and after my daughter had been severely bullied in school, I will offer no apology for being overprotective as a mother.

I knew that I was right, and I knew that after the attraction with the asshole ended, that I would not need to say the words "I told you so".

He spoke to her like shit, and as he did not drive, Faye had to do all the running to him. I offered that he could stay ay ours because she had a double bed in her room, but he would have none of it. I cannot imagine why!

I offered so that I could try and gauge him, but I think he was aware of this and flatly refused. We were having dinner with a couple of friends who were visiting, and Alex was invited so that I could get my friends opinion of him as well just to make sure it was not just me. If they thought he was quite normal, then I would drop my guard, but they did agree with me that he was weird.

Faye went to pick him up and he arrived with bed head, and a dishevelled, unkempt look about him along with his usual odour foul body scent. His unclean strong armpit smell was pungent, and it hung around the table making the whole room smell putrid!

I was also aware that Alex used drugs, smoked a lot and was a heavy drinker. My word! What a catch! And to say that I thought my daughter could do a lot better was an understatement. It baffled me what on earth she saw in him. Faye has always kind of picked the bad lads that treated her less than favourably. I wondered if she wanted someone that treated her like her father was with me. Someone that was not very romantic with a controlling nature and not able to show real emotions. Maybe she witnessed that and thought that it was how it was supposed to be, for in her little world growing up, that was the norm.

The day after we returned from holiday, Faye went off to see Alex sporting her new suntan, and we had made the arrangements to collect our adopted dog who was going to be on a flight coming over from Cyprus.

Ajay and Ruddy horrible had been posted off to Cyprus for two years, there are a lot of rescuers out there already, but my friend Ajay had instantly joined their ranks and became very proactive in helping to find homes outside of Cyprus. She would fund raise and obtain donations; she also spent her life savings on getting these animals off the island and into loving forever homes. I called her husband Ruddy (Ruddy horrible shit) because he was physically abusive and controlling with her, he pinned her up against the walls spitting obscenities in her face and tried to strangle her on more than one occasion. Yet she had to go on like everything was fine and hide the bruises. I could not stand him because she had told me of the abuse, and I could not say anything because it would make things worse. I hated him, more so because he acted like such a gentleman around everyone and was soft spoken, a wolf in sheep's clothing and a narcissist; he was charming but behind closed doors, he was deadly. He was also Jack's gym buddy and they used to train together and were thick as thieves.

On a warm, summer's evening, we drove to the collection point at the airport to collect our first dog since losing Lara five years earlier. Anne and her husband had given the biggest donation because they knew that this boy was going to a loving home, and that he had landed on his paws! This little crossbreed had been dumped by the highway in Cyprus and left for dead after being hit by a car. The rescuer who had found him said that as she drove past, he just "did not look as stiff as the rest". She drove to the next exit and turned around to go back for him. They named him Lucky because he had survived with only a bloody nose and a bad case of dehydration. He was well fed but obviously had been mistreated and to this day, he is still submissive and runs at even a slightly raised voice. I renamed him Alfie and we set about settling him in.

Jack wanted a dog to run with, but I should have known from when we had Lara that he never really wanted the mess and the care that goes with the status of having a dog. He did not like walking the dog if it was raining, and if I suggested anywhere muddy or going off for a long walk and take a picnic, I was met with excuses and reasons not to. It turned out that Alfie was older than first presumed but as he was found and rescued, they can only go by certain factors such as teeth and their fur. In any case, Alfie was not fit for an hour worth of running so was of little use to Jack, Jack was the one that wanted a dog years ago and I took over with the care, it felt like déjà vu because now the same was happening again.

It was decided that we would adopt another dog that seemed fitter and lived outside in a porch in Cyprus by a family who already had twenty or so cats in their house, and so having a dog inside was out of the question. Isobel arrived two weeks after Alfie, she was a good runner, and had the stamina for it. But obviously when you run with a dog, you do have to allow the dog to stop and pee! This was an annoyance to Jack, and one day while I was walking the other three, I saw Jack coming back from his run and caught him dragging Isobel while she was trying to pee. I told him when I got back home that it was out of order, and that I did not want him taking her if that was how it was going to be as I did not consider it to be fair. A dog's walk is their time too. He was not happy, but I think that was because I had seen him do it and felt that I was telling him off, oh well there, there! What I wanted to do, was forbid him from taking her out at all, but as it transpired, he paid little to no attention to the dogs he had so desperately wanted anyway.

He had previously set up a fitness club on the new build community social media page, and from what I understood, it was going well and consisted of mainly women. The first year in the house had been lovely, until the rescuing of the dogs had commenced, and I added two more small ones because I felt we were in a position with a big enough house and garden to accommodate them.

The cold shoulder treatment from Jack intensified after the arrival of the last dog, Charlie, but Jack was rather fond of the second little terrier girl dog called Rosie. These dogs would play a pivotal role in the next few years with them becoming my sole focus on breathing other than my daughter.

Just after we picked up Alfie and he had settled in, there had been a massive argument over Faye's questionable boyfriend, and I was beginning to lose the plot because Faye refused to see reason and did not want to heed any sort of warning about Alex the asshole.

I arranged to take Alfie down to meet Anne and her husband, as they had been the ones who made it possible by donating such a large amount of money to fly him over. I was only staying there for a couple of nights and as it was July, we were fortunate enough to be able to sit in the back garden and allow their dog and Alfie to get to know each other. We walked them for miles, and it was good to spend time with my extended family members as the visits to see them became few and far between now that we lived further away, but texting and phone call contact remained the same.

On the day I was to drive home, it was a Friday and Jack sometimes finished at lunchtime on this day, but not every week. As I was literally just about to get on the slip road heading north bound on the A34, my mobile rang and I pulled over in a layby to call Jack back. He informed me that Faye had gone.

"Gone? What do you mean gone?" I asked.

He said, "Well, I came home early from work and found her loading up her car with her belongings, the mother and sister of Alex were also in the house helping her!" My reaction was that the equivalent to an atomic bomb going off in the car. I told him I was just getting on the motorway and it would probably take me the three-hour drive, if not more to calm down!

My thoughts on the drive were that of guilt because I had pecked her head about Alex so much that now she was rebelling by moving in with him and his family, who from what we had been told were less than favourable. The argument in the kitchen was too much for her; maybe she had been sat there thinking, *Fuck you two. I will do what I want!*

All I knew was that there were only two people in this world that could hurt me in a monumental way, and they both had done it in the same manner, packed up and moved out without a word. *Like father like daughter,* I thought. "My God how could she do this to me?" But the simple fact is she is her father's daughter for being silent and planning without remorse, but she was my daughter in having the strength to do it. She knew that striking me in this way would hurt the most. I always told her that I would never put her out on the street and that I would never boot her out for any reason. I wanted her under my roof to protect her, but in doing so, I drove her away. This was a life lesson that she and I both had to learn by. And I had to allow her to get this out of her system and hope that she would eventually come back.

She was not living with us when Isobel arrived or the third dog Rosie, in fact I bombarded her with phone calls and angry pleas to come home or at least let me know that she was okay. But I heard nothing from her for seven months. The same amount of time that I had been gone after Mum put my bags on the doorstep when I was sixteen.

It was shortly after Christmas that I got a call from Faye. The first phone call, she was very tearful and apologetic. The second call on the following day, she asked if she could come around for a cup of tea. My heart was in my throat, I wanted her to come home so badly that I could hear my heart pounding as if it were about to burst should she suddenly changed her mind. She gets her stubbornness from me, and everything will be done, but we will do it in our own time and only when we have got something out of our system. But as I was told at the time, she will come back with her tail between her legs when she is ready and not before. I did not want her tail between her legs; I just wanted her home.

But I could never have prepared myself for the time when she was ready to talk about what happened while she was away. And I still NEVER once felt the need to say "I told you so". It was not relevant because all I wanted was my little girl back where I could be there for her. I understood why she had made the decision to leave because I had been relentless in trying to persuade her that asshole was bad news, and that nothing good would come of it. For his part in it, her father was cold and blamed her for things that were not always her fault, he told her to stop crying all the time as he could not accept that he was responsible for making her cry too. The man is cold and emotionless at the best of times, but to suppress the emotions of the two people he once claimed to love was unfathomable. To this day, I find it impossible to cry for no good reason. I hold it in and bottle my emotions because that is what twenty-even years with him made me into. I became a product of his making, and this was something that I desperately wanted to change. I wanted to be free to let my emotions flow as they needed to, but instead I had learnt over the years to suppress them.

I know my daughter, the same as any parent does when you spend every waking hour you can with them while your husband is away. I knew that something was wrong. When she arrived to move back in, she looked tired and drained with dark circles under her eyes from evidently not sleeping well. She took to Isobel straight away and said that she was such a beautiful dog, and that she would be her favourite if she had the choice. I think all my dogs are beautiful because they all have their own personalities, and all of them have issues after their traumatic lives in Cyprus. But Isobel was more the size of Lara, and Lara had been Faye's best friend when she was going through the hard times in secondary school. It is a bond that no one can break, so Isobel became Faye's dog. By the time Charlie dog arrived in April 2014, my marriage was well and truly dead in the water. It had been for a while. I was still acting like a dutiful wife and being a doormat in a last ditched attempt to try and salvage what I could of a sinking ship, whilst trying to stop my own anchor (my mind) from dragging me down to the depths. I could not fathom how someone could become so cold but still claim to 'always love you'.

The weeks became lonely and depressing because I did not understand what it was that I was doing wrong, why Jack stayed in camp all week every week and stayed away as much as possible. He had left the regular army in 2012 and drifted from job to job ever-since, none of them suited him.

He would sometimes come back on Friday nights, but I swear that he only came back to reinforce the fact that he hated and loathed me. I had grown my hair long and my lovely hairstylist Daniel (who is one of my best friends) listened once a month to my sad little life story that unravelled more each time that I saw him for hair appointments.

I had started losing weight due to the nauseous feeling that I had in the pit of my stomach twenty-four hours a day. I dreaded hearing the door handle being flung down, as if in a mood before he entered. Jack had told me that I could leave my job to set up my craft business, which I was a dubious about, but I went ahead. I knew that he would somehow use this against me in the future, I just did not know how or when. For now, I would sell things that I made online, and to family and friends. It was slow going to start with until I was asked by one friend to make a few things at once! Which to me was brilliant news! She just kept finding plaques that she liked, and I would replicate or design my own and personalise them for her with the names of the people who were to receive it.

I was in my element and I loved being able to get up, walk the dogs and then work from home. I even began to do a little bit of running with them! This was all short lived as another of my dreams was about to be ripped out from underneath me. In February of 2014, and before my crafting had really taken off, I flew to Southern Ireland to stay with my Auntie Lin who I had not seen for thirty years. After chatting with her on the phone, it was decided that I would make the trip and look for any potential houses to buy, with the order from Jack to find a quiet cottage. He did not intend to live anywhere else with me because his decision had already been made. I just did not know it. I think he was pleased to ship me off out of the way.

It was amazing to see my lovely auntie after all those years, and so good to catch up with her news. She told me about the death of my uncle who had passed away after fighting a brain tumour, and how she could never leave the little bungalow that they had shared, it would destroy her as all her memories were there, including my lovely cousin Sarah growing up. We spent the weekend talking, and I drove us into her local town in the hire car that I picked up at the airport, Lin had caught a bus to meet me so that she could direct me to her little house.

I spoke briefly to Jack who sounded distant, the conversation was short and I was not comfortable with the tone of his voice which seemed irritated and impatient. Something was amiss, but he was so distant these days that I really did not want to piss him off by asking. I cried, and I told my auntie about the situation. She offered amazing cuddles and made me feel better even if it was for a short period of time, I enjoyed that night in front of her coal fire in the living room. I was so lost.

It was painful trying to get through every day after waking up with an invisible mallet smashing my brain in a few times before I had even got out of bed and reached for the coffee pot. Only to realise that coffee did not wake me from the nightmare, and the eggshells that I walked on did not fade away, they only increased in density. I felt like I was swimming in a sea of emotions that I could not understand because there were too many of them, and I was unable to locate the shore. I could only tread water and hope that one day the tide would take me back in so that I could once again walk on solid ground.

The reality of it was that I was not looking forward to leaving my aunty or going home. I liked my house now that the place was homely, and everything was in its place. I was proud to have my first dishwasher, and a lovely kitchen with all the crockery and accessories that I had collected over the years. It was all now in its place in the house that Jack built. The house that Jack so readily tore down.

As always, everything came down to money. Not only was I about to lose the first house that I waited years for, but I was about to lose my daughter and a shadow husband.

I landed back at the airport on a chilly evening in February 2014, but the reception I received from Jack was even colder than the temperature outside. As I came through the arrival gate, I could not see him in the crowd of people waiting. I was about to text him to ask if he was stuck in traffic, when his face appeared sheepishly from behind a man.

It was completely bizarre! It was like a different man had dropped me off and a stranger was there to picked me up. His face displayed a look 'I don't want to be here'. It was clear that something had happened in the two nights I had been gone because it was like a light switch had been flicked off and there was nobody home except this shell of a man. He was gone. I had no idea what could have happened. I was no longer in the equation, and the person I had left as I boarded a plane was now devoid of any emotion. The transformation of the person that I left on Friday did not resemble the person that met me on Tuesday. There could be only one reason for this occurrence that would manifest itself eventually, but for now, I waited.

In the car, he tried to make small talk, but I had felt my heart crack after witnessing his repulsed expression at my attempt to kiss him on the cheek in the airport, and now all I felt was the rejection. I just wanted to get back to the house and see my daughter and dogs. And I wanted him to be gone the next morning and go and hide in his camp that he valued so much, I could then try and process whatever it was that had just transpired.

On one of the rare weekends that he was staying in the marital bed, he had one of his usual moods on him, so I did not want to talk. Charlie dog has always been the one that I could not prevent sleeping on the end of the bed. He has always done it, and that can sometimes be the problem with rescue dogs, once they get into a habit with one family, it is sometimes difficult to retrain them. Jack went to move Charlie a bit further down the bed. But Charlie picked up on

Jack's demeanour and growled and bared his teeth at him. The dog was protecting me, but at the time, I thought it was just a quick reflex to the fact that Jack had tried to move him. It is common knowledge that dogs pick up on someone's mood. And at this present time, Jack was being a complete bastard to me. Charlie had picked up the vibes when his mum had been crying whilst sat slumped on the bathroom floor quite frequently. And therefore, he is always sat with me and very rarely leaves my side. Wherever I go, my dogs go too, especially Charlie.

I had been chatting on messenger to a friend called Alison whom I had not known for long, and she was one of those types of people who, although I had never met her, she was willing to listen to my tale of a failing marriage. I was chatting to her in one of my darker moments while alone in the house, and yet again sat crying on my bathroom floor when she said something that totally slammed it home! Something that I already knew but still needed to hear from the horse's mouth. I wanted to hear these words from Jack to get the closure that would draw a line under it. She said, "Elise darling, I hate to say this so bluntly, but your marriage is over!"

Faye was still working at her job and was not home a lot of the time, but she spent it in her room watching DVDs or on the internet whilst doing her crafts and chilling out. If Jack was in the house, she was always told not go on the internet so much because the more devices you have working at once, the weaker and slower the signal. I felt it was yet another reason to pick a hole in her and make her feel unwelcome in her own home. She did not sit downstairs with us much, and I could not that say I blamed her; no one wants to sit with a room that feels like Mister Frost had visited and coated the walls. As kids, Darren and I used to say that Jack Frost had visited when the first frost of winter had coated everything white; this was one of Mum's sayings that we carried into adulthood.

I later found out that Faye stayed upstairs because she could not cope with what happened every time I said or did something, Jack would fire dirty looks my way, like I had just annoyed him by breathing.

Finding that out hurt monumentally, and I still had no idea why I repulsed him so much. I had taken to getting changed and ready for bed in the bathroom out of sight. I started wearing sleep shorts and a T-shirt to bed instead of knickers, but now, he made me feel like I was an object of discarded waste. He would look at me as if his skin would burn if I touched him. Sex was a thing of the past and had been for the whole of 2014 and way back into 2013.

I had originally Googled PTSD and some of the symptoms were resonating a little with the way he was treating me. We had always had a healthy sex life, right up until the holiday in summer 2013 and after Faye had moved in Alex the asshole. It was after Jack got the fitness sessions up and running that things started to change. We attempted a couple of times to be intimate but the last time it ever happened in September 2014, he got off me and said, "I can't."

I was so ashamed and embarrassed because it was me that had instigated it. In my attempt of make or break, it broke catastrophically. I crawled in horror to the bottom end of the bed so that I could cover up with the duvet and face him. But I was so broken that I could not even look at him. I had made the effort and showered and then put on some nice underwear, and although I am not the smallest of people in all fairness, we had more sex when I was a lot fatter with short hair (because he hated it in his face).

It was a catastrophic failure and the realisation hit hard. He then attempted to talk. But I was so numb that even my tear ducts were failing me. I could not even cry. He sat up on the end of the bed with his back to me and told me that we were detached. I replied that I had tried everything I could to save what was left of the marriage, but I could not fix something when I was the only one trying. I suggested that he should seek help for the PTSD, but he replied, "You'll be surprised how little of the PTSD that it is."

Then while I was in the middle of a sentence, he shouted at me, "What do you want from me?"

I just replied, "I want my husband back."

And his response was that "man has gone, I am not him anymore".

The truth is that I had known this for a long time. I knew that the man who had been the Jack that I had married had made his last appearance back in Mallorca in 2013. Even his own daughter did not want to be around him anymore.

This was one of the last times he stayed in the same room as me, which I was thankful for because I could not go through that humiliation again.

On another ridiculous show of fake unity, we had been invited to a wedding of one of his work colleagues from the new job he was at. I did not want to go. Because I was not working and only crafting from home to earn some money, so I made the card and a couple of wedding gifts. I wrapped them nicely with little keepsake cards. I thought that because they were handmade and personalised that it would be a nice original gift in the shape of sewn hearts and a lovely plaque with their names, the wedding date and a little white dove either side.

I made the effort, and I wore a lovely linen Jade colour dress because that was what I had been informed the colours were, green or blue. Faye and I had practiced doing my hair with straighteners like we had lots of times before for the Regimental mess dos. Only this time, there was an air of complete sadness that had been whitewashed over to disguise the heartbreak I was feeling. She did my hair in ringlets and I wore simple makeup that was more than I usually wore, but not overpowering. Jack came up to the top floor where we were just finishing up and asked if I was ready.

Faye said to him, "How beautiful does Mum look, huh, Dad?"

But all her hard work was unappreciated and went unnoticed because he just said "yeah" and looked away. Faye looked at me and she could see the pain in my eyes, and that I was fighting back the tears. She was hurt too. He was so cold, and now she had witnessed for herself that he was just not interested, and it appeared that he was just going through the motions. I hated him for being this way in front of Faye. I thought to myself, *How fucking dare he and who the hell was he anyway?*

Faye and I were both devastated at the lack of emotion from this person that was in the house only when he had to be, and that was thankfully not very often at all anymore. I preferred it when he was not there because then I was not going to be shot down in flames and made to feel like a useless idiot that he despised. I often wondered why he did not just end the torture for all of us and bloody leave. He refused point blank that it was PTSD, and he insinuated that the problem was me.

Chapter 19

The Last Christmas

We arrived at the wedding of his work colleagues and I knew absolutely no one, but I have the ability talk to anyone about anything, and that is one thing I am proud to say I can strike up a conversation. Just as well really, but all the years of practice came from being left to my own devices at the Mess dos where Jack could go and talk shop with Regimental buddies.

I saw two ladies that looked like they might take pity on a woman who knew nobody and did not know anything about the people or the job that her husband was doing, because he talked so little about anything to me anymore, so I did not ask. The little group that I had latched on to were deep in conversation about their place of work and I was like a duck out of water. In the Regiment, I knew generally what was being discussed, but here I knew nothing. I asked general questions avoiding what ranks they carried because I really did not want to know, or what job they did because all I knew was that Jack worked on a camp that was to do with medical stuff. He had shut me out, and it was not until this day that I had become acutely aware of how much. I mean for fuck's sake an Escort would have known more than I did! He would have had to tell an Escort something about himself and she probably would have known more than me! It was a ridiculous situation that I found myself in and only deepened my loathing of this man.

He went off to get cups of tea, and on his re-appearance, I had to pretend that I was his wife who was pleased to see him. When realistically, I had begun to loath his ways and I felt like a complete dick head! It was like they all knew something that I did not. I brushed off my pride and drank the barely warm tea that he had delivered before disappearing off to speak to his mate, only to resurface when it was time to go into the reception hall when we were all called in.

I had been seated in-between Jack and another man whose suit jacket ended up with more of my mohair shrug on it than the shrug itself! Jack was not impressed with the fact that his jacket looked the same, but I could not help that the seats were packed in like sardines on a starvation diet! Everything I did or said just annoyed him and he had no patience with me, his daughter or the dogs. His presence was toxic, and it made me feel like I was to blame even though I had done nothing to provoke his anger. After the ceremony, we were ushered into the big hall where they were to serve up the posh food in this posh bloody hotel that was set in stunning postcard surroundings. Joy!

During the meal, Jack was quiet and made no effort to laugh and joke like the Jack of old times. He used to be life and soul of the party and well known for his hearty laugh that was infectious. Even in the company of the lad he worked with that was his 'wingman' as he called him, there was no jovial banter. The mood on our table was sombre; he made zero effort whatsoever. Again, I was made to feel that this was my fault just with the looks he gave me. Bloody hell! What had I ever done to deserve this treatment? I just could not understand it and I was wondering why he had even requested me to attend the wedding at all.

It was to keep up the farce and sham that he was a good hardworking man who had a wife that suffered with depression. He would never admit that the depression his wife suffered was as a direct result of his gaslighting and narcissistic controlling ways. This treatment was about to be stepped up a gear or two just to seal the deal and make it look like he ended the marriage because of me. Of course, none of it could be his fault; he deludes himself that he is a good man. Doing charity work does not make you a good man. Being a good person throughout your life makes you a good person, and then that justifies a good reputation, not covering the bullshit underneath by coating it with candy and painting it bright colours to throw people off the foul stench underneath. One day, someone will knock him off that pedestal that he has put himself on. But I do not want or need to be there to see it, because I really do not give a shit what happens to him. Karma will do her work. The truth is that I know the nasty person that he truly is, and attempts have been made to stop the writing and publication of this book on more than one occasion.

After the wedding photos were finished outside and I had left the gift on the hall table along with all the others, (which I never received thank you for, from any of them) I was standing with the same two ladies as before, when suddenly and with no warning, I was kicked on the back of my Espadrille. I turned to see

Jack with his hands in his trouser pockets and a look of foreboding on his face like he really did not want to touch any part of me with any part of him, which was fine by me because I now put him in the same league as Delores, a first-class toxic bucket of poison who treats people like shit once they have drained the person's life force. After he barked his order "come on, we're going", I made my apologies to the ladies, and then had to run up the hill after Jack who was walking like he had the devil chasing his ass! Oh yes, I forgot that the devil was me and he did not actually want to be seen with me even though I was dressed in my lovely Joe Browns linen dress with sequins and floaty hemline.

In the car, he pulled away down the long gravel driveway like he had a pressing engagement to get to, and then slowed a little whilst looking at me which I caught out of the corner of my eye, so I looked back at him. I was bloody horrified at what came out of his mouth. He said, "That was a beautiful wedding, wasn't it? It kind of invigorates your own."

What the actual fuck!

I wanted to punch his face for him, I wanted to scream and ask him what the hell was he talking about! Instead, I decided that I could not be bothered with the drama or the argument that would ensue if I gave him the satisfaction of answering. I just did not want to be with him in the car, or in the house, but I did want to know what was going on. I constantly thought all along that it is just screaming 'affair'! But I knew that he would never in a million years be man enough to admit infidelity as it would ruin his perfect little persona that he had built for himself. He still believes he is a good person, and that we were just two people that wanted different things. So, after his little statement, I gave no answer and just sighed; I had nothing and no words to give. He had broken everything that defined me and thrown away the key after locking it in a box and throwing it the back of the wardrobe. He stole my dignity, my self-esteem and belittled me at every opportunity. My aura had disappeared a long time ago, my light had gone out and I was to blame because I allowed him to peck at me and erode my confidence until there was no doubt that he could control what mental abuse I was to accept as he dished it out.

Since this iceman cold shoulder treatment had started, as I said before I had begun getting clothed and changed in our little bathroom and I would tuck myself in the corner as much as possible so that I showed no skin at all. This is what our marriage had come to. I did not want him to think that I expected sex if I got changed in front of him in the bedroom, and quite frankly, it was my dignity that

I was trying to preserve after the last horrible attempt that ended with the ultimate humiliation of being told that he could not finish it with an orgasm. "But you did so what is the problem?" He had barked at me.

Why torture me with this bottomless pit of fork-tongued nastiness? I still do not understand why he did not just leave and call it a day instead of putting me and our daughter through this abuse. Faye had asked me one day how long I was willing to endure it.

I had lost myself. I did not know what I was to do next and I had no idea of what would happen after the house was sold. So, I concentrated on getting through every day, which dropped down to every hour because he had chipped away at me so much and been a cold heartless bastard for no reason. Well, no reason that he was going to suddenly grow a pair of balls and admit to. Little did he know at this point that I had cheated on him years ago and nearly left him for the Corporal. I knew the signs of infidelity were clearly there; it was only him that believed he had successfully pulled the wool over my eyes. The only difference was that I was never nasty or impatient with him. I had stayed with him and stuck it out. When what I should have done was run and take Faye with me. Hindsight is such a wonderful thing in one way, but it is also a curse with the ability to break you when you know that you sacrificed a life with someone who would have loved you the right way, only to waste years on someone who thought of you as a consolation prize.

My self-esteem was rock bottom, my confidence, and my ability to look half decent every day had done a Houdini. It was gone; every ounce of my being was in a place that was unfamiliar to me. He had made me feel like I was subhuman and not a woman at all, and that no man would ever want me now. I found it a struggle to get through every day knowing that the one person I had spent over a quarter of a century with, was now the person that was putting me in the darkest place since Darren died.

And then, the email arrived in my inbox, as if not talking in person was not hurtful enough! He was now mailing it in! He had verbally said a few times "it would turn nasty if we ever split up". And he had been saying it quite frequently just lately. Initially, the email was a shock at first, but then I accepted that this is how he works. He does things the coward's way instead of having a face to face. He will pen it down, so that he has it in black and white and creates a paper trail. Everything is about evidence for him so he can use it against whoever he is attacking for a later date. He used the excuse of emailing it because any attempt to talk face to face was pointless and that I would not listen, and it would be futile anyway because he had made his mind up and what he said goes. It had always been that way and I was left with little to no say in the matter.

It was started off like it was addressed to one of his work colleagues or his boss, Dear Elise, please find enclosed…

The email was a lengthy one that had obviously taken him some time to write, and clearly, he had the previous months to think about what he would write. He cared not of how this deliverance would be received because he did not give a shit about me or my feelings anymore, he cared nothing about Faye's either. He wanted what he wanted and fuck the rest of us.

He had probably rehearsed the deliverance of it a thousand times or more. He will have fretted over it and covered all angles to make sure that everything was said that he needed to say, but also that it was said in a manner which made him look like it was in my best interest when realistically, it was all for his benefit because he was pulling all the strings. All this trouble had been brought into the family because of the bullshit that he had managed to keep covered over. He failed to mention the woman from his running group. I would have had more respect for him if he had told the truth.

Dear Elise, I have met someone else and I am leaving you. Bosch! Job done!

But the bullshit and lies continued so that he could save face so that his daughter would not hate him. Despite later being shown evidence of the affair, the denial carried on which was an insult to mine and Faye's intelligence, because I knew all along. And I am good with it. It was not the affair that bothered me, it was the fact that he thought I was too stupid to know.

The email was telling me that we, not him, had fallen out of the love tree a long time ago. And yes, looking back, he was completely correct. But at the time while I was reading it aloud, all I could think was, *How the hell does he know how I feel?* Again, a form of control because he TOLD me that was how it was!

But I had fought to save the marriage, and up until a certain point was even still convinced that he was suffering PTSD. I still have an old phone that I was using at the time with all the text messages that went back and forth between us. I always told him that I loved him, and that I wanted to help. There was one message where I had clearly had enough of being the mat that he wiped his shitty boots on as he came through the door until he exited back out of it a couple of days later.

It was clear in the texts right back to February 2014 that he no longer felt anything, which again, threw into question why stay so long and not just end it. I had initially felt that I had invested so much time in him and we had been through so much together, that I did not want to start all over again. The thought of being with someone else was just unthinkable! I had joked a few times that I could not imagine having to do online dating. In the reply texts from him, he had stopped saying that he loved me too, which I found heart-breaking. He would always evade speaking and would say that he missed the call from me because his boss was running him ragged or another excuse. I grew tired of waiting for phone calls and texts that never came. When the chemistry is gone, history does not matter.

Before the shit had hit the fan, I had called him when he said he was taking the recruits to a camp on the coast, he was furious and we ended up in a heated argument! He wanted to know why I kept trying to contact him and that he was far too busy to talk (as was always the case). I was under the impression that married couples did have a conversation every now and then, and when they practically live apart, it is not healthy to ignore each other for obvious reasons.

Faye watched this all and witnessed nearly every tear that was shed. I could not hide my puffy eyes even if I wanted to, especially as it had been going on for months now. There was one weekend that he came back to the marital home and we did nothing but battle it out all weekend but achieved absolutely nothing.

The resolution was always that it was the end, and nothing that I said or did would make an ounce of difference. He stayed in our bed but for the last few times, there had been no intimacy or even kiss goodnight. This man was no longer someone I knew. It was like he was a shape shifter that had been possessed by a nasty demon. He was yelling at me every few minutes, "Why are you not asleep yet, for God's sake go to sleep!"

This happened nearly every night that he was in the room, like he had something else he wanted to be doing (possibly checking his mobile but I had no proof). All I knew was that I was sick of having his control over me and being spoken to like I was a piece of shit. I used to lay there thinking to myself, *Is this really my life and how it is going to be forever?* Surely, there is more to life than having someone's boot on your head! He was not happy with just controlling the recruits, because he still felt the need to have full control over me and Faye. He wanted me asleep so that he could reply to messages on his phone no doubt.

Quote,

The Narcissist;

The abuser does not want their deception discovered, so they will say and do anything to divert this attention. No matter how much they say they love you, they will turn on you with hatred. They will attack with lies, threats and rage to discredit you and intimidate you.

They will manipulate you with guilt, mind games and deception, and they will expect your tears and apologies for their crimes.

This is exactly the treatment that I came to expect from him every weekend he was in the house, the dirty looks were endless and all I had to do was open my mouth. I buried my head in reading the Fifty Shades trilogy and in doing so, it probably made things worse. Because then I started thinking that I wanted some excitement instead of the shit that I was getting from him.

On one of the Saturdays that Jack was in the house, he stood behind the butcher's block, with his back against the kitchen work surface, his arms were crossed and his posture told me that there was a defensive statement inbound. We had not really spoken much the evening before, and I was putting my coat on to head out of the door to a craft shop for a couple of things so that I could hide away in my room while he was around, and it meant that I had something to do. I did not plan on spending much and was using the money from something that I had made previously for a friend. She had ordered another personalised plaque for a couple she knew who were getting married, so I needed a couple of supplies to make it special for them.

While Jack glared at me, I asked him what was going on. He proceeded to tell me that he had met Faye in the local supermarket, and he had told her that if he was in the house, she was not to be! Faye had met a new boyfriend two weeks previously and was spending a lot of time at his house, but this was basically telling her that she could not come home at the weekends! Therefore, forcing them to practically live together after only two weeks! I was horrified because she had not been back in the house long. Faye had settled in a new job and met the new guy there. It was not fair on the couple to be forced into a situation that they had no control over. It was ludicrous! But Jack's mind was made up! I could not argue the case and was given no choice whether I liked it or not. Our daughter was being forced out at weekends! She had been staying with Mark because of the intense atmosphere in the house anyway, but to be literally forced was a different kettle of fish. The uprooting and discarding was indeed, well under way, and he was executing his plan.

I told Jack that if we could not find a solution to what was going on between us then we would have to do some soul searching, and I left for the shop because I wanted to cry. I did not understand how he could do this to his own daughter, and I knew that this was the next step in his plan of phasing out his old life. The fact was that he was moving on, and Faye and I were surplus to requirement. He was discarding people one at a time claiming that he 'couldn't be doing with them' for whatever reason he came up with. Even one of his best friends did not stand a chance and Jack cut contact with old Regiment friends. It was like he was cleansing himself of anything and everyone that was to do with his old life so that his new one would start afresh. The old one now just annoyed him.

I knew that I would be next, this had been coming for years and the end was near.

One evening after being reprimanded in bed as to why I was not asleep again, I turned my back on him completely as I could not bear being in the same air space as him. He had slept most nights in Faye's bed now that she was practically living at her boyfriend's. I was used to Jack staring at either his bloody laptop or his phone all the time, and I had learnt to ignore it and let him crack on so that I could not be accused of invading his personal space. In all the years we had been together, I can honestly say that I never once felt the need to sneak a look at his phone. Faye later said to me, "Well maybe you should have, Mum!"

We spent an awkward Christmas day with a cloud over us and an atmosphere that even the proverbial knife could not have sliced. I cooked the dinner, while he played on whatever game on the Wii there was to play with Faye's boyfriend Mark although Mark himself was not a big gamer, he made the effort but the strain in the house was uncomfortable. In my heart of hearts, I knew that this would be our last Christmas as a family; it was over. But I kept going with the hope that a divine intervention would suddenly smack him on the head (or more desirably Thor's hammer, because that would have put more of a dent in it). I wished he could see what a complete dick head he was being.

We had opened our last presents as a family and I had received the last Christmas card that read…my darling Wife, the last twelve months have not been easy, but I would never have made it through without you, All my love as always.

I had searched for a Christmas card for him for weeks before, but to no avail, I was not feeling it! I would stand in the aisle and observe other ladies picking out various cards to read the verse inside, then putting it back and repeating the process. I struggled to feel anything this Christmas of 2014 because I was just done. Done trying to save a shitty marriage, done with crying, done with being stared at in public because my eyes were constantly red and puffy, done with being treated like an option and done with his unawareness that his daughter was witness to how big an asshole he was capable of being!

Unfortunately, there were no cards with the word CUNT on it. I would have had to make one in big bold black letters, so I settled for one with a little cute dog and a blank inside. Blank because then I could write with big letters, I KNOW YOU ARE CHEATING! But I wrote the usual Happy Christmas love you shit instead, knowing that there was absolutely no meaning behind my words. I felt nothing, and he had made me this way. I had died a thousand times and cried several rivers over a man that seriously did not give a shit about me or his daughter. Well, no more, I was done.

Now…I waited.

Chapter 20

My Friend the Streetlight

Although realistically, Jack had mentally left the building a long time ago, it felt like he had wanted to make sure that he personally hammered the final nail into the coffin of our marriage. The torture continued with his arrival at weekends to drive my sanity and wellbeing into the ground as far as he could before finally deciding that he was done with me. Then he would deliver the final blow and say the words.

In a brief phone call, I told him that I wanted to give him some headspace and he could be in the house alone with his beloved laptop. I had found a place that accepted the dogs. It was a campsite in Dumfries and Galloway, and I was going for a break away the second week of February 2015. Truth be told, I could not think straight, the fog in my head refused to lift while I was still in the house. I felt like he had tied my brain up around the detritus and what was left of a life I had always hoped would be a good one. The rug was being pulled from underneath me, I still did not know why for certain, and hoped that my suspicions would prove me wrong.

After Christmas, and up until the inevitable departure, our life carried on pretty much as it had done for the past year and a half. The cold shoulder and the obligatory dirty looks. We were all sitting in the living room one night pretending to be a family. Faye and I were crafting, we were making pompoms and silly things for some project or another because that is what she and I liked doing. Due to the life that we had lived previously, we are close and always will be, so the little mother and daughter smiles and a bit of banter between us is how we roll. After she passed a bit of gas, which I must admit could have won a number one prize for the smell it created, all hell broke loose and our peaceful (although on edge) evening was shattered with monumental repercussions! Jack kicked off that she should have gone outside and done it and then started on the "now she's got a fucking attitude" line.

Oh, my days! It was all totally uncalled for and he was acting like he had never created such a stench himself! I remember the foul odour that was caused by eating army ration packs on exercise for weeks at a time, but I had to put up with it and accept it as the normal procedure after he got back. He had zero sense of humour, and even less patience if that was at all possible.

Faye left the room in haste and stayed in her bedroom understandably. I was then subjected to the verbal attack that I was always on her side and that he was sick of her attitude. Although a lot of the time, the attitude and mind games were coming from him and he was projecting his anger and frustration onto us. I wished that he would just fucking end it and be done with it. I had spent nearly every single weekday night on the phone crying to Denise, she was extremely tolerant and listened to me, and she cried with me on more than one occasion. Bless her I love this woman to bits. She was my rock right from the minute I met her in 1995 and our friendship withstands the test of time. I would do anything for her. Denise is my person, and she was/is the one person I know that I can call on in my time of need, and vice versa.

I felt that he was deliberately going out of his way to cause arguments so that he could then say, "I do not want to be in the house." Denise would ask me how long I was going to go on like it.

My answer was always the same. "I just try everything but nothing I do is right. I am just a doormat that he treads on every time he sees me."

I cried often, and I used to sit in the garden with the dogs trying to fathom out what I could try next. I decided that I would say nothing, because doing so meant that he had nothing to be pissed off with me about. I crafted and made a little bit of money, and just stayed out of his way. I found a part time job with a family in a nearby town, and she was willing to take me on even though I explained in my email that I would be moving soon due to selling the house. I did not know at the time where I was moving to, but that it would potentially be Wales. I had decided on Wales because if we started afresh, then maybe we would have a shot at saving things, in the earlier days of putting the house on the market, he even kept up the bravado of viewing houses with me and fooling me into believing that he was willing to try.

In the end, the viewings stopped too; he just wanted to get the house sold as quickly as possible and was willing to take a loss of profit to do just that. At night, I would lay for hours staring at my new best friend, the streetlight on the main road shone through the gap in between the houses on the opposite side of the road. I was not sleeping, and the cause for it was because the texts between us were so hostile now. I had enough of him accusing me of being the nasty one, when all I was doing was defending myself against his fork tongue and trying to get through each day.

I would stare at the streetlight every night, because it reminded me that I was still human and that there was a big wide world out there for me to discover as a single person. I did not need him in my life any longer because all he had brought was stress, misery and heartbreak. But first, I had to go with the flow of the emotions that were pouring out of me, cleansing my body and mind so that I could rebuild slowly when the time was right.

At around 4 am when the housing development was silent, only the early morning flights and the ships could be heard, as they drifted up the shipping canal. Strangely, I found their nightly arrival comforting, because it was the only sign of life I would see for another few hours. The gentle hum of the engine could be heard long before the little light on top of the mast shone over the tops of the houses and rolled on past like a little beacon of hope, only to disappear a few minutes later, leaving me alone once again with my remaining friend, the streetlight.

Those were my darkest days. I felt numb and lost, but the loneliness did not creep in until the sun rose to wake me from my broken sleep. I wondered how I could get through the days because I felt so lethargic, but thankfully, I had the four dogs to focus on, they needed their walk so it was them that kept me grounded and gave me a purpose every day.

While I was staring at my streetlight one night, I heard an owl off in the distance and found great comfort in his little night cry because I believed it was my reincarnated brother Darren whom I had not heard since we lived in Germany. I still find comfort in that my brother is a wise old owl and comes to hoot every time I am in total despair or in a dark place. He always said that if he went first, he would find a way to haunt me. That Owl is my comfort, and I had not heard him since we lost our beloved collie cross seven years previous.

I now realised and had accepted that things were never going to be fixed, and what was happening to me was the grieving process. I was grieving because my life as well as Faye's had been turned upside down and brushed aside like we were meaningless, and Jack wanted nothing more to do with us. He stopped coming to the house at weekends and said he was staying in camp, wherever camp was. He seemed to have washed his hands of us, and only seemed to remain in contact regarding material things and finances. Rather that, than his mistreatment and bullying!

I loaded my little car for my trip up north and Jack was there when I left, but he had only 'popped back to say goodbye'. I could never have imagined that meant literally…and for good. He gave me a half-hearted kiss, as I drove off with our rescue dogs; they were to become my saving grace. He waved as I drove away, but I could not help the gut feeling that it would be the last time I would have a kind word out of his mouth. I felt that he was only actually there to make sure that I left.

I was relieved to be going somewhere other than my own house because it now only represented heartache, despair and loss of direction. I had no idea how this had all come about or why, and I had no sense of why I had allowed it to get this bad. I could not analyse anything while I was confined to the same four walls because of the memories. It was like someone had flicked a switch and turned off ninety percent of a fully functioning machine, only to let it rust and buckle under the pressure of a sinking ship. I was done, I needed to sleep and I needed to try and recharge some sort of brain battery power without the knowledge that the door handle could go down at any given time and the devil would appear and burn my skin just with a look.

I had arranged to see my friend Ajay who now lived further up in Scotland after my four nights stay in the caravan. But for now, I would be tucked away on a holiday park in Dumfries and Galloway in the middle of February, so it was unlikely to be a warm weather vacation. I had driven at a steady slow pace because I needed to reflect a little on the events that had led to this point, and I needed to breathe. As a result of his coldness, I was convinced that Jack had someone else, but I had no proof, and quite frankly I did not care because I just wanted to be free from him. I also knew that he always had a backup plan and would have thought long and hard about how he would execute his escape.

The receptionist was welcoming and had a smile that would melt any heart, but her smile faded slightly as she looked me squarely in the eyes. She donned a concerned expression which was a little alarming to me. I thought that maybe my bank card had been refused, but it had not. I made it clear that I wanted to get into the caravan that she had handed me the keys for, and that I was a bit tired from driving. The truth was I was scared that if I stared at her for any length of time, she would see the pain in my eyes. It oozed from my very soul to reveal that the one person I had put all my trust in had seen fit to break my resolve a little bit at a time, and now I was the shell of a woman who used to be full of hopes and dreams. But that was all gone, and I would have to change my sails.

The receptionist was quick to ask was I okay, she said that she could see that something was wrong, and did I want to talk about it? The last person I would tell anything of my troubles to was a stranger whom I had just met, but I appreciated her concern very much. She told me that people come to stay when their relationships were breaking, or indeed already broken. I was bewildered how she could possibly know! I had not said a word of what the problem was, but I suppose it could possibly be written all over my face. It was grief, and maybe to others that had experienced this pain themselves, it was all too evident.

Faye and Mark were driving up to stay for a night or two the day after I booked in so at least the dogs and I would have some company, and maybe we could all have a chilled-out time as we were temporarily away from the impending fallout of a failed marriage. I was so looking forward to seeing them without any outside interference or pressure. We would be able to speak freely and say what we truly felt with no atmosphere!

I had been upgraded to a proper chalet with heating by the owners because the weather was particularly bitter, and I had booked a glamping pod as it was cheaper thinking that it would be an adventure; all I wanted was to get away from Jack to clear my head.

Here lies one of the problems of the time, my thoughts were not with my comfort, they were with just being in a different location other than where all the pain had been inflicted. I did not feel at home in the house that Jack built and then pulled down in such a monumental way.

The first night was unbearably cold because I could not find how to turn on the heating and I did not want to go up to the farmhouse and wake everyone up to find out. So, the dogs and I cuddled under the throws and blankets that I had taken for them to sleep on as they were not allowed on the furniture. We shivered, and I ended up rummaging for the warmest clothing that I had in my suitcase and slept with my woolly hat and gloves on. The dogs were not impressed with me, but I just could not find the heating controls, and after we went to bed and I had turned off the gas fire in the living room, the temperature plummeted. In hindsight, I should have stayed in the living room!

Faye and Mark arrived the following morning and brought alcohol and cigarettes. I had avoided both until recently, but the pressure of what was going on in my life became too much, and after ten years of not smoking, I relented and found it to help but I certainly did not intend to continue it any longer than I deemed necessary.

The man from the farmhouse came down after I asked at reception about the heating, bless him it was simple, the controls were hidden behind a mirror in the bathroom! I would never had thought to look behind it! Even Mark had looked and could not find any sign of it.

We settled in after walking the dogs along the shore but getting onto the beach was impossible at the time of day that we ventured outside for a walk because the tide was in. I did not particularly want the dogs getting soaking wet, as it was so cold, and I could ill afford for them to get sick.

We drank a bottle of wine and even though the TV was on in the background, we talked about things in general and tried to play a game of Monopoly. Jack called, and in a brief conversation, it was only to tell me that the house sale had been agreed. He had agreed to a considerable loss in the asking price purely because he just wanted it sold and be done with it. I knew that this would be the end but still hoped for a ray of light because I had no idea where I would go. I felt like a nomad already when all I had ever wanted was to settle in a house for more than a couple of years. Faye and I were really done with moving, and our futures were now in the hands of the person we had followed around for years and gave up friends for, now he was throwing us out with the rubbish.

After the call ended, I broke down a little, it was a frequent occurrence that Faye and Mark had been witness to, although Mark still did not know what to say to me, so I tried to avoid crying in front of him. Faye asked me how long I was willing to put up with the treatment that her Father was inflicting on me. The truth of it was I did not know because I still loved him in a small way. But I had built a brick wall around my heart, and I would not break it down for anyone, I was in self-preservation mode. I was totally numb and felt nothing except the love for my daughter and the dogs, then all that was left was the house brick heaviness that I carried in my chest twenty-four hours a day.

After more wine, I accidentally let slip that I had been unfaithful twenty years ago. Faye took it very well after I explained my reason why, the fact that I never felt wanted or appreciated by her dad, I was just wife of and part of a trophy family that was there to keep up the image that he was a good family man who worshipped his girls. Bullshit.

We got quite drunk and despite what I had confessed to Faye, she said that she was not really surprised because now she was now old enough to understand what he could be like with his mood swings, and his temper was sometimes uncalled for. After many tears, we eventually got into bed and looked forward to our bacon sandwich in the morning.

It had snowed during the night, but because I had left the heating on, we had not noticed that the weather had changed so dramatically and now we had a blanket of snow to walk the dogs in. They did not seem to mind at all because I had purchased them coats with fleece liners, so they hardly noticed apart from their cold and wet feet! We walked further along the shoreline and came to the entrance of the Estuary before we decided to turn back because it was bitterly cold, and we had enough of being wind swept.

Faye, Mark and I spent our second night talking again but with less drinking because of their drive back home the next day. They left after a night that was spent not sleeping very well at all, I could not sleep because I knew I would feel the emptiness after they had gone, and Faye could not sleep because of the worry of leaving me alone. I only had another three nights, and it would be a long week, but I also needed the time to think and leave Jack alone.

We ate breakfast together and they loaded up the car to head back. I reassured Faye that I would be fine. I had made it this far and would have to just accept whatever would be thrown my way and deal with it no matter how hurtful it was. She left with a heavy heart, as I stood with my shattered one in my throat. Faye was the only stable thing in my life; she and the dogs would be the things that kept me going. I did not want to rely on her as heavily as I did because she was watching the crumbling walls that were now crashing down around us, with no remorse and at a great speed. It was out of our hands, and there was nothing Faye or I could do but be crushed by the bricks that were thrown on top of us.

I took the opportunity to write a long letter to an old friend from the regiment who I had not seen for years. She had battled with breast cancer and came out the winner, so I thought it was about time that I wrote to her as she likes to get mail the old-fashioned way. I tried to describe the tale of woe, but I could only tell so much because as I wrote the words on the paper, it became real. Talking about it was only words, but physically writing it and seeing it on paper was a different feeling altogether. I told her some of what had been said and done. In previous texts we had exchanged, she could not believe that it was the same person she and her husband had known for so many years. I have heard the same thing time and time again and it was unfortunately the same person causing the pain, but it was for his own gain, not mine and his own daughter.

On the fifth day, I vacated the chalet after I cleaned it thoroughly with the hope that the owners would be pleased that they did not have someone who had just abandoned the place in a mess. All the years of housekeeping has taught me to be respectful of anyone's home not just my own, and I used my own cleaning products to make it smell nice. My dogs are as clean as I can get them, but I am still paranoid, so I probably go to extremes.

I drove straight up to Ajay's house which was an hour further up north, with the little guys that she had helped me to adopt in the back seat of my car ready to meet her for the first time. I was so excited to see her after six years, but I could not hide the dark rings under my eyes, the puffiness was prevalent so she would inevitably see how bad the situation was. I pulled up onto her driveway and got out to ring the doorbell. She flung the door open like it was made of paper! It was a heavy-oak door, and she is only a small woman, but her excitement was a very welcome surprise. She came out to help me to get the dogs out of the car to bring them inside and meet her four dogs that she had brought over from Cyprus, along with her cats that she had rescued.

We introduced the dogs one by one and to our delight, they all got on well which was a massive relief considering that we had eight dogs of varying sizes between us! We set about catching up and drinking red wine which I am not a big fan of as I prefer the pink stuff, but it was a sociable drinking time, and it was lovely to be in her company after so long. She wanted to know everything about why the lady that was sat in her house was "a shadow of her former self", as she worded it.

I was happy to tell her what I knew, but it became apparent that she was as baffled as I was, apart from the obvious answer and the same conclusion that I had drawn. Her suspicion was the same as mine, that there must be someone else involved in the background. No one acts that way without someone else waiting in the wings. We talked into the small hours because neither of us slept much due to the nature of what our husbands were subjecting us to. It is difficult to sleep with one eye open and switch your brain off if the men were around to treat us like shit, so I was hoping to get a good night's sleep while I was staying with her. Although I secretly knew that it would be broken because that was how it had been for a couple of years now. I cannot remember what it is like to sleep all the way through the night anymore, even to this day.

The next day, Ajay and I walked the dogs on the hills before she drove us into her local town for some lunch. The streets were cobbled, and it was very pretty, but my head was so mashed with my life in tatters that I do not remember which town it was. I brought Faye a few trinket things from a little boutique and some sweetie things from an old-style sweet shop which was full of all the old-fashioned sweets and candy that time had forgotten.

Then we ventured across the main road into a café, the smell of the toasted sandwiches was very inviting to say the least and I was feeling my tummy rumble as we ordered some food. I had not been able to eat properly for weeks and the weight had started to come off, so I was pleased about that small achievement, but it was falling off too fast. I was living on Weetabix and energy drinks. I had no appetite and had to force food down my throat most of the time. The toasties arrived with a side salad and it was just enough of a light lunch to fill the void in my ever-decreasing tummy, I was full quickly! We carried on chatting about the things we had started discussing the previous evening, but all I wanted to do was cry, and this little café was packed full of attentive staff and fellow lunchtime companions. Besides, crying would not solve anything, and my embarrassment would cause more harm than good. I had learnt a long time ago not to show too much emotion in public and so, I suppressed my tears.

On the drive back, Ajay was very empathetic, and we agreed that we had both come a long way from the two women who had met in Germany six years ago. We both had no idea what was going to happen to us, and we both were extremely emotionally numb. She knew that her husband had cheated the same as I had always suspected Jack. She knew Ruddy was a monumental flirt and acted like butter would never melt in his mouth, while all the time he was inflicting his mental and physical abuse on her. She said that he had pinned her on the floor one night, and once again tried to strangle her while spitting in her face.

We talked about our days in Germany and the rescued dogs we now cared for, and the houses we had both waited for that we were about to lose. She wanted to fight to keep hers but could not afford it on her own. Ajay's house was a beautiful cottage that would have suited a family and she loved it, but our futures were now thrown up in the air and we were both scared. Me more so because Ajay had been through a previous divorce and lost everything the first time, so she knew what to expect, and I think this made it slightly easier for her to start preparing herself mentally. She has always been an inspiration to me because she had already been through so much, and she stood strong and proud and ready to face whatever was coming her way. I hoped I could find it within myself to gain some courage to get through what was coming my way. Divorce would be inevitable; it just had not been said yet.

I had called Jack during the next day, but it was a call that was cut short because his tone told me that he could not care less that the youngest dog Charlie had run off across fields for half an hour this morning, or that Ajay and I were hoarse from shouting Charlie's name. He said that he was too busy to talk and that I should just go and spend time with Ajay and forget about things.

This was the last time that we would speak relatively normal on the phone. He asked why I had to keep calling, again, his icy tone was the reason that our ship was inking, he had created an iceberg and our Titanic was on its way down.

It was at this point, that I started to hate him.

Chapter 21

The Cowardly End

After two glasses of pink wine that I had brought from home, Ajay and I sat in her living room eating pistachio nuts and making the best of a bad situation, but we ended up talking about the two main people in our lives that were causing us to feel so shit about ourselves. This was supposed to be a joyful reunion but instead it was clouded and overshadowed by two wankers! Tears were shed, but we decided that we had to sort ourselves out one way or another. It was 16 February 2015. I knew that there would be no Valentines card or gifts waiting for me when I arrived home. I did not buy him one because he no longer had my heart and certainly did not deserve it!

There would be no miracle cure for the marriage; it had been dead in the water for a long time and we had just been floating on a ship that was doomed to sail ever again.

Ajay suggested that I should call him on her house phone after I made the decision that I wanted the truth, I had no mobile signal and it was around 9.30 pm so going outside to obtain a signal on my Sony was not an option due to the fact it was bloody Baltic outside! I called Jack's mobile and he took his time to answer the call, I failed to ask why because I had a more pressing question that I wanted to ask so I just came out with it. "Okay, you really need to tell me what the fuck is going on? No bullshit, no lies just tell me!"

His voice was low when he replied. "I want a time out."

I said, "Okay, that is fine, but what are we talking about here, a trial separation or divorce or what?"

He replied, "I want to call it a day."

So, there it was, he had finally said it. The only thing that pissed me off more than anything was that he then said, "My God, you had to push it!" Okay, so he deflected that on to me as well! Like it was my fault after twenty-seven years, he could not have told me to my face. After all those years, he took the most cowardly way possible to tell me that he wanted to end it. I had one word in my head; it begins with C and ends with T. The only other thing I recall saying was "I cannot believe that you are doing this over the phone".

I was already sitting on the floor staring at the snow settling on the rooftop of the house opposite, so I did not fall to my knees with grief-stricken horror. I felt a pang of relief that the wait was over, and I wondered what the hell had taken him so long! Now, the wait for the truth would begin, because eventually the truth does come out. I will not bullshit you it was not the lie that offended me, it was the insult to my intelligence that pissed me off.

The call ended with the agreement that I would be back at the house the next day, and that we had to talk face to face regardless of whether we wanted to or not. I gave Ajay her house phone back after I sat with her at the dining table. She had been downstairs waiting for the fallout and expected me to return to the kitchen in floods of tears. I went back downstairs and to my own surprise, I felt like I had done my grieving. And all that remained was the numb sensation that chilled me to my very core. I was cold and physically shaking from head to toe. Shock does some weird things to your body, and at this point my fight or flight mode kicked in to keep the vital organs and breathing going. Internally I was breathing, externally I must have appeared to be about to go and jump off a bridge.

More wine!

Ajay gave me yet another glass of red wine which I took a mouthful of and instantly regretted it as a sharp pain stabbed my temples. I leant forward with dizziness that I had not felt since the call from the consultant to inform me of Darren's death.

I set about trying to calm my thoughts, which was totally the worst thing that I could have done at that moment. But I could not help it and I had a desperate need to know the ins and outs of the whole situation. Why would he be so cruel for two years and then end it the way he did?

I could not get my head around it, but hopefully, it would be resolved at the house tomorrow, I doubted that I would be told the real reason for his departure, but time would only tell. The truth will be out.

Ajay and I went to bed around midnight knowing that neither of us would sleep, but we had to try. I tossed and turned all night with his words spinning in my head. My thoughts were of Faye and what this would do to her, I cared not about what he had done to me because now it was over, and after we had talked and said what we needed to say, I was hoping to gain some clarity as to why he was doing this. Faye was expecting it, but that did not mean it would not hurt her. I despised him for this.

I watched the big snowflakes landing and settling on the rooftops outside the bedroom window and wished that I were one of them, because then I would melt away and would not feel the heavy chest pain that I was experiencing at the present time, because it would all eventually be gone, and no one would know.

The pain did not match that which I felt after I lost my brother, that was a full body heart and soul pain that was immeasurable and unforgettable. This was just a pain that meant my heart was in my throat and I felt as if I could vomit at any given moment. But I would not allow this pain to consume me for any longer than I considered long enough to realise that we had been over a long time ago. I refused to give him any of my energy reserves; he did not deserve that from me or the situation that he had put us in. This was him being selfish and he owned the moment, but from here on in, I would control the rest of my life! I could now make one for myself that was not built on a lie, nor would it contain the stress and drama that he was so capable of creating.

I had been awake literally all night! I had not even dozed off or drifted in and out of sleep. I was wide awake all night over thinking. I knew it was done, and I knew that there was nothing that I wanted to say or do to change it, any attempt to would be futile and a complete waste of brainpower that would be better used for looking forward and getting my shit together. Firstly, I would have to look for somewhere to live!

I got out of Ajay's spare bed and showered in her house for the last time, I knew that I would probably never be able to come back because she and Ruddy horrible were splitting up too.

I was not in any fit state to eat anything, but coffee was very welcome as I just wanted to get the dogs in the car and head back to the house, I would be leaving it soon enough so I would try and spend as much time there before the inevitable upheaval of moving yet again. My stay with my lovely friend Ajay had been cut short, and as much as wanted to stay, I had to get back and get the ball rolling as to what was to be the plan moving forward.

I had thought the days of moving would be a thing of the past, but at least I knew exactly how to prepare and pack. Ajay and I said a very emotionally charged goodbye on the doorstep of her lovely cottage in West Scotland, and I hit the road. It would take me three hours and the TomTom said that I would be back by 9.30 am. I did not feel the need to drive fast and chose to sit in the slow lane most of the way so that I could take my time. I just wanted to be invisible, and as my life was no longer going to be lived at one hundred miles an hour, I could do what I wanted and go at my speed. Jack found fault with my driving along with everything else. I would not miss that!

I had three hours of driving and obviously, my mind wandered over the previous two years and the time we had spent in the UK after leaving the army life. Our detachment had begun the minute that we had driven off the ferry on our last return from Germany. He had never been the most patient of men and I could not cope with living on eggshells anymore, so I was interested to see what he had to say for himself.

For the briefest of seconds, I stared at the central carriageway. I then spotted a low heavy bridge that would be an easy option if someone were thinking of ending it all. There was simply no way that he was worth that, no one is worth taking their own life for, especially not someone that was capable of such cruelty and believed that it was acceptable to behave that way and that it was normal. Why would I hurt my dogs in that way? Not a chance would I ever do anything to harm them, they mean so much more to me than he did. And why would I leave my only daughter with the one parent that she had never seen eye to eye with or really been there for her? I am made of stronger stuff, and this hurt did not rival that of Darren, this was a blip, and I would recover from it, and probably recover quickly because I had fought and done everything that I could for two years. There was no more fight left. He could go, and I could move on.

I made a couple of stops to let the guys have pees and I went for coffee of the strongest style I could find! I was exhausted but caffeine helped, and I carried on and took my time. I arrived at my estranged house at around 10 am to complete emptiness. My first job was to get my laundry done and see if there was any cleaning to do, but there was nothing. It looked like he had not even been there. So, I took the dogs for a walk to stretch our legs, and then had a bath.

Faye was at work but was texting to see how I was, and I know that in all this wreck of a marriage that my daughter is my rock, and she loves me regardless. I waited for what seemed hours for Jack to arrive at the house; I was not looking forward to seeing him. In fact, I was completely dreading it and wanted the ground to open and swallow him, not me. He sent a short text saying that he was picking up a microwave meal, so now I knew that he was on his way.

My heart sank to the very base of my soles on my feet. I did not want to have this conversation and just wanted it all to be over as quickly as possible. At this point, I felt a cold sweat cover my entire body like a spirit had walked in the room and come to protect me, my hands were cold, I felt light-headed and my temperature was making my face flush.

He walked his bike through the back gate and leant it up against the shed that he had built after we had laid down the flagstones. We had designed the garden from scratch and a lot of time, money and elbow grease had gone into it, so to have the knowledge that I would not be able to enjoy it was enough to send my head spinning. He came through the back door red faced and soaking as it was tipping it down. I did not bother to hand him a towel because I did not want to go anywhere near him; I did not even want to be in the same room! I detested the way he was with me and his daughter and I had mentally shut my true self away in Archimedes for protection. I had left enough of myself on show to fight whatever battle was coming my way.

I moved out of his way so that he could use the microwave after he told me that he had got me a sweet and sour chicken. These were the only words to leave his mouth since his arrival, and I was not at all surprised that he could find nothing to say after what he had said last night. I wanted to tell him he was a prick and that I hated him for what he was doing but I kept my mouth shut.

He heated his food and started mine on the time shown on the packet, which was about four minutes, but I had no intention of eating it anyway. He sat down at the dining table in our kitchen without making any eye contact. I stood facing him while positioned behind my lengthy butchers block from Ikea which was the one thing I had always wanted. He barked at me to sit down and eat! Rage entered my body, and I swiftly replied by saying, "You are not in any position to tell me what to do anymore!" He looked at me with a wide-eyed stare as if that was the last thing that he had expected me to say, maybe had not considered that fact. But I was not going to live under his boot any longer; he had made the decision to walk away, so I made the decision that I would not be governed, the doormat days were over. I was no longer his to dictate to, he had now forfeit, and he would never tell me what to do again, I was done with his shit.

After he had eaten, I had gone up to the living room with a cup of tea knowing that I would not drink it because tea does not solve everything, and this occasion made me want to vomit.

He sat on the couch without so much as looking at me. I asked what on earth was going on and how had we arrived at this point to which he replied, "I will always love you, but I am not in love with you, and I just do not fancy you anymore!"

While he was saying these cruel words, he was gesturing with both hands and his fingers were spread wide the same as all the numerous times he had done over the years while he was angry at Faye or myself, like spreading his fingers made it absolute and there is no compromise or argument. It is what it is according to him, what he says goes and that is the end of it. The next words out of his mouth were just another sign of his ignorance to the magnitude of his actions and total disregard for my feelings. "Just move on!"

I said, "But I do not really want anyone else." I guess at the time I felt that I would have one last stab at seeing if there was still a human being in him, but again "just move on". Like it was that easy and it would all be forgotten in the morning. Twenty-seven years. Just move on.

I was numb before he had said that to me but once again, my inner red mist made an appearance and I asked, "Is there someone else?"

To which he replied, "No." But he did not even look at me as he replied, which spoke volumes. He looked at the carpet instead. I knew that he was lying; there could be no other explanation for his insufferable cruelty. He was not man enough to confess and never would be. He and I alone know the level of cruelty that he is capable of.

I had told him all the years that we had been together, if I ever found out that he was cheating, that I would deal with her first, and then I would deal with him. He was protecting someone I could feel it. There was no way that he was just walking away; he was not capable of being a single man. He always had a backup plan, and he had never been without a woman the entire time I knew him. He dumped someone to go out with me and there was no way he would be on his own, he did not know how to. But in the last two years, my feelings about him going off with someone else had bothered me less and less; if this were the case, she was bloody welcome to him! My grieving was done, and I had more than accepted what has happening because I had foreseen it for years. I would not fight for him; he was not worth any more of my time on this planet.

My gut instinct was screaming at me, but there was no way he would admit it, this was a coward who does not claim responsibility for his actions. He instead chooses to talk and bullshit his way out of it, blame everyone else and use tactics to cover it up.

Somehow, we managed to agree to stay mates as he said through a cracked voice, "I cannot lose you as a best friend." I knew that it would not remain the case, and I knew that I could use that statement to my advantage if I ever needed to call upon it. Tough shit, mate, I am gone!

He slept that night in the spare room which used to be Faye's. Originally, I had asked if he would be staying in the marital bed, but his demeanour was cold and unforgiving, so I was grateful that the answer had been no. He was adamant that he would be in the spare room and I was okay with that as I could not stand the thought of him anywhere near me anyway. I was too tired to discuss anything more and we went our separate ways in our own house. It was the beginning of the end, but I now at least had closure. Even if he had not given her up and admitted the truth, it would surface eventually but for now, I wanted to sleep.

The next morning, he got up and left after a brief "see you later". I was thinking, *Yeah whatever!* I certainly do not intend to fight for something that departed a long time ago, I would need to focus on taking care of the dogs and myself because if I went down into depression then no one would benefit and my daughter would suffer, so I made a pact with myself to be as strong as I could mentally.

The minute he left, I felt totally liberated. I remember thinking, *I can breathe now!* The controlling entity that had been so dominant in my life was now gone and I felt like a demon had been exorcised from my body. The fog in my head started to clear and my thoughts were not of ending my life, they were thoughts of *Now I can live my life the way I want to!*

I can speak to whom I want to and smile at silly things that I would never had noticed before because I was so focused on not embarrassing him or saying anything that would get his back up. I learnt to see things through my eyes as an individual not as a married woman. There would be no more criticisms of my driving, or stress when I went out shopping. That feeling of being free was overwhelming and I knew that eventually I would embrace it, but before that would happen, I also had a couple of desertion issues to get through, as they would be the same as grieving.

I looked in the bathroom mirror; what I saw was a broken woman whose eyes were red and puffy beyond belief. I did not recognise the person staring back at me. The person staring back was the shell of a former life of worry, stress, anxiety and depression. Now I started to see it for what it was, and I would get through this for Faye and my adopted dog's sake.

After I gathered enough strength to venture out because I needed dog food, I got in my car and drove the short distance to the closest supermarket. I was so light-headed from the night before and the conversation that ended a quarter of a century. I could not focus properly on what I needed from the shop. I knew that money would be even tighter now, and my appetite had left the building a long time ago, so I just got some energy drinks to keep me going. My trolley was empty apart from the big tray of twenty-four cans of food for the dogs and a bag of dry food for them. I wondered why I had bothered to get a trolley in the first place, but I had no energy to carry anything let alone tins of dog food. I wandered around the store knowing that the countdown would commence now as to when the house sold, and I would no longer be visiting this store. I had to decide what my next move would be and where would I go.

I walked slowly out of the building and crossed the car park with my focus being on my feet. My legs buckled as I very nearly fell to my knees and cried. I had to stop for a second to regain my composure and wondered if what I had just experienced was in fact an anxiety attack? I had never had one before, but I suspected it was because while I was inside wandering around, I had to look directly at a fixed object and count to ten for fear of running out of the store and making a scene because I did not want to be in there! My head was spinning, and my hands were clammy. I was very conscious that people were staring at my swollen eyelids and red puffy face, and that if I looked directly at anyone, they would see straight into my soul, and therefore would see the pain that was swirling around inside of me.

I had never been in a room full of people but felt this alone. I wanted to scream but do not like drawing attention to myself and did not need nor want to explain to anyone that my life was now a road that I would be walking alone. Except for Faye, but this was also unfamiliar territory and sadness for her to deal with too, so I decided that I would do damage limitation and only show her so much. No one could help and I had limited friends who would know what to say or do. Denise was on the other end of the phone twenty-four hours a day, but I did not want her to be burdened with my troubles, as she had her own life. I segregated myself and started closing myself off temporarily while I repaired some of the damage done to my sanity. I would deal with the shattered pieces of my heart, my pride and my dignity later. For now, I switched into my

Archimedes for protection and worried about just breathing and taking each hour as it arrived. I could do this!

I managed to get to my car that I had parked right at the end of the car park. Unloading the items slowly…I remained calm and drank something before I passed out in a heap in Tesco's car park! I did not like to leave the dogs for too long as they were feeling the strain of everything that was going on, and it resulted in pee accidents because I was their alpha, and if I were suffering, they would sense it. I did not want them to be out of routine too much but unfortunately, it would be a bumpy ride until I could figure out what my plan of action was. It would take however long it took and I could not foresee when or where anything was going, but I would not give my dogs up if I could do everything to avoid that happening.

Jack and I remained in scarce contact by text and it eventually became as hostile as he had predicted, and I am sure he will have been proud of the fact that he was correct, and he did turn even nastier. I just defended myself. But in my eyes, I did not believe for one minute that it was all my fault! They say that a narcissist blames their victims and projects their wrongdoings on their victim. I had never researched the word narcissist until three years after he left, and I had been divorced for two years. It popped up on one of the social media sites and the only reason that I took an interest was because the phrase rang true in my eyes. And in any case, the main one I found funny was "it is better to have loved and lost than to live with a piece of shit that makes you bloody miserable for the rest of your life".

One of these phrases read; to a psychopath's target, the sudden breakup seems to come out of nowhere. But this moment has been carefully planned for some time. They have been spreading lies and gossip about you, quietly convincing others that you are unstable and ruining the relationship. They use the story to groom the next victim and distract friends from their obvious cheating. You will find yourself replaced in a matter of days. (I had already been replaced it was only him that believed his own bullshit lies that he had not been cheating.) His perfect life with another woman would unfold. While I was running around desperately trying to repair things, he was laying the foundations of his new life with her.

The psychopath will not break up with you like a normal human being; they string you along until the bitter end. They deem you as 'Crazy' and 'Jealous', gleefully eroding your entire identity as they prance off with someone else. They do not just break up with their targets, they use it as an opportunity to watch you press the self-destruct button; physically, emotionally and spiritually.

The only way to go is no contact. (If possible, although when there are children involved it can be impossible.) This means no texts, no calls, no emails and no social media. Otherwise, you can guarantee that they will do everything in their power to make you feel crazy or threaten you.

The good news is that when a narcissist tries to make you doubt your intuition, it means your intuition was causing them trouble. Psychopaths seek to psychologically destroy anyone who may threaten their illusion of normalcy to the world. The abuser (and this is exactly what it is, ABUSE) does not want their deception discovered, so they will say and do anything to divert this attention. No matter how much they say they love, or loved you, they will turn on you with hatred. They will attack with lies, threats and rage to discredit and intimidate you. They will manipulate you with guilt, play mind games and deception, and they will expect your tears and apologies for their crimes.

Do not stay updated on people who hurt you without remorse. You do not need to know how they are doing. Get rid of them on social media and avoid torturing yourself with what they are doing with their life, nothing good will come of it. They do not care, so why would you?

I am not an asshole, I am a teller of unfortunate truths, and unfortunately for one person, none of this is fictional. I will be the worst person in the world because I have not written shit about one person, I have written the truth about a shitty person; there is a difference. But I cannot lie, and why the hell should when he persisted to peck for years after he left?

If you focus on the hurt, you will continue to suffer. If you focus on the lesson, you will continue to grow, and you will learn that letting go of that bag of shit will be the best thing that you ever did after you have accepted that it is over, and it was probably over a long time before you saw the train wreck arriving.

My train wreck was always in the back of my head, it had finally happened as I had known it would all these years, and as I spat out at him by text one day during a texting war. "I wish you had left before we bought a fucking house!" He could have paid me off and made things simpler by letting me go. I could have moved back to where family were so that I had some sort of support. But no! Instead, I found myself in a part of the country where I would have to start all over again and risk losing my daughter if she wanted to stay near her bloody father. That decision would be hers alone, but I started looking for houses and I told him that he would have to assist me with a mortgage once the marital house had sold. Then once I had moved and found a job, that I would then take over the payments.

After the last conversation in the living room, and the last microwave meal he would eat in the house, Jack had told me to "move on", so I did as I was instructed. And I did it in true rebellious "fuck you, pal" style that proved I could still pull a guy or two, and that I did not need Jack's put downs, and I certainly would not be controlled any longer!

Did you know that narcissist spelled backwards is asshole? Hey, if they can make shit up, so can we!

There was a song out at this current time and the words were "girl, you're amazing, just the way you are". I knew that Jack had never thought this about me. He had never looked at me with that 'look of love'. I longed for someone to want me in this way but knew that I looked like shit because the person I was now getting divorced from had tried to break me. I had to rebuild myself before I could even begin to love myself, let alone love someone else. Looking or feeling amazing was a long way off. I wish I had known years ago that this man would stunt my personal growth and dull my sparkle; he had clipped my wings and made me old before my time.

He made it clear that he thought that I was not attractive; he solidified this by not being properly intimate for two years. To say that I was in desperate need of some male attention was an understatement. So, I had been recommended to join dating sites.

I had driven down to see Anne a month after he had left. She had very kindly read my cards and gave me some crystals to work with because at the time, I was convinced that the marriage breakdown was completely my fault. My cards read:

The Scythe = Sharp break from someone or something.

The Moon = Growing good fortune, new ideas.

The Rider = Good news, renewal of your love life.

My central card was The Heart = Love is important and will turn out well.

The Lily = Something is flowering, new beginning in professional life (and here I am writing my first of many books).

The Flowers = You are looked after, improvement after a long period of unhappiness. (Well, it's funny that should be said!)

And finally, The Stork = Stagnant matters will be resolved, an event.

Chapter 22

Leaving Under a Whopper of a Cloud

Singers write their pain and feelings into their songs. Poets write their sonnets, and writers put their thoughts in books and blogs. This story is my version of how I released my pain, and indeed my joy. Joy at having lived the life I had and survived it with only two regrets, the first being that I had not left when I had the chance in 1997. And of not listening to my gut instinct in July 2005 when I felt that I should go home to the UK and see my brother. I always knew that that letting the Corporal of 1995 go and be happy with someone else was the right thing to do. The second, well, it is something that I have learnt to live with.

After I had said goodbye to the Corporal all those years age, I told myself the same quote to try and convince myself that it had been the right choice. "Why have cotton when you can have silk?" Of course, I knew that I had let the silk walk out of my life. But I stayed with the cotton.

I believed that I had made the right choice, and letting the Corporal go was the fair thing to do, even though I always think of him and wonder where he is and hoping that he is well and found love again after his messy divorce. Did he meet someone and fall in love? Who knows, but I did hear through the military drums (not jungle drums lol!) that he had remarried and was happy. I found that heart-warming, as much as it was a bitter pill to swallow but I was glad that he had found happiness. "I had the silk and set it free, the cotton however eventually wrapped itself around my neck and hung me out to dry." For the silk was the Corporal, and the cotton was the scratchy man that I remained with. Oh well, another lesson learnt!

I did as I was previously instructed and I moved on, I did it quickly too. I would hope that you would not judge me too harshly in my next actions. You see when someone goes from having a healthy, active sex life to absolutely nothing overnight, it is a monumental shock to the system especially when you have no confidence left in your entire body. I was left feeling unattractive and that no one would want me based on what the abuser had drummed into my brain.

Two weeks after he left, I joined dating sites. Not nice ones as they are more commonly known as 'shag sites' as I later found out. But this was all new to me and I had a lot to learn! (Yet another book!)

I had chatted to someone that appealed to me, and as I quickly learnt it was only a one-off thing, but it would serve a purpose. I had been without sex for what seemed an eternity! I was so naïve and really did not have a clue on how bad things were in the singleton world now that I was classed as a single woman who was heading down the divorce route.

I did not actually know what to label myself, single, divorced or just misunderstood. But I always told the truth on my profile and said that I was living alone and going through divorce, but that it was recent event s in the early stages. The one-night stand guy was my way of flushing out the last disastrous time with Jack. I just wanted a different memory of sex other than the last failed attempt with Jack because it sealed the fate of the failed marriage. He had given me permission by telling me to 'move on' seconds after telling me that he loved me but was no longer in love with me, and he just did not fancy me anymore. Cruel words from someone that were not needed to be said. I thought he was full of shit and knew he had never really loved me if he had been truthful; he was only ever capable of loving himself. I do not think that he expected me to move on as quickly as I did, but like I said previously, I was done with his treatment years ago and saw no reason to waste any more time worrying about him or what he thought. And besides, I had needs that I wanted sorted out.

I had met a friend with benefits that suited both of us; his name was Darren. We had so much naughty fun and he taught me that there was absolutely nothing wrong with me, he always said that he could not understand why anyone would leave me with the appetite that I had! And he did not mean the appetite for food! But not everything is always about sex, there had been none for a long time and that was why I needed Darren! He pointed out my best assets and became obsessed with my pert ass as he called it! He enlightened me what sort of things that men of today are looking for, and how they treat women. He was the one to inform me of the way things are online and how bad it can get. But he lent an ear if I was chatting to someone and I needed to ask what on earth the other person was talking about.

In these early days of online dating, I became acutely aware of how out of touch that I was! Someone asked me if I would Golden shower him. I had no idea what the bloody hell that was and was horrified at the answer that I got from my trusted friend Darren.

We saw each other frequently and talked often by text. He became a good friend as well as a nice distraction, we knew our boundaries and that it was not going anywhere, it was only the fun that we needed. But it started with Darren, and over the past few years I began to collect knowledge, the kind of mind-blowing knowledge that would fill another book and tell of online dating horror stories and experiences. That book is also well under way and the notes are full and ready to type up! Brace yourselves! *The Hitchhikers Guide to Being Single* is my third book.

So, I was no longer a dating site virgin! I had entered a world that I could never had prepared myself for, I never wanted to be single let alone date other people. I had told Jack that I did not want anyone other than him, but in truth, after I had read the fifty shades trilogy, I knew there was a bigger world out there and that I had been bored in the bedroom for a while. I wanted that first kiss feeling, and the sex that followed it. I wanted to play the field and live a little, and maybe be more confident in my ability to catch the eye of men. I wanted to know that I could still attract the opposite sex after being oblivious for so long. I had already lost lots of weight and I knew that more would drop off by the time I was finished. There is nothing better than 'the divorce diet'! It was as though I was shedding a few layers of skin. Like a butterfly shedding its chrysalis. I became aware that my self-worth was trying to escape. I was breaking free as an individual now, and no longer part of a two-man team where I had been the one following and never leading. Now I felt that I could be myself and start to shed the layers that had bound my true self inside this shell of extra weight, and the burden of being a wife to someone who no longer cared.

It would not be an overnight transformation. Due to the length of time that I had been embroiled as two, it would take time to completely detach myself and regain the person I was before I was married. I like to laugh and joke, and I wanted to be like that again. It would take a further three years to achieve this goal, but I got there. In the meantime, I was sending my friend Ajay in Scotland all the gossip on messenger and telling her that my first one-night stand guy had a massive cock and knew what he was doing with it! I decided that as we were both telling each other our darkest secrets that I would tell her that I had cheated on Jack twenty years ago. I was very graphic because I was single now and I would not hold back, I saw no reason to after being confined and restricted for so long. I wanted to live my life in that proverbial fast lane for a while because it was more exciting. I had been in prison for years so why the hell not!

I told her about the little things that bugged the shit out of me over the years about Jack, his bad habits that drove me insane! We exchanged our horror stories and tales of the lives that we had led with these men. I revealed so much over the internet that I should have known it would not be secret for long. We agreed to delete our conversation as we went, but unbeknown to me, her husband Ruddy Horrible had suspected her of cheating because he found her fishy account. (Google it, but it will be in my next book!) He also went through her laptop to gain evidence of her infidelity. What he found after hacking into her account was the full conversation that we both dropped ourselves in the shit with.

I received a text from Ajay saying that the shit had hit the fan at her end and that I should expect it to roll down the country to reach me at any given time. Her husband, or ex-to-be, was a twat! Like I said, I named him Ruddy Horrible with good reason! And this was tame compared to what I wanted to call him! C and ends with T. Ajay said that he had screen shot the whole conversation and was threatening to email it all to Jack. I told her that I believed he would do it because he and Jack were best buddies in the gym on camp, so I had no doubt that he would send it without fail, he had nothing to lose. It would also be used against me to file for divorce, because I had revealed my secret it would give Jack leverage and grounds for divorce as adultery. What he would fail to mention was that he was doing the same and that was his real reason for leaving. He had stuck his paraphernalia in another, and clearly enjoyed it so much that he would hide it from everyone and just discard his life instead. Everything was used against me and Faye, nothing went untouched in his attempts to discredit me, and blatantly lie to his daughter.

Ajay said that she did not think Ruddy would be so cruel, but I knew that he held no allegiance to me; his loyalty was with Jack. So, I was not shocked to receive the text from Jack one morning while I was at the only housekeeping job I had. "I have just had a text from Ruddy, is there anything I should know before I read the email?" I did not get a chance to reply quickly enough before the next text arrived where Jack asked, "Did you see someone else in Yorkshire?"

To which I replied, "Yes." Technically, I had never lied, because before now, Jack had never asked.

I was not going to lie. I did not see the point, he had already left me, so it was cards on the table. I had never been asked by him whether I had ever cheated, but I would not have lied. I probably would have told the truth and accepted the consequences. Jack had always said he would probably have forgiven me (maybe because he knew he was a dick to me) but who knows, and who cares now anyway it is all water under the bridge. That ship sailed such a long time ago now that it matters not. At the current time, we had agreed a five-year financial agreement. We had met at the Costa coffee in the bottom section of the food court in a well-known location which I am unable to mention (because of him). He had cycled since apparently, he claimed that he had sold his car to support me. But I refused to listen to that shit because he sold it as he wanted a BMW, and this was just another way of making me feel guilty over the fact that he had calculated every single move he made. He was not just making this up as he went along, he will have planned this and made sure that he came out of it looking like he had done the right thing by me. Plus, he had been shedding his life for months, so the car would obviously go in the end because it was his old life that he no longer wanted.

This meeting in Costa was the last time I planned to ever see him again. I told him that as soon as we agreed on the sums and we had both signed the agreement that he had printed out, that he would never see me again. And I meant it.

I knew he was hiding something! He had a certain look when he was lying. He slurred his words slightly and would reprimand me if I tried to correct him or finish his sentence when he clearly was not capable. It was like he had someone else's tongue in his head never mind their bloody teeth. It was all civil and sort of amicable while we signed, and he explained that he would pay certain things if I would pay the others. I was not working many hours and had little money, but I would eventually find my feet and get myself sorted. I did not want him to have any hold over me whatsoever. It was a tense conversation, and I kept my resolve right up until he asked me how our daughter and the dogs were. Then I lost the fucking plot!

Discussing our daughter and the dogs was not on my agenda, and in my opinion, it was taking it down the 'familiarity breeds contempt' route. I was not willing to discuss them to the one person that had destroyed our lives. I raised my voice and people stared as I did it. But I raised my voice because it was the one thing that he hated. He hated drawing attention to himself. Remember the

Accident and Emergency room whilst waiting to view my dead brother? I wanted him to know the magnitude of the events that he had created, and I wanted him to know that the minute I walked away was the last time he would watch me do so.

I had heard enough, and as we had now both signed the useless piece of paper that would only serve as his blackmailing leverage in future, I stood up and put my coat on with my back to him. My back was also to the crowd that who were now aware that something was not right with the couple sat on the edge of the coffee shop seating area, and the raised voice was from a woman who had clearly had enough of what was coming out of the man's mouth. As I finished zipping up my Parker, he said, "Do you want me to walk you to your car?" All I could say was 'no' because he was the last person on this green earth that I wanted to be in the same air space as at the present time.

I picked up my bag, put it over my head and across my body. Then I picked up my copy of the piece of paper that was signed as it sat beside a cup that was still half full of the coffee that I was unable to physically drink without vomiting. I felt the tears waiting behind my eyelids, I felt bile in my throat and I felt like letting the dam open and allowing the water works to flow. But I refused to let him see me cry. He had seen enough of my tears that he had induced, and I would not cry anymore in front of him. I set off walking away from him without saying goodbye, and without looking directly at him. I did not see the point in looking at him because my eyes were incapable of giving him anymore pleading looks. I had no reason to want to look at him. I just wanted to be anywhere but near him. He was a stranger. I get on better with complete strangers and find it easier to talk to someone I have never met. I very rarely look anyone straight in the eyes anymore and always found it difficult anyway. My eyes and facial expressions give too much away.

I walked away after telling him that he would never see me again. I walked away and did not look back. After twenty-seven years, he said nothing, not even goodbye. I have no idea if he watched as I walked away and I did not care. He had broken me for the last time, and I was determined he would never break my resolve or my strength to carry on. I did not consider that he deserved to have that power over me. At that moment, I decided that he would NEVER see me again, and that I would eventually cut contact and cut him out of my life completely. No one would treat me the way that he had and get to remain friends.

I know my worth, and he did not deserve it any longer, the Corporal had been correct, Jack had never deserved me. Now it was done!

I had the will power to walk away and suppress the tears for as long as it took me to walk the length of the shopping centre and up to the top car park. I was scolding myself for parking this far away because I had a lengthy walk and had to pass lots of shoppers on the way, but parking where I had, had become a habit. I would always park in the upper car park because there were more spaces and I usually prefer the walk as opposed to squeezing into a space when others are waiting to drive past. I like to park away from the busy parts of any car park and avoid parking next to a car that has child seats in it, purely because a woman smacked her car door off mine once without even saying sorry and leaving a massive dent! She had clearly underestimated the size of her ass and just carried on with strapping in her youngster. She was not someone that I would have messed with, but she did not even see me sat in my car waiting to get out of the door she had just dented.

It took me approximately seven to eight minutes to reach my little black Corsa. I had parked her in the centre of the car park and was glad to have put my backside on the seat to hide my face from any onlookers that would witness what was about to happen. I really did not expect the dam to burst as violently as it did, but as I sat processing what had just occurred, the floodgates opened, tears flowed freely from my already puffy eyes. Then my crying turned to sobbing with the obligatory sudden deep breaths. In the time it had taken me to walk the distance from the coffee shop, I had counted five times that I had really had to stop myself from falling to my knees and sobbing uncontrollably on the shopping centre floor. But somehow, I had managed to maintain my relative calmness, until my butt hit my car seat. I did not and would not humiliate myself because of the cold-hearted prick that I had just left standing alone.

I assumed that he had text Faye, because no sooner had I let my tears flow than she was calling me. He would have said something along the lines of "make sure that your mother is okay" or told Faye to call and make sure I had not jumped off the bloody roof! There was no way he was worth an ounce of any more of my time, I was done. I had literally cried rivers of tears and if I shed any after today, it would not be because he had broken me. The tears would only fall now because of the situation that I found myself thrust into. An open road of thoughts and unfamiliar emotions. He left our daughter to pick up the pieces of the life he had smashed to smithereens without any explanation or apology, and Faye was there to pick up the fragments of my broken shell. My heart was locked away encased in ice, in the back recesses of a compartment that I had devised deep within myself when he showed signs of departure three years previously. I had prepared myself for the inevitable a long time ago because I sensed it so far back in the early days of moving into the house that Jack built.

I never thought this would happen to me, and I know Faye never wanted to be the child whose parents were not together. She was devastated at the thought of not sitting at the dinner table together anymore. Although that had not happened properly for around three years, but it was now final and would never be happening again. This crucified Faye.

In the coming days, I focused on not crying too much, my eyes were sore and puffy enough without adding to it. Faye told Mark that she was staying with me for the week and bless her heart, this was so difficult for her. She stayed to support me in my nights of getting used to idea that my bed was now going to become very empty for the foreseeable future. She slept next to me while my troubled mind refused to let me sleep until I could physically no longer keep my eyes open. I had night terrors of being eaten alive, trapped in a cave with certain death imminent. The days were long, but I walked the dogs for as long as I could without the cold weather eating into my bones. I felt drained and weak, and I knew the recovery period would not begin until the divorce was absolute, and not until I had found somewhere to live where I would be able to settle down on my own terms. I needed a forever home; somewhere I could start again and settle with the knowledge that I would not have to move unless it was my choice.

For his part, Jack kept his word for the time being and supported me financially, because the mortgage still needed to be paid until the house was sold, and as he was the one that left, it fell to him to do it as I was not able to get a full-time job when I would be moving again.

Faye was forced to go back to stay at her boyfriends after five nights because he could also be controlling of her, and he wanted her back, and although I missed her, I knew that I had to get used to being alone with the dogs and take responsibility for me and them. I set about looking for houses to buy that were cheap in Wales because I wanted to run for the hills and get way from the control of Jack. I wanted to get right away from him and have nothing to do with him. I wanted to salvage myself so that I did not lose the plot and be somewhere that he could not reach me. Unfortunately, I still needed him to secure a mortgage because I could not do it myself and renting with four dogs would be nigh on impossible.

After leaving the dogs with Faye and Mark, I drove four hours to Wales to look at different houses. I did this journey about five times and stayed at budget hotels to keep costs down and allow myself the time to think whilst driving and be able to look at a few houses at a time.

I chose Wales because I have a cousin there, and some good friends. I thought that being that far away from him would allow me some peace. But it would become evident that he would continue to peck at my head wherever I went.

I ventured as far as Barry Island once because I had chatted to a bloke named Tony, and although I knew that he was a prick, he was a distraction and he let me stay in the hotel with him. That was an awful experience, and it opened my eyes to how callous people can be. I was only there two nights and I could not wait to leave on the third day after viewing five houses that were totally unsuitable. I left the hotel room on the last day and went and sat by the water. It was cold but I had a thick coat on and wrapped up as much as I could. I sat on one of the many benches along the boulevard to mull over my life and take stock. Before I knew it, I had sat there for four and a half hours. My train of thought was a blur. I do not recall anything that I thought about.

I missed my daughter and my dogs now! So, I knew that if I moved this far down, seeing Faye would be very few and far between visits and that was my main reason for sitting so long. I knew that I would not handle the distance away from her; we spent too much time together while her Father was off playing soldier and it would be unthinkable to not see her.

I had to find somewhere quickly as the house had now sold and I was under pressure while the necessary actions to hand over the townhouse were under way. I stumbled on a stone built terraced house at the bottom of a rather large hill and called the estate agent to see if I could view it inside. By chance, the agent was around in the area and I was informed that she would be on her way as quickly as possible.

When she arrived, she was very polite and let me in in a hurry. If I am completely honest, I know that I was not thinking clearly at this stage, because I did not actually know what I wanted or where I wanted to be. I felt that I did not belong anywhere in the country. I had moved around so much that it became impossible to imagine settling anywhere. I found this very upsetting and I was not clear in my head of what I should be doing regards looking at this house. The fact is that I only saw the superficial. I did not see the work that would need to be done to the place to make it habitable to bring it up to any sort of living standard, or anywhere near it!

I was so lost. But I tried to remain focused, this house was one monumental mistake that would also lead to the life that I needed to be in. This mistake would be the despair of immeasurable depths.

I was lost enough to text Jack and tell him that I would go ahead with this house. Fatal mistake, but it turned out to be a necessary evil. Just to say those words was sort of a relief in one way, but in the other way, my good little chimp on my shoulder called Jester was shouting at the top of her voice, "What the hell are you doing? This place is a shit hole, and it is situated in a shit hole!"

Then my other naughty chimp on the other shoulder who I call Eejit was saying, "Yeah, do it. It's not so bad and you need to get a roof over your head." Within days, the ball was rolling, and Jack B had secured the mortgage that I would take over as soon as I found a job. IF I found a job! There was nothing around except for a local convenience store and a post office!

I drove back up north and set about packing up the house that Jack and I had bought, built together and called it home, and then he had torn it down.

I recruited a friend that had been in the army and now lived with PTSD along with other mental disorders. I had met him online on some shitty site and we had become friends, but not friends with benefits as I had already got myself one of those. I thought that he was a good friend and he helped me to take shelves off the walls and dismantle the garden chairs and furniture. He enjoyed helping me out because I did not have a drill and did not want to buy one just for this event. He had planned to drive the lorry that I would be renting to relocate to Wales, but as I could not give him a definite date, he turned on me and voiced his anger at Faye because she protected me, which then resulted in Jack asking me who he was!

It was a drama I really did not need at this present time, and despite that, I had given him a few things that I would not be taking when I moved, he failed to take this into consideration after I could not bring myself to argue on the phone with him. I gave him a gas barbeque including the gas canisters, he also had some wood and other items that I no longer wanted or was unable to take to Wales for lack of a garden. After several phone calls that I refused to take from him after he kept shouting at me because I did not know my move out date, I handed my phone to Faye as he was calling me yet again while I was at hers. We were making plans to get the move underway in a couple of weeks. He had threatened Faye and said that he would never hit a woman, but that he could quite happily smack her one. He told her that all he was getting out of this was 'fucking friendship'. The simple fact was that I was not in a mental state to deal with him, he wanted more than friendship and I just did not fancy him that way. I did not find him attractive, but naively I assumed that he was okay with just friendship because that was the first thing that I had made clear when we started chatting. Up until this point, we got on well until I could not give him the date that I would be leaving my house.

I was gutted that he was able to turn so nasty when he knew what I was going through because he had been through a divorce himself and he had daughters that no longer spoke to him. In any case, I let go of him and his drama and blocked his number so that he could not contact me. He lived an hour away and I had given him fuel money when he had come down to help, I also gave him the gas BBQ that had only been used once in the three years we had lived there because Jack could not be assed with doing them, and Pete did not refuse when I offered the BBQ! In fact, he could not wait to get it in his truck, and he took it with no questions asked! I was quite glad that he was no longer around. Although he had never stayed more than two to three hours, I was glad when he was in his truck and on his way. I had underestimated the effect that someone with posttraumatic stress would have on me in my vulnerable state of mind. I was drawing on my own reserves of mental strength to get through each day, but to take on Pete's attitude was just too much.

I had thrown Jack's belongings in the boxes that he had left in the garage. We only communicated when we had to. He refused to show me a picture of where he was living and claimed that he was renting a room after he had left camp. I did not believe him but did not push the situation because I would only torture myself with the thoughts of him on someone else's bed and living in her house. He told Faye that he was living out of food banks and cried uncontrollably once saying that he 'Had nothing'. This really bothered me at the time, and by text, I asked him if he was eating, to which he replied yes that he was eating. But I was mindful that he had chosen to live this way. We were now a separated family that was living the best we could under the circumstances that he had created. Did he want pity? Or just to portray a message of "look at me, I am suffering". I had to ignore it because he had to take responsibility for his actions. This was all his doing.

On one of my afternoons of packing up the house, I threw in my collection of all the blue letters (the folded free letters) that he had ever sent me from all the operational tours. It was a ten-inch pile of letters full of sentimental words and forgotten love. The memories that we had shared of each tour right from the first Gulf war in 1991 up until Kosovo in 2002. I had kept them together all this time with a few elastic bands around them, and they were in order of the years and tours with numbers one to whichever was the last letter of each tour on the front. Those numbers signified the order that they had dropped on the doormats of whichever house I/we lived at, or indeed which post bunk it flew into. I had left the big wooden box of all our family photographs until last, the truth is that I was dreading sorting them into piles of three like I had done with CDs, his, mine and Faye's.

There were quite a lot of photos of the fatter woman in dresses that made me look so much older. Someone had once said to me, "You are old before your time, and you look like your mother!" I had stayed fat because I did not know how to maintain a healthy diet and get my ass moving more. Plus, Jack claimed he loved me when I was fat, so I grew comfortable and complacent. I threw any photos of the two of us in a pile that Faye said that she would take, but I insisted that they should go in one of his boxes.

He would deliver his empty boxes into the garage, and I would fill them with his belongings, but when I say fill them, I did not pack them neatly. I just threw it in, and I did not care if something got broken or not. I threw stuff in there that meant anything to me as a family because now I would make my own memories without him, and so the old shit had to go. When Jack had left to go play soldier on all his departures, I always made a habit of changing the furniture around and changing small things so I could make the space mine, so that after he had sat on the couch the night before leaving it would not be a constant reminder that 'Jack was here!' Because now he was not. For good!

I wanted my own space, and I just worked through the days, weeks or months until he was back. I had spent a lot of wasted years wishing my life away whilst waiting for a man who never really came home. So, throwing things out that were no longer required was a cathartic and easy thing to do. For I had done it so often that this time, I knew whatever was left would only be the furniture and things that I had chosen and would have to keep for the foreseeable future, because I would not be able to afford to replace it all, but then I am not one for just 'discarding' for no apparent reason. That is things that I hold dear, and more so…people!

There were plaques that I had made and items that he had brought me back from numerous times away on tour or on exercise in Canada, but I did not want any reminders, so I gave up everything that I valued just so that I would be able to move on and close the old book.

The one thing I found extremely difficult to part with was the Marriage certificate. I received a text from him one day telling me that he needed it to start the divorce proceedings, and that he needed to know my thoughts on what grounds he should file it. Initially, he had suggested that he would file it under the Adultery that I had committed twenty odd years ago! I told him that they would not consider that for relevant grounds at this late stage and after the fact, and they would probably laugh at it. Desertion was my suggestion because it was the truth, and he had only found out about my infidelity after he had deserted me. Trying to make me look like the reason that he had fucked off was not going to work in this instance. He should have put it as adultery by himself because that would have been the plain truth. But instead, he had tried to pin the blame on me for something that happened years ago.

I was about to give the chest freezer to Pete when the text had come through about the marriage certificate, and at the same time, it was said that Jack also wanted the chest freezer! I felt that I was being watched and that Jack knew my every move! How on earth would he know that I was giving away the chest freezer? I asked how he knew, and he replied that the neighbours were watching. But the estate was quiet during the day because most people worked. I thought that maybe he had driven past or someone he knew had done so, but it was irrelevant because he wanted the bloody chest freezer apparently for when he set up his own place. Oh yeah, he was setting up his own place all right but not the one he was telling everyone!

Eventually, I gave up trying to fathom out who was reporting to him what I was doing, because I really wanted to just focus on getting myself and the flock out of there and away from his poisonous tongue. And eventually, it would become clear that it was not the neighbours.

Chapter 23

The Money Pit

The town house was sold, the keys were no longer mine and I had handed them over to the estate agent in July of 2015. Faye, Mark and I had loaded up both the trucks that I hired from a place in the centre of the city. It was the biggest vehicle that I had ever driven but it was a challenge that I rose to and I really enjoyed.

I had said goodbye to my friend who lives locally after she came to see us and helped us three pack up the vans. Donna and I cried, I found all this so heart-breaking, but there was nothing that I could do. It was out of my hands and there had been no going back. Yet again, I was giving up my entire life, friends, and faced being separated from my daughter for long periods of time because of my need to get away from him. We could only park one of the trucks on the drive at a time because it was a skinny drive and although I could not stand the noisy Nigerian neighbours it did not mean that I wanted a confrontation with them now just as I was leaving.

I could see on Faye's face that she wished that I were not moving so far away, and that also reflected on Mark's face that his girlfriend was so unhappy. She did not try and talk me out of it though as she understood that I needed to be as far away from her father as possible and supported me with whatever decision I made.

The last thing that was loaded in the second truck was my bike, it had been in the shed since I had adopted the dogs and was no longer used, but I refuse to give up anything that I form an attachment to, and my bike is one of them. I was never one for hoarding and I always clear out anything that I cannot use, but I have never been good at throwing away things I cannot afford to replace or indeed, anything that bears a sentimental value, unlike some people that feel the need to replace things even if they are scratched just to make themselves feel better. I brought my bike in 1999, and at the time, it cost £120.00 which was paid in monthly instalments because we had so little money and hire purchase was the only way. Jack also got a bike, as did Faye, which he taught her to ride in the back section of the house.

My bike was the one thing that I have managed to hold on to all these years and my point is that I do not just give up on things or people unless it is a lost cause. I have never ditched anything just for the hell of it. He replaced his bikes five or six times in the time I had just the one. That was always the difference between us in that was raised in an environment where we had to make do and mend until Mum could afford to replace, where his upbringing was totally different.

He knew that I had blokes around after chatting on the dating sites, although I had not slept with them because I was seeing Darren and I saw him often enough to not bed anyone else. And all I can say is thank heavens for that little fit guy! Because he was that one that built my confidence back up and made me feel wanted. Even though it was doomed to go anywhere other than fun, it was a welcome distraction at the time in my months of need. I was fond of Darren, but I was in no position to start getting attached to a man that only wanted me for sex and could not commit to anything else. But it was noted and assumed that I was sleeping with the people who I chose to invite around for a brew. Of course, I would be all the slags under the sun to someone who only saw things from his perspective because I had been living in the house that HE was paying for. This would be to deflect the attention from what he was doing. And it was not his business now that we were no longer anything to do with each other. We were not two good people that wanted different things; we were one good person being sold out. As the other goes off to lead a 'blessed' life while paving over the pain that he had caused.

My world was going through some massive changes and I did not know what would happen from one day to the next. But I knew that I am a survivor, and I would get through whatever mud and rocks were thrown my way. If I were temporarily buried underneath, it would mean that I was under there planning my next move. But while I was under, I would be allowing myself to heal and recover before rebuilding with those very rocks that he had thrown at me, because of the mentality he was displaying, there would be plenty of mudslinging too! It would be said, "You did this, and I paid you that!" Always about what he had given!

I would be okay, because I had no choice in the matter.

The day arrived that we would be driving to Wales and on to whatever awaited me there.

The couple who had brought the townhouse had been extremely impressed by my standard of cleanliness, I had cleaned room by room and shampooed the carpets so that they were spotless and there was no trace of my dogs ever having lived there. I keep my homes clean anyway regardless, in fact, I am always cleaning as it is my job as a housekeeper and it is something that I excel at.

I do not remember feeling sad at leaving the house, I was sad that it had all happened so quickly and now that it was over, I knew the road ahead would be extremely bumpy. I would have to ignore the verbal abuse that would be thrown at me. The one thing I was certain of was that brick wall I would hit at some point. I would remain strong until I felt that it was time to allow myself to slump into a form of grief for the loss of twenty-seven years, for it was no longer the path I was on, but I knew that I would have to grieve for it in order to be able to let go. Not grief for him, but grief for the years that I could not get back. A lot of life lessons in those years, and a lot of experiences that would ensure that I was mentally capable of going it alone.

Faye and Mark were in one truck with two dogs and I was driving the other. Mark drove the other while Faye took in the scenery. We stopped a couple of times to water the dogs and I would buy the coffees on the four-hour drive down to the house that I had found. To say that I was anxious was a complete and utter understatement! I was terrified, and in my heart of hearts, I knew that I had probably made a grave error in getting Jack to start the mortgage off on this place as I knew that to settle in Wales so far south of my daughter was going to break me.

We pulled at the Estate Agent in the town of Neath. I had called ahead to say that we were on our way with a rough time of arrival. I had allowed time for my dogs to have time to pee and for our coffee, food and toilet stops too. I brought most of the provisions for the week because I had caused such an inconvenience to Faye and Mark who had given up their week to help me.

On arrival at the house, I cannot describe how I felt. My stomach was so full of knots and I felt despair from the minute we pulled up along the curb side. I got out of the van, and we were all exhausted and just wanted this to be over. My world was in tatters and I did not actually know which way was up or down. Crying at this point was futile, because I had made this decision thinking that I would be able to settle here.

I had the keys to what was my first house on my own, subject to me taking over the mortgage payments as soon as I could find a job. The house stood above the pavement as we climbed the ten or so wonky stairs up to the front door with the stone-built wall either side of the stairs to support the grassed lawns. To look at it front on, it was pretty and quaint. I guess that was what attracted me to it. That and the fact that I was under pressure to find somewhere and the need to be away from Jack where he had no say on any part of my life anymore.

I inserted the key into the lock, but before I turned the key, I turned to Faye and said to her, "You will either hate it, or you will love it." I knew which one I felt already, and I hated it! Now we were stood outside, it meant that it was real! I had to at least give it a go. Faye looked at me with anxious eyes; her beautiful, big, brown eyes told me she knew that I would not stay for long.

I opened the internal door and was greeted by the musty and unused odour that I had smelled when I had entered the house before. I could not keep travelling the four hours just to view a house that I had felt pressured into buying. I was forced to leave the brand new one I had just come from. This one was a stark contrast to the new and secure house I had left behind.

We walked in slowly, and the first thing that I spotted in the living room just off to the right of the fireplace, was a dead mouse. Spiders with long, spindly legs were dangling in every available spot, and cobwebs hung like fishing nets. I hid my tears that were bubbling under the surface. I wanted to fall on my knees and sob uncontrollably and wail, "What have I done?" But I just voice my opinion about the mouse and spiders and ascended the uncarpeted stairs. I hated Jack so much right now, but I forced that unholy thought right down into the pit of my stomach for future processing.

The house was cold as it had been uninhabited for a year. The storage heaters would be something that I would have to try and get going later because although it was warm a warm July outside, it was freezing in the house! There was so much undergrowth and trees on the hill in what was supposed to be my back garden that the sun would stand no chance of penetrating through any of it.

There was no fence to keep the dogs in. If I let them out in the back, they would just disappear up into the woods and probably never be seen again. I had thought initially that maybe I could get someone to fence off part of the garden, but that would take time and money, neither of which I had.

The hill was vast and carried on as far as the eye could see. Faye and Mark were looking at the kitchen when I came back downstairs, I could see the looks of horror on their faces. There was no light fitting and just bare wires hanging down from the ceiling. I did have a light fitting that could go up there and once I had found it in one of the many boxes, Mark duly did the job at hand; bless him he did help as much as he could, as did Faye. It was a light fitting that I had saved because I had brought it in Germany, and I could not replace it. I had left my big rotary washing line from Germany too and I resented that I had to give things up that I had saved for the house that we eventually put down roots in. I was angry because I had planned it all for years in advance, and he had ripped it all to pieces. I know that it is not wise to become attached to material things. But I had it in my head that if it was all in its place, then things would not need to be replaced so much and money would not be spent unnecessarily.

I still felt that urge to not even unpack the vans and drive back up to north with my tail between my legs and say I am not leaving my house and you can give me the bloody keys back and piss off with your sale of it!

At this stage, doing that was obviously out of the question.

Faye and Mark stayed with me for the week, and on the second day of unloading the trucks we had carried, and accidentally dropped my tumble dryer on the steepest part of the stone steps leading up to house. It weighed an absolute dead weight and there was only enough room for one person going up the stairs backwards, and one person climbing to hold the bulk of the weight. Either side was a wall with no room for errors. Unfortunately, it was Mark that bore the heavy weight and I went up backwards. Faye was waiting at the top to help me with the lifting, but Mark and I had already let it slip to the side and onto the wall, it was scratched but I did not care much, we just wanted to get it into the house. I tend to not be too precious about items that can be replaced through the monthly insurance that I took out when I purchased it. Hopefully, it would still work and dry my clothes, I really did not care what damage there was to it cosmetically. This would have been an instant drama queen moment if Jack had been there. I could see it now. "Oh for fuck's sake, can you not be careful!" That would have probably been followed by huffs and puffs and an atmosphere that only the devil could cope with. I was glad that anything that happened now was down to me, and if I did not feel like getting irate about something that was not life threatening, then I refused to get stressed! It was now my prerogative to control my emotions and my own thought processes. And I liked that!

Once both the trucks were unloaded, we parked them just up the road out of the way. We were living with a broken toilet and no hot water, the toilet cistern was just not working, it was completely knackered and therefore the only way that we could use it was to flush our waste away by pouring a bucket of water down it. This worked effectively but I could not live with this long term for hygiene reasons.

The power shower worked fine but the whole bathroom was a very depressing olive colour, and in such a dark room at the back of the house, it was a foreboding room. Showers were taken quickly and not enjoyed very much due to the state of the old-fashioned bathroom suit that also was green. I intended to paint this room, and quickly!

I had observed the toilet when I viewed the house, but the viewing was so quick and I was not really looking properly due to my head being all over the place at the fact that my marriage had ended so abruptly, and the unplanned event that I was forced to house hunt in the first place! So, I did what I always do, I saw a project that I would attempt to make good with as little money and resources as possible. But this was totally beyond my capabilities of renovation. It would take thousands of pounds to make this house in any fit state to live in comfortably and to my standards.

Jack had previously suggested that he had found a static caravan for £70,000 and maybe I should have considered that. How insulting, to think that I would even entertain a static caravan was such an insult after he had known me for so long how the bloody hell had he presumed that I would be open to such a suggestion. This made me hate him to the core.

By the end of the second night in the house, I had made a definite decision, I text Jack and my exact words were "get this shithole back on the market". He had internet and access to the relevant ways of making this possible. I only had a dodgy signal on my mobile that meant that I had to go out of the front door to even pick-up normal texts, so using the internet was kept to a minimum anyway because of the lack of mobile masts nearby, and the rolling hills surrounding the valley. It was extremely frustrating. He texted back immediately to ask why, I reeled off a list of reasons why, but I omitted to say, "Because this is your fault!"

I would never have looked in Wales if it were not for the fact that I had a cousin in Cardiff, my friends in Bridgend and I had stayed in contact with a couple whose house was still up for sale with a lovely fishpond that Jack had envisaged having his hands in (or so he said, because he never had any intentions of living there).

David and Christine lived further along the road only about five minutes away, so I had let them know when I had arrived with my daughter and her boyfriend. They helped unpack a couple of boxes and I tried to remain calm when they came to visit. But I could feel myself welling up inside and the control over my emotions was failing, I could feel it. Whilst making tea for everyone, I broke. I broke into a fit of outpouring and complete and utter despair.

I wailed in the kitchen in the arms of an older man with his partner stood beside trying to comfort me too. I cried so hard because I did not understand how I had reached this point. I was stood in a kitchen that was nowhere fit for purpose, and I was looking at two people I hardly knew and the previous time I had seen them was with my husband stood beside me. We had stayed in contact because I had fallen in love with their little cottage. They were selling up and moving to New Zealand and it was their house that I wanted above all else.

It was a breaking point that left me with a snotty nose in front of David and Christine, and with my daughter crying into the shoulder of Mark who was trying to console her. I was a broken snotty, emotional wreck and I did not know which way to turn. At that point in time, I was unable to be strong for myself, let alone anyone else.

Mark told me afterwards while we were outside smoking cigarettes, that my outburst had left Faye feeling totally helpless, and that she was at a loss as to what to do. I had not intended to upset my daughter and tried to avoid being upset in front of her. My outburst was not something that I had any control over. That pressure cooker needed to explode, and I could not predict when it would go. I had not expected a simple task of making tea to be the trigger mechanism.

I did not know what to do myself, all I could do was fight my way through each day and deal with the different emotions that came flooding in with the sunrise. I had usually held it together in front of Faye but on this occasion, I just felt so desolate, isolated, ousted, hurt, angry at Jack, let down and scared. I was scared! I had no income and was living off the verbal agreement monthly money that Jack paid into my account. Once the house had been sold, he controlled the amount that I received and would later tell me that I came out of it better than he had. Bullshit. Of course, he would say that!

The trigger point for this outburst of tears and uncontrollable sobbing was because we had been talking about when I was last at their house, it was to view it with my soon to be ex. He had seemed interested enough while we were with the couple, who were now stood in the living room of 'the money pit' as I had called it because it needed so much doing to it. Napalm would have been cheaper!

He had seemed genuine enough because he was a very convincing actor. He was playing along with a part that he had no intention of ever fulfilling. Within a week of it going on the market, the For Sale sign was back up!

I had briefly met the lady next door, and she had lent me an extension lead for Mark's drill. Little did I know that we would become the best of friends as we had been thrust into the same area of Wales through no fault of our own. And so, she enters my story as my lovely Dilys.

Faye had unpacked my craft room boxes, and in her kind little heart, she had tried to make it so that I had at least one room that I could feel a little at home in. I was impatient and snapped at her that she should not have bothered with it so much as I had absolutely no intention of staying any longer than it took to sell the house. Bless her, I felt terrible afterwards because she only ever tries to help and instils a positive attitude towards most bad situations. "Right, Mum! Come on, we can go and put beds together so that we can all sleep a bit better tonight!" She commanded, and I obeyed because I really did not know what else to do with myself, and we all needed a good night's sleep.

Mark and I had driven back up North to return the hire vans, while Faye stayed in the money pit with the dogs. It was a hell of a day. We set off early morning and drove the entire journey with one stop for food and water. After dropping the vans off, Mark's mum had picked us up to take us back to her house where she had made some food for us before we set off back down in our cars. We had left the cars at the back of her house for safekeeping.

I set off slightly before Mark so that he could catch up with his parents and spend a bit longer with them, but I wanted to get back to Faye and relieve her of the dog sitting duties. She had no way of getting anywhere except walk across the bridge over the bypass to the local shop, which was literally a small convenience store for the very basics. And she needed food!

We all did what we could to make the place look a little like a home, but I really had no interest in unpacking boxes, and refused to make it too homely because I would never class it as so. I had asked Jack again to please source a local plumber and a carpenter to come and give me quotes on repairs in the house. The plumber was the main person I needed to call on because the house would never sell with the broken toilet, and the bathroom in the shambles that it was. The carpenter was a friend of the plumber, and they arrived at the same time which was very convenient. I showed Andrew the carpenter the wood floor in the master bedroom because it had a massive bow in the corner under one of the windows. He looked at it, and then put his hand down the gap saying that it had collapsed and would need to be replaced, but that it was not going to fall through any further than it had already. He left, and shortly after so did Johnny the plumber, both saying that would be in touch with a quote. Johnny said that he would be back over as soon as he could, and that I should have a look around the local B and Q to see which tiles and bathroom suite I could find within my budget. This was being paid for from the proceeds of the first house, so technically, I was using it for the purpose of securing the sale of this current house by improving the bathroom, painting the place was next on the list!

The evening before Faye and Mark left, we had ventured to a pub in the nearest village, it was a nice meal, and again, I paid so that I knew they had something decent to eat as opposed to the fish and chips we had so frequently eaten over the last few days. I really could not stomach any more chips! In fact, I had only eaten to appease Faye, but in truth, my appetite was still under question and I still wanted to throw up at the thought of food. I was still suffering with the anxious feeling that took over my body and crippled me, but it did not cripple my ability and will to carry on regardless. I was determined to do this shit, and to come out of it the better person.

The dreaded morning that they were due to leave had arrived. They both had to be back at work on the Monday, so they left on the Saturday to do all their laundry and then they could get some rest on Sunday before returning to work. Bless them they had grafted to help me in the week they were with me, and I did not really know how I was going to ever repay them. Faye was crying before she even got in the car, and Mark did not know what to say except "goodbye and you know where we are".

As they drove away, Faye looked back through the rear window waving. I waved back with my heart in a million pieces. I had not had this feeling of wanting to fall to my knees for real since my brother had died, but moving away this far was my doing, and I had to suck it up and deal with it. Why was I watching my daughter drive away? I knew that I was not going to see her for a while and that left my heart in my throat.

Yet again, that man had brought about a chain of heart-breaking events that would eventually spark a fire in my soul, a fire that burned so hot and angry that it inspired me to write this book. A fire that would burn so fierce! My fight for survival was now in my own hands and it would be my drive to push myself at all costs. He would not break me! But for now, I would have to keep it as amicable as possible until the money pit was sold. And, for future reference. I did not feel the need to speak to him about anything other than what was I needed to survive with my 'my moving on'!

As I turned to go back into the house, I saw a friendly face coming towards me, a face that spoke a thousand words. She said, "I know that look, I have said goodbye to my girls so often that I know your heart is broken." Dilys stood and offered a hug, which I accepted gratefully because now I did not feel so alone in a village that I knew nothing about. I was eternally grateful for that hug and her timing had been perfect!

She had been out food shopping and it had been fortuitous that she arrived back home just as Faye and Mark were leaving. I considered this a sign from my guardian angel. Darren was watching over me and Dilys and I were meant to cross paths. We still discuss those days and how lucky we were to have found our friendship in such a dreary place, under such dreary circumstances. Darren had delivered a friend in my time of need, and Dilys needed of a female friend too because she lived with a nasty piece of work who was a control freak!

I may not be God fearing, but I believe in my brother.

The friend I had made in Dilys was to be my saving grace. Even with her strength and support, I still felt despair. We became nigh on inseparable apart from when it was time to sleep. She would retire next door and we would see each other at some point during the next day. Dilys hated me smoking but I still did it as we chatted on my doorstep before she went home. I let the dogs out for pees on the front lawn and we said our goodnights. I vowed that I would quit as soon as I was able to, but for now it helped. I can write about my friend with a heartfelt fondness because she is very much still in my life. She is such an amazing lady and an inspiration to me because despite her age she just ploughs on and keeps herself fit and healthy and looks nothing like her true age. She kept me going for the two months while I was living in the money pit, and I kept her going too!

I write with admiration and a warm glow in my heart for my fellow Aries friend because she had been to hell and back at the hands of her ex-husbands and was still standing! We swapped stories while drinking tea and she listened and offered good advice. She also told me some home truths which I was appreciative of, there are not many people who can be as honest with me, but I needed all the input that she shared with me. My most valued piece was "hold on to that anger, because it will be that strong emotion that gets you through".

Dilys had questioned me and we had deep conversations every evening. She asked me to tell her what had happened to the marriage. Why did I think the marriage fell apart? Did I suspect foul play?

I told her what I knew, and explained what had happened, but that despite my suspicions, I had no proof. I knew that he was trying to pin stuff on me that was not my fault.

She drew her own conclusion, and she was convinced that there would be a third party involved. I told her that I did not care if there was. He was someone else's problem now. I just wanted him to let me get on with my life and stick to the financial agreement because that would be paying my rent/mortgage from now on. If he were to stop paying it, I would be in trouble. All I had was an agreement that was not worth the paper it was written on, and his unreliable good word to fall back on. His good word that would be used as leverage to control what I said or posted on social media. He was so concerned about being badmouthed that I was unable to post anything for fear of the threat. "If you post this or do not stop anger voicing, then I will stop the money!" He saw what he wanted to see and did not even consider that there was an ex or two after his sorry ass. It was not about him unless it was straight after he had left.

But he was able to post exactly what he wanted, and I just never saw any of it because I had blocked him ages ago. And it got worse as the years went on!

We would sit night after night in my stone-built house freezing! I tried to get the storage heaters working, but they were set to come on in the day but not the evening! I had put money on that account to see me through, but it was hopeless to try and heat the place because I could not figure out how to change the timer. Instead, we would sit with woolly jumpers and thick socks to try and keep ourselves warm. It was August but we were wrapped up like it was midwinter!

The only time that we were genuinely warm was when we were walking our dogs up on the hill behind our houses. It seemed to rain constantly because we were not too far from the coast, our town of Resolven, was half an hour drive from Neath or Swansea, but we might have well been on the seafront because it was so wet and miserable all the time which did not help our moods. My wood furniture in the living room began to grow mould from being so damp in the house with no heating. I knew that I would have to bin some of it because it would be ruined if I did not get out of the house soon.

Dilys was a biker chick. Even at her age of sixty-five, she would get on her motorcycle and drive off up the dual carriageway on her travels; she was fearless. This is how she inspired me so much.

It was also how she had come to be in Resolven. Because the control freak that she lived with was also a biker and offered her a place to stay when she had nowhere else. They had met on the plenty of fishy site and seemingly got on in the early days, so he came to her aid.

Dilys had come from a family with money. She talked of a yacht, housekeepers, butlers and chauffer's, along with nannies. She painted a picture of a grand lifestyle in a beautiful mansion with her sister and parents. She and her sister had attended private schools.

But one year after her parents had passed away, the families accountants invested badly, the inheritance was put in all the wrong places and a substantial amount was lost! Which left little for her and her sibling.

Dilys had been married three times. She has two grown up girls and now has grandchildren too. So, this was how she understood my pain as Faye and Mark drove away from me. One of Dilys' ex-husbands had been extremely physically abusive to her, but she had been mentally strong enough to have escaped him! The nice man that she loved a great deal blew his own brains out in front of her in their farmhouse, and the third was an ex-soldier who used, abused and took her for every penny that he could screw her over for! He was, by all accounts, a flirt who would shag anything he came across, and loved himself more than anyone else. The farm that she lost on account of this man was the one that broke her heart. Dilys had kept livestock and when it was sold, she had to rehome most of her animals. The dogs went with her to her new place courtesy of fishy bike man, but she had owned horses, chickens, sheep and a goat.

Every morning and evening, Dilys would walk her dogs up on the hill without fail and quite often came back in the dark! I used to crap myself looking out of the landing window at the dark forest out the back! Let alone walk undeterred in it! Most of my nightmares have always been about being lost in thick woods and not being able to find my way out of it, so knowing that anyone could walk right up to my back door from the hill scared the shit out of me and I grew to dread the nights there. Anyone could lurk and you would never know that they were there. (Maybe I have watched too many things on YouTube about strange things lurking in the woods lol!)

I did venture up there one afternoon after we had arranged it the previous night and confirmed by text that we would meet on the middle path out the back of our houses, as is transpired, I had taken the wrong path leading up and ended up on the wrong track! By the time I actually caught sight of Dilys' red Hunter wellies in the distance, I was in a panicked state because the light was fading fast! We had talked on our mobiles trying to determine where each of us was, but it took around half an hour before I became aware of the mistake I had made with the pathways. It would be easy to get lost up there as I found out. The conifers made it darker in the forest quickly under the canopy, so by the time we reached Dilys' back door, it was fully dark. Bless her, she was so calm and did not let the darkness get the better of her. That was the difference of her growing up in the countryside, and me, a townie.

I had transported the few plants that I owned, and they were situated on the front windowsills because that was where the light came in. Two of the bigger plants were not doing so well because there was no room for them by the window so they were on the way out and I did not think that they would be going with me when I moved again. Dilys very kindly gave me a cut off; it was her money tree plant. I remember exactly where we were standing as she handed me this adorable little plant with its shiny plump leaves. We were by the back door that I had practically fallen through to get out of the woods quicker! As she handed it to me, she said, "Always keep this little guy alive, nurture it, feed it, repot it as needed and it will ensure that you will always have enough money to get by." That little plant is now huge! It lives in my living room window with as much light as it needs, and I treat it with the love and care to make sure that it survives. I have also given cut offs of this lovely plant to people who expressed an interest in how lovely it grows. I tell the back-story of my pride and joy plant that signifies two lost souls in stone built terraced houses in rural Wales, and the friendship that endures.

I had ordered a phone line from BT before I had arrived, but now that I knew I was not staying I refused to accept the connection and asked the postman to send it back and say that I had refused to take collection of it. No point spending money on it when I was not going to be there.

Two weeks after the money pit had been put back on the market, and several viewings later, I had an interested party! The plumber had redone the bathroom suite in the plain white that I had chosen so that it was clean and fresh. And I had help from a lovely village man who needed a bit of extra tobacco and beer money. He was an absolute legend and cause no bother at all and just wanted to help me get the place painted and cleaned up so that I could sell it. Again, this was a man that Dilys had hired to do odd jobs too, so he came by way of recommendation. When we had finished the painting, I gave him the ladder that we had used because I did not think that I would need it anymore. Watching him walk away on the last day gave me a sense of pride because now he had something that would benefit him more than me; he needed it to help with his odd jobs he did for the people in the village. I missed him after he was no longer visiting; he would sit on the storage box out the front and smoke his rolled-up cigarettes with a fresh brew, and he was happy with his quiet life of doing these jobs to help people out. His name was Martin, and I will always be grateful to that little, old man.

The interested couple came back to view the house twice. She had stood on the front lawn and said that she loved the quaintness and character of it, and that she could see its potential. Her partner was a builder and on the second viewing, he was already knocking down walls and adding log burners! Fantastic! This is exactly what this place needed other than a bomb to level it! All I had to do was wait for the confirmation that they wanted it, and then I could start making an escape plan.

I was already putting out the flags and throwing an imaginary street party at the fact that she seemed so keen and had fallen in love with the place. My budget décor freshen up had worked!

The kitchen was still dark and dingy, but I explained that I just had not got to that yet, and that it was the biggest job that would have to wait. They still got the ball rolling with their plans to buy and renovate because she wanted to be nearer to her parents.

I did not want to know the ins and outs of their lives, but they had a dog and she had two children that they were raising together. We exchanged numbers so that we could cut out the middleman estate agent and communicate with each other directly. Which was a blessing because I eventually sold her the bed that had previously been Faye's, and the furniture that I had decided not to take with me, she got it all for a fair price.

Because I detested being in the horrible kitchen so much, I only fed the dogs and made whatever I was going to eat in there, mainly Weetabix and tea! I still drank lots of Lucozade, but I ate little.

I had no running hot water for the duration of the two months that I was there, so I had to boil the kettle a couple of times to wash up with. It was such a primitive existence from what I had come from, but I did manage. The first night in the house, we had put the emersion on for the hot water to wash up with, but we had gone to bed and forgotten to turn it off! During the night, Mark had got out of bed to investigate the loud banging that was coming from the airing cupboard, only to find that the water was at boiling point and it sounded like it was going to explode! It had sounded like a steam train on approach!

I was too scared to chance it after that and just managed with the kettle because it was enough water for washing the dog's bowls, and the power shower was my source of washing myself.

Dilys arrived one night with two pots of culinary heaven that sent my taste buds into overdrive! She placed then straight in the kitchen as I set about getting out the cutlery and two plates. My friend stood with a big grin on her face and told me to start helping myself! This amazing woman had made curry that she had started preparing the previous day and brought it as a surprise because she noted that I had not eaten a hot meal since Faye had been gone.

It smelt so good that I was not going to argue with her! And, she had gone to so much trouble that there was no way that I could refuse. She said, "I will tell you what is in it after you have eaten some of it!"

Now I was worried!

But I did as I was told because the smell was making my mouth water. There was enough in those pots to last us three nights. The next evening, I plucked up the courage to ask my friend what was in it. She started with the main spices and ingredients which included dried apricots, which were the one thing that I really enjoyed as I have a sweet tooth, then as a last ditched attempt to evade what the meat was, she told me chicken! For a minute, I nearly believed her, until she started laughing!

Then, she blurted it out, "It is goat!"

Initially, I was mortified that I had just eaten it, and now I realised that after eating it for the last couple of nights that the goat was well and truly dead anyway, and there was no going back. But to add to the story, she told me that she had to make the decision when she left the farm because the poor goat was the only thing animal that she could not find a new home for. It was getting on a bit, so she shot it herself. And the rest is as they say history. Poor goat I will never forgive myself, but I can honestly say that I did enjoy the curry, nonetheless.

I had not been at all surprised that my stomach was so welcoming of the food that my friend had cooked up. My plate was not overloaded, and I was careful to eat slowly because I knew that my stomach would not handle it after all the months of not eating. It would have to be retrained to accept food gradually. But the positive that I could draw from this was that my allergy had completely cleared! I had a rash on my entire body before the train-wrecked marriage had taken place, but now it was all completely cleared up. So, when I did start eating again, I could weed out whatever it was that I had been allergic to.

You got to love Dilys' outlook on life and her courage.

While I was waiting for the house sale to go through and all the necessary wheels were turning, I made myself busy looking to the future and trying to sort out where I was going to live. This would prove difficult with four dogs even though they are clean I did not know how this was going to pan out. Jack had originally told me to get rid of two of them which I refused to do. Now this was something that I was going to have to consider if it meant that I could find somewhere to live further up near Faye.

I scoured the internet, and Faye was also looking from up her end for places to rent that would allow pets, it was when the people were informed that I had four dogs that we were told it was a problem. I cried and I knew that getting another mortgage would be impossible, plus I did not want to be beholden to the Jack bastard up north, so renting was the only option that I had at this short notice. I could only give a rough timeline as to when I would be moving because of the legal processes that go with selling a house. Dilys introduced me to another friend of hers that did removals, and he visited with his wife to give me a quote. He was stunned to see that I had already been there for weeks and had not unpacked one box. I only had out exactly what I needed, and I lived out of two suitcases of my clothes and washed them as I went along. To say that I seriously was in a hurry to leave was an understatement.

I had made it as comfortable as I possibly could and had put a rug down in the living room that I knew would be going to the tip as soon as I left. I wore cheap slipper boots in the house with furry lining that were two sizes too big since I had lost weight, and I wore three pairs of socks to keep my feet warm. I used the time alone to try and come to terms with the things that happened even though I was still unaware the real reason why it had. I had to stay emotionally strong, but I did cry a fair bit. Not because I was lonely, just because I felt so betrayed, and the fallout did not just affect me it really affected Faye although she did not really talk about it, it was her way of coping. I have never felt such despair and helplessness and at this point, I wanted to fight for survival. I just did not know how. I had done the flight part, now I would be prepared to fight.

Whilst I was in Wales, I had no idea what was happening in Faye's world, or what was being said and done to justify his exit strategy. This was not something that I wanted to dwell on, but I knew that Jack had the capability of hurting our daughter through his own selfish actions and words without remorse, if he wanted to do something, he did not care what impact it would have on her. I had not been there to support her as I was four hours away, and this bothered me greatly, but not for much longer before I would be within her reach.

Also, while I was in Wales, I had been logging on and off the fishy dating site that had brought about my little friend with benefits before I left. I had also chatted with a man called Paul from it too, and he had called my mobile the very same night that we had been attracted to each other on fishy. I wanted to meet him from that first phone call, and he was someone that I was instantly attracted to just from his profile pic and voice, his voice was so nice. I wanted to listen to him speak face to face. The second call came the very same night after he had told me that he was single and lived alone. Then he said his conscience had got the better of him and he had to confess that the girlfriend he claimed that he did not have was asleep upstairs.

I was livid and totally gutted on that occasion, but we still stayed in touch after I left despite having never met. This sort of thing would be a lesson that I would learn time and again; it made me more mindful of not believing that what they were telling me was the truth. He hurt me repeatedly, but only because I was naïve enough to believe his bullshit.

He texted me one night quite late while I was watching TV in the freezing living room and about to go to bed. Paul said that he wondered how I was doing and just wanted to chat and could he call. We spent an hour on the phone catching up and I told him how my time had not gone well in Wales and that I was moving back up.

He told me that I was his one biggest regret, in that he had let me go and not actually met me. But we planned to meet when I was back up north, and he would come to see me for a drink. He said that he had lots to tell me and that I would probably stop talking to him after what he had to say. I pressed him to tell me, but I was not expecting the response that I got.

He started explaining that his girlfriend was ill and that she would eventually leave him, and in this, I presumed that he meant she would pass away. He said that his first wife had died of cancer but that they had divorced mutually before she had passed. He said that he had no children and that he just had never been fortunate enough in that respect.

Like a fool I believed him, although I remained open-minded. We just left the arrangement that I would contact him by text when I was settled, and we would go from there. But he was talking of going for meals and meeting regularly and that he would make the excuse that he was going out with the lads from work and staying out for the night. I was not comfortable, but I had done nothing wrong as we were only chatting, and what was a drink between two friends.

There were lots of chats going on with the guys from fishy, but none ever amounted to anything because as expected, they were mostly married and cheating, or just wanted pen pals that were willing to send naughty pics so that they had wanking material. (This is in the third book about online dating; it will open the minds of the saints let alone normal sensible people!)

One guy that I did have a connection with was someone that had served in the same regiment as Jack. We got chatting on fishy after I commented on his uniformed profile picture, as I used the army uniform as an initial way of opening a line of communication. This time it worked, and we chatted about stuff in general before getting to the subject of where we lived and that we were only half an hour from each other in the valley. I told him about the house and my situation, and what had happened after I left Germany. He told me that he would cook if I brought the wine, and that I could stay in his spare room and bring the dogs with me.

He was great and was originally from the south, he had served two years on a posting to our regiment. I was fearful that he was in touch with JB and I asked him not to tell him that we had met if he was, because there was nothing to tell, nothing had happened except spaghetti bolognaise and cheese and onion crisps, washed down with a couple of bottles of wine. His reply was a welcome one. "I am not in touch with him and have not seen him for years. Plus, he is not my brother, and I would not tell him anything anyway!" This was music to my ears. Then he said, "I am just playing big brother and looking out for you as a mate, because you are very broken, and I would not take advantage of that!"

He also worked out the amount of army pension if it had been paid as a lump sum for the twenty-two years that I had been married, it would be a considerable amount. I kept this rough calculation in my head for future use, but right now, I had to take small steps just to be able to bloody breathe let alone think about fighting that battle. He urged me that I should fight for it and secure it in the future because I was entitled to it.

I left my new friend feeling a little bit lost, the link between us was only that of being in the same regiment at the same time, and I felt comforted by that. I knew that in time, I would discard anything to do with being near the military, but for now, the link was too raw and I had too many friends from those days in Germany that I was not willing to let go of.

I had reached a very painful decision that I would have to try and rehome two of my dogs. I cried uncontrollably for days, but it was proving too difficult to rent anywhere with all four. Now I really loathed Jack!

After adopting them through rescue groups, I reached out into that social media community and leaned heavily on their contacts in the UK to try and find the best solution, I would not part with my guys if I did not feel the adopter was not right.

I wrote an emotional plea searching for help, and through eyes that were filled with tears, and a heavy heart that was breaking yet again in a such a short space of time, I pressed the 'post' button. I told the truth in my post and it was met with heartfelt good wishes and lots of support. But I was completely broken. I hated Jack enough already, and now, I was about to lose two, if not three of my dogs in order to be able to move on.

After lots of messages on social media but no real forward progress of finding forever homes, I suddenly got a message from a lady who made the clouds of doom lift, and the sun shone brightly for the first time in years! Call it divine intervention again, but the message read "dear Elise, I have a house coming up for rent in Cheshire in a month if it would be of any interest to you. And I do not mind if you keep the dogs or if you still decide to rehome, but the back garden is secure with a lockable gate".

She had attached the pictures and the estate agents contact details. And it was perfect.

Considering the way that I had been living recently, this house that she was offering was a place that I could call home and be warm at the same time! And my guys would be safe with me forever.

I fell to my knees and sobbed! Because for once my prayers had been answered in a positive way. I could not lose my dogs, it would break me and this lady named Donna had just prevented both these things from happening. I will always owe her a debt of gratitude.

Chapter 24

Back to Cheshire with My Guys
September 2015

Three weeks before I was due to leave the money pit, I drove back up north to stay with Faye and Mark for a few days to break up the time I had left until I was loading up the removal trucks. I had arranged to meet a guy that I had been chatting to off the fishy site, but it was not Paul. This bloke was not really my type and had smelly breath, but after having a drink with him, I said that I would see him again after I had moved back. I was still too trusting of these people.

In all honesty, I did not know it at the time because I was still learning about online dating, but I was still so naïve to the ways of the men on these sites, I stupidly thought he was okay. But what he was doing was grooming me and making me believe that he would be seeing me on a regular basis to see how we progressed. In fact, as I learnt time and time again, all he was doing was feeding me bullshit stories of what he thought I wanted to hear.

My head was spinning, and I knew that I should just focus on the move and getting myself on an even keel before trying to meet anyone. I guess at the time, I just needed a distraction from the crap life that I was in at this current time.

There were people who stuck by me, Gerry, although he was severely depressed himself and could only offer to be on the other end of the phone, which was enough. Denise was my rock as always and she was still my go to person in my varying emotional states. Anne was there to a degree, but I could feel her slipping away, perhaps because she did not know what to say to me. Nothing anyone could say would make things better and I had to deal with this alone. I had to sort my shit out. And that would not be for a long time yet.

My mum was on the other end of the phone if I needed her, and she listened to me as I broke time and time again. My dad however was nowhere to be found, but nothing changes there. He has always been so hen pecked by Delores that to expect any help is a cause that was lost years ago. There were not many people from the Regiment that knew or could understand what had gone on because I was being monitored on social media and I dare not post anything because Jack would make it about himself even if it were not, so I was careful not to post anything derogatory. Bloody hell it is my account! And I was still being controlled from afar! I felt spied on and my hands tied around my back. I resented that he had done all this and yet I was not allowed to talk about it. Not on social media, but I was forbidden to talk about it in general. I did of course ignore this and all his warnings because I considered myself as nothing to do with him! Besides which, there was a whole other side to what he was posting, but I will get to that!

It seemed that if his wrongdoing was not mentioned, or he was not being accused of anything that he had done no wrong. I detested that it looked like I had been deserted through something that I had done. I know that people are quick to judge because I have done it myself, that the person who was left, must have deserved it for some reason.

When Anne visited before I left Manchester, she had shared a quote with me that said, "Taking your ex back is like putting a piece of shit back in your asshole!" I laughed hysterically at this because it was so poignant at this stage and I so wanted to share it publicly to say that I was never going back there with him, that I was done the minute he walked out of the door for the last time. I always said that he would never get a third chance if he left again. But I knew damn well that the threats would arrive by text about stopping the spouse maintenance agreement, I was not working yet and still living off the money from the sale of the first house so I would have to remain civil and do nothing to poke the bear.

I spent a week with Faye, and we tried to chill out under the circumstances, and it was good being with her after the weeks in my solitary confinement. Although I would really miss Dilys greatly when I left, I knew that my place was near my daughter and there was greater opportunity of work near the town that my new home was.

I made the arrangements with the estate agent to view the property knowing that I already wanted to rent it. I only needed to see what furniture I would be able to fit in. After leaving the townhouse, I still had most of it and there would be things that I would not part with under any circumstances.

My new address was a good omen to me as soon as I was given it, I felt blessed, because it contained the word Tudor, and the number seven which is my lucky number! I had been born while my mum and dad lived in Tudor Avenue and it seemed to bring a sense of familiarity and comfort for some reason. Bizarre, but true.

As I pulled into the road, I liked it straight away. I would need to work on the feeling of being closed in on all sides because I had never lived in a close before, but the size of the house and garden were perfect! The front lawn needed some tender loving care; it stood out like a sore thumb! But I like gardening and I would make it beautiful by the time I had finished with it. I was mentally redesigning the lawn and the border areas with flowers and shrubs while I waited for the estate agent, when suddenly, and without warning, there was a face at the passenger window! The next-door neighbour on the other side of my new driveway was tapping on it to get my attention without making me jump because I was staring into space. After the dogs had calmed down a bit, he announced that just wondered if I was here for the lady across the road, her husband had unfortunately just passed away and he wondered if I was here for her. He was being vigilant! He just wanted to know who I was and why I was parked in my little car with four dogs on the driveway.

I explained that I was here to view the property before moving in, and that I was waiting for my son-in-law to arrive to view it with me when the estate agent arrived. He seemed all right with my reason for being there and went back into his house via the back gate.

Mark arrived shortly after and we talked about how Faye had been and how she was coping with the divorce imminent and the knowledge that her parents were no longer together. She was devastated was the truth of it, and no one knew the reason for the split. No one knew yet. I was positive that there were people who knew why. But they were not my friends to ask the question, and they would never tell me now that I was the 'estranged wife'!

I detest that word as I was not the one acting bloody strange.

The two-bedroom house was the perfect size for me and the dogs, I could envisage the spare room with my crafting things set out on one desk, and perhaps a writing desk for the books I wanted to write. The landlady had already told me that the previous tenant had left furniture behind as she did not know where he was or what had happened to him, he had just disappeared into thin air! She asked me if I wanted any of his furniture, but I respectfully declined because I had all my own out of the four-bedroom townhouse, and I knew that I would not be able to bring it all with me.

The previous tenant had left behind a massive fridge freezer that stood in the corner by the back door, to find a milk carton of milk that looked like it had been there well over a couple of months!

It practically jumped out of the fridge begging for escape! The fridge was quickly slammed shut and I wretched at the smell that penetrated my nostrils. The smell was fouler than foul and was one of those smells that made me wish that my sinuses were been blocked.

The back garden was indeed secure enough for the dogs and I would not have to worry about my guys escaping unless they sprouted wings or jumped the six-foot fence, although I would not trust Bella not to attempt it as she has long and agile legs. There is an oak tree in the bottom of the garden and two sheds, the in front was more of a lean to with sides and a door, someone had apparently built it for a motorcycle as there was a massive metal thing that had been concreted in for the use of attaching a chain and lock.

The back shed was full of car and bike parts that seemingly the tenant before had left, but I later found out that he had kept himself pretty much to himself and none of the neighbours knew him too well apart from being pleased that he had finally gone.

On further questioning, my neighbours revealed that he had been a nightmare, there had been police raids for drugs, and he had his young boy and a boxer dog living with him, but neither had been cared for by all accounts. He used to leave in the middle of the night and not come back for hours or days and was apparently always piling his furniture in the centre of the living room for cleaning purposes and did it meticulously! Possibly to hide the evidence of drugs because bleach was often smelt.

He kept bad company and one of his friends was caught staring up at the young girl in the house attached, it had made her very uneasy and understandably so! My friend next door said that she often gave the dog biscuits through the letter box because it was hungry. There are scratch marks on the wall on the landing where the dog obviously needed to get outside and not be cooped up all the time, poor thing.

Viewing the house gave me a sense of calm, because I knew that I would not be far from Faye, and the surrounding towns would be more beneficial for me to gain housekeeping work. I told the landlady that I was extremely happy and would love to be able to move in as soon as possible! But by law, she had to the previous tenant another couple of weeks to see if he would surface and I would have to hang on until his time was up. The locks would be changed at that point because he had his chance and had blown it. We later found out that he was incarcerated courtesy of Her Majesty's Prison for being part of an armed robbery gang! It would also explain why the neighbours in the close took a long time to get to know me. It was a lonely time when I first moved in, but I totally understood why.

I left after spending the week with Faye and Mark. I headed back down to the money pit and to my lovely friend, Dilys. The drive back was not a pleasant one and I did not want to go at all, but I had no choice. I was extremely proud and grateful now that I had solved my problem of somewhere nice to live; it was light at the end of the tunnel.

I arrived back to a smiley and pleased Dilys who had been on her own for the week because the bloke she lived with was in Bavaria sorting out things for them to move over there. I think he had driven the four days it took to reach the house he had brought and transported his motorbike over as well as taking other stuff in his van. So Dilys was ready for my company by the time I returned. She was gutted that I would be leaving two weeks before her departure to Bavaria, but she was pleased that the little house in Cheshire had fallen into my lap and that I could take my dogs.

She had offered to take Bella to Bavaria and care for her, but I did not want to part with any of my dogs after the bad starts in life that they left behind in Cyprus. I wanted to make sure they have a happy life with as little stress, drama or upset as possible. Even though I had moved them to Wales, and they had witnessed so many tears from their human and they sensed my utter despair at times; they were always there for cuddles because they needed reassurance too, which I gave freely. I gave them no reason to be fearful that I was going to leave them.

I so wanted to settle, and I believed that settling with my dogs on my own terms could only be a good thing from now on. I wanted the fur-babies to feel loved and not feel like I was going to abandon them. I would have to go to work but once we were settled and in a good routine, they would know that I was coming back. The unrest that I felt whilst living in the money pit was worse than all the tours of duty. I felt angst twenty-four hours a day and very rarely slept. I had a constant nauseous swirling feeling in the pit of my stomach which made me not want to eat. I must confess that feeling has come back while I have been writing because it had dredged up the memory of it all.

But now, I have it in black and white, I feel lighter and in a better position to deal with the feelings. I am six years on from it, but I held on to the thoughts in my head to be able to write it. I burst the bubbles in Archimedes who can soon retire! Writing is a good release and a way of letting go of the negatives for good.

I sold my beloved butchers block and my oiled wood dining room table that came from Germany, along with the benches that sat snugly underneath it. Faye's long white TV stand that had been in her bedroom in the townhouse had to go too unfortunately, as did a bookshelf that I did not think I would fit in. I proper hated selling my butcher's block! I am not good at giving up things that I had waited a long time for. I was bitter and twisted about losing my first house, but it was bricks and mortar that held nothing except bad memories. I hated Jack.

I made one fatal decision one day when I was in one of my 'get rid of evidence of the past' moods! While searching for something in the unpacked boxes, I came across my vinyl records. I had around 150 seven-inch records dating back to *Maid of Orleans* by Orchestral Manoeuvres in the Dark. Mum brought me it after I broke up with the boyfriend Karl who she had loathed so much, it was an unexpected gift to cheer me up and I had kept it all those years.

I had a lot of twelve-inch remixes varying from Bros to Alexander O'Neill. I had treasured my vinyl, but I simply had no storage space in the next house, no record player, I really had a proper bad mood going at the way my life had just been dropped from a great height, so I loaded up my car and I drove to the tip in Neath. My little car was full of any items that would remind me of a life that had been controlled by someone who cared little unless it served his own purpose. My Toyota sewing machine that Delores had given me many years ago, I launched it with such a force that it bounced practically from one side of the skip to the other. I hated the woman for taking my dad and making him a jellyfish with no backbone to stand up to her, not even for his own son (when he was alive) or daughter's sake.

Then, I made the biggest mistake I had made since allowing the Corporal to walk out of my life. I threw my records in the skip! All of them! Except for the *Tears for Fears* Four Leaf Clover that I could never bear to be parted from. I did this action without hesitating because I would not have gone through with it otherwise. To say that I still regret doing this is an understatement, but I do know that there is no place in my house for them anyway. Binning my records still does not sit well with me but there is nothing I can do about it they are long gone. Chins up, it was time to look forwards not back, never look back for too long because there are only ghouls in the past, and I refused to let them affect my future. Just keep moving forward a little at a time.

Dilys and I went shopping a few times while we were waiting around to leave the stone-built houses that we despised. She is/was a crafter like me, the only difference was that she makes amazing jewellery, bracelets and keyrings with beads and she had added little dogs to mine and owls on Faye's. We filled our time as best we could because we did not know when, or if, we would ever see each other again. I knew from moving around so much in the army life that even when you say you will see someone in the future it is not always the case because life gets in the way, and we both were moving to totally different areas. I mean Bulgaria is not a five-minute journey! It is four-day drive or booking a flight and neither was something that I could even think about right now.

While I was away in Wales for these two months, I was unfaithful. Only in the sense of that I was unfaithful to my hairstylist. I have visited Daniel methodically, and without fail, once a month since November 2011 and I missed him terribly. He had listened to my tale of woe with regards to what was going on in my private life, and he has never held judgement. He was/is an ear that listens, and he remembers everything. He is now one of my true and trusted friends, and a staple part of my life. After all the years, we have been through a lot together. And I still see him once a month, he is the only luxury that I afford myself because I always adore the blonde colour tones that he mixes for my hair and never fails to deliver the personal touch. I would not be without him, and I refuse to change to another stylist. I drive miles to see my cherished friend because he is more than worth it. I missed one month without him and was traumatised!

In these times of bad things happening, I needed consistent people in my life, for example my daughter. She has been there through thick and thin despite our differences, and the usual differences between a mother and daughter that we found ourselves arguing about, but we have always been together. She is my ultimate best friend with unfaltering devotion to a mother when I feel like I have let my daughter down on certain occasions.

Then there is Denise.

Denise is my go-to person and my total heartfelt number one trusted sister not by blood, but I know that she is completely with me no matter what happens, and I am with her, always.

The day arrived for my extraction from Wales. Mentally, I had those flags out and I was throwing a street party that would rival the Queen's golden jubilee! Craig, who was recommended by Dilys brought his mate Dominic to help. They arrived early because before we could even start to load up the two removal trucks, the guys had to take out the living room window for my couch to be moved out of the living room the same way it had gone in, it was just too big to go in or out any other way. They had that sorted in no time at all and before I knew it, the trucks were loaded and ready to go.

We worked like trojans and there was no time for hesitation. The guys were moving my belongings with the intention of being back with their families the same evening.

We had started upstairs and emptied one room at a time so that I could clean the rooms and shut them off one by one, old habits die hard and that is how we used to do the march out of every married quarter that we vacated. In this situation, it worked well because I had dismantled everything and cleaned as much as I could in the days leading up to the big move.

Once everything was loaded, and the house stood completely empty, Dilys very kindly made cups of tea for all of us while we had a breather before setting off. Craig and I negotiated the quote that he had previously given me for the removal because as he said he was "more concerned with getting you back to your daughter".

The lady who had bought the house had been in touch by text because I had sold her Faye's bedroom furniture, and it was now staying in what was to be the little girl's room. I sold it to her for a very fair price because I could not take it with me. She texted me to wish me well and good luck! I also wished her well in her new house because heaven knows she was going to need it!

All I had to do now was say goodbye to my friend.

Craig leapt from his seating position on the back of the truck and said, "Right! We are going to get you home to your daughter!" This alone brought tears to my eyes. Dilys and I looked at one another because we knew that this was it, and it was unavoidable. She would also be leaving in two weeks and I would be happier when she was out of there too. She had made me promise to start eating, and we vowed to stay in touch. If I make that kind of promise, I intend to keep it, even if we do not hear from each other for a while I stay in touch with my best mates as much as possible.

Obviously, life takes over, things happen and people drop off the face of the earth for long or short periods of time. This does not mean that they do not think of each other, it simply means that they have a life. But a sign of true friendship is when you do eventually pick it back up and it is like you never parted. This happened to Denise and me; we lost touch for twelve long years!

Before Craig and Dominic drove away in their separate vehicles, Craig had advised me to take a certain motorway, which I forgot instantly because I was focused on saying everything that needed to be said to my friend. Craig had said his way would be quicker! I had already typed my new address into google maps and was ready to go so I did not want to change the route when I had more pressing things to concentrate on.

I was waved off by a tearful Dilys in my rear-view mirror. I too cried whilst I drove away from my friend. She had been my saving grace and my guidance throughout the last two months, I certainly knew and understood that we were two strong women who had kept one another sane! My lovely Dilys who I had no doubt in my mind that I would see again. We held a bond of friendship that would stand the test of time. I would never have got through that difficult time without her, and our paths had crossed for a reason.

As I rounded the bend just up the hill, she turned and walked back to the concrete steps that would lead her back into her empty house. I lost sight of her, and I prayed that she would be all right, and I swore that I would let her know when I arrived up north. We would speak and stay in touch and I had no intention of abandoning her. Despite our age difference, we had got on so well from the start and our friendship would endure no matter what.

I sincerely hoped that she would find some peace and happiness in Bulgaria, because she was so deserving of that. I wished the best for her after everything she had been through (another book).

And all the tragic events that had been bestowed upon her. On the passenger seat of my car sat the little naked teddy that she had given me. We had written our favourite little sayings on them and then exchanged as a keepsake. Those teddies were a crafting idea that were probably meant for children, but on this occasion, they serve as our personal keepsakes of a friendship that was born under gloomy clouds and came out smelling of roses! Little reminders that Dilys and Elise were there for each other in dark times.

Dilys, my friend…we made it out alive!

Chapter 25

My Little Sanctuary

I had ignored Craig's advice and driven up the same motorway that I always had, the last few of these journeys had been full of doubt and fear, this one would be the last time. It was a positive road to new beginnings, and one that I was confident would put an end to my nomadic lifestyle. I was desperate to put down roots and be able to settle in peace, and although this house was rented, the landlady Donna told me, "It is my house, but it is now your home, and you can stay here for as long as you want to."

This made me cry. Absolutely priceless! No one had ever said such kind words, but she knew and understood my situation completely from having been there herself.

I had stopped twice on the drive up north because although my dogs are excellent travellers in the car, even they could not hold their bladders and the need for water for four hours! I text my half-sister, Eva, with a message for my mum that I was okay, and that I would keep her updated on how things were going. I know my mum worries, but she also knows that I am more than capable of looking after myself. It is a comfort to know that she has got my back though and I think we all need our mums at certain times in our lives when we need a bit of support.

The two pit stops that I had made were done swiftly because I knew that Craig and Dominic would want to get my belongings unloaded and be on their way back to their families, which I fully understood. I arrived in the close where my new home was to find them waiting for my arrival, and I was questioned as to whether I had taken Craig's suggested shortcut because I had taken longer! But I could tell no lies, and on my deliverance of justification being that I could not deprive my little guys their pees! It proved to be a suitable reason and was duly accepted.

The unloading took less time than the loading. They worked like trojans and before long, I was watching the two trucks disappearing out of the close. By this time, Mark had arrived and was drilling my hose to the wall so that he could do some jet washing of the garden, he was eager to help in any way. This lad was a grafter, and I really appreciated that he would just find things to do and crack on with it knowing that I was here now, and that his girlfriend would be a lot happier now that her mum was on their doorstep. The truth would later escape Faye's mouth about how he really felt about me, which made me feel completely gutted because he had acted so genuine and I had not planned on being an inconvenience to him.

My gardens would be a work in progress as time went on. I planned to make both the front and the back look like they were loved and cared for. I have never been able to keep my hands off a garden if I can see it for the full potential. I would plant bulbs and make it pretty. Patience and time would be required, but for now, I started by cutting back the bushes, tidying leaves and mowing the front lawn!

It took a while to get it painted but I decided to start with the bathroom, the previous tenant had painted it grey and it was too manly and looked dreary and depressing. I painted it white with the belief that it would be uplifting first thing in the morning and that in itself set the mood for each day!

As I unpacked the boxes that we had dumped in the spare room, I found my dinosaur aged laptop. Now, this thing was over ten years old at this stage and it failed frequently to support any internet signal, emailing took so long that I could have run over to the other side of the country and got back before it had finally sent it! Maybe I should have launched this thing in the skip in Neath!

It fired up eventually and I set about looking for a job with an agency whom I had been registered with prior to my world being set on fire sending me running for cover.

I tweaked my CV adding the last two years of history, which consisted of impending divorce due to marriage failure. Shit happens and I would be fine once I had secured work and could look at getting on my feet by myself. What had happened was a blip and I was positive that it was for the greater good. It had been two years of hell that I could never recover, but he had not broken me!

I sent job applications to another agency with whom I would have to make a trip into the big city to register and take all my relevant documents for the purpose of their records. It was the turning point, and it would lead me to a family who would eventually become mine because I would remain in their employment for longer than any job I had ever had.

It was now October; the months were drifting from one to the next and I was making good forward progress in securing a job because I was registered with one agency, and an appointment had been made for me to make the trip to register with the other. One of them would prove fruitful because there were jobs advertised that were relevant to my housekeeping abilities. I suited and booted, wore simple makeup, and made a huge effort to look professional because this agency span the length of the country and I wanted to make the best impression to them. That would then reflect on to potential clients because I had been vetted face to face. I plotted my route on the trusty Google maps, fuelled up my little car and hit the road.

Just as I pulled into the very cramped car park, my phone pinged with a notification that indicated it was my little friend Darren to check in and see where I was and how I was doing. With his sixth sense of usually knowing that something was wrong, he timed this right because I was on the up, and I would fight my way back to normality. He informed me that he had decided to get in his car and drive to my new location for an afternoon of fun and catch up. I told him that was out of the question because I was currently on my way to an important interview!

He was not dissuaded though and told me to give him a name of a pub that was close to my house because he would go and chilled out there while he waited for me. He was exactly what I needed right now, a familiar distraction with no complications. In fact, he was the only uncomplicated thing in my life right now!

The interview went well, and I disclosed that I was about to go through a divorce, but that it was not going to affect my work capabilities and if anything would only drive me to work harder! The lady who interviewed me was kind and understanding and told me that she had a vacancy in a very affluent town, and that the family were lovely. She recommended that we would put my CV forward and see if they would be interested in me. I left the building feeling elated and so positive that I practically skipped down the street to where I had left my car. I text Darren to say that I was on my way and left the city in a hurry, because I was scared of the trams and never knew which way they were coming from!

I was greeted in the street next to the pub where my little friend was sat casually enjoying his pint. He walked up the road but quickened his pace as he saw my car in front of his. It was so lovely to see him and get a cuddle and kiss that meant we were pleased to see each other, more than six months had passed since we had set eyes on each other, and for me, it was nice to see a friendly face with who I could be myself and we would have a laugh. I asked how long he was down for, he said until midnight! We had hours of fun and frolicking and it took my mind away from the last couple of months that I had felt were mentally challenging. I had needed a friend, and as always, he had been there.

The winter of 2015 was a particularly difficult one. I had a roof over my head and my only focus was to hunt for jobs and care for my dogs. Everything else seemed to be a blur.

I found the back garden to be a good place for reflection, and I would sit on my wooden sun loungers and pour out the tears that flowed so freely. I had hit the same brick wall after losing Darren, except my brother was my whole reason for wanting to fight my way out of the situation and the depressed state that I found myself in. I did not want to succumb to my mind ruling my head like his had succeeding in doing. He had wanted to end it. I did not for the sake of my daughter and dogs. I was made of stronger stuff, but I would allow myself the opportunity to cry because I felt cleansed afterwards. I was emptying the bucket of toxic waste of twenty-seven years so that I could rid myself of the memories and negative thoughts. I would not listen to anyone who dared to advise me how to deal with these emotions that I considered to be natural, and my body's way of repelling the bad stuff.

I found it to be a dark time, but I knew that it was a necessary evil that had to be allowed so that it did not eat away at me and fester. I think being a housekeeper applies in most areas of my life, because I like organisation and order. Denise and Ajay were my two people again, because while I was busy falling apart about running a house with four dogs, they would instil confidence in me and tell me that if anyone could do it, that person would be me! But I was second guessing at times and wondered how the hell I was going to manage. But of course, in my fiery Aries fashion, I would do it and I would fight with every ounce of my being to excel and thrive.

The last civil text that was exchanged between me and the estranged Jack would be October 2015. He texted to tell me that we needed to meet because apparently, I was putting Faye in the middle. I had no idea how I had allegedly done this, but I refused to bow to his commands. He failed to see that I was no longer any of his concern and I would never do anything that he commanded. I just wanted him to leave me alone, Faye was now an adult and we had no common ground to argue over.

Faye had disclosed to me on one of her visits alone that she and Mark were not getting on, she hated that he had so much control over her, and she had to lie to him to be able to come and see me on this occasion because she wanted time alone with me without his glare piercing through her. She had needed a day or two away from him. We talked about what she planned to do, she knew that she would leave eventually and threw out into the universe that one day, I would get a phone call to say that she was on her way and to get the spare room ready!

This day did indeed arrive, and before I knew it, she was living with me and getting over the boyfriend that she had just left after two years. He had read her diary one day while she was at work. It revealed that she had gone to visit an old friend from school in Germany, one of the very few school friends that she had stayed in contact with. Again, she had to lie to be able to get out of the house for some breathing space; her only downfall was to document the visit in her diary. Mark had thrown a fit of angry jealousy and packed Faye's car for her. Packed would be the term that would be loosely described as thrown it all in as he had brought it out of the house. Her job was close enough for her to walk and on this day, this was exactly what she had done. She went home to find the front door locked from the inside, and her car piled high with as much of her belongings as possible piled into her car!

An argument ensued because he believed that she had been unfaithful (which she had not) and I received the call I had been expecting. She called in at her father's before leaving the area, and then headed to my house further down the motorway. Her commute to work would now be a lot longer than before because she stayed at her job until she could find something more local. She was making a new life for herself just a few months after I had started mine. But now, we had one another to support, and my roof over her head would be exactly that with no fear of her ever being thrown out! I would never inflict such cruelty on my own daughter and now I felt such a relief because now we could move on and protect each other from under the same canopy. I had my girl back, she had her mum, and the dogs were overjoyed at having both of us!

Faye and I celebrated our newfound freedom by inviting her best friend to stay on the weekends that he was available, and we would walk to the local pub. With the assistance of alcohol, lots of shots and cigarettes, it was now our time to live and be ourselves as mother and daughter, with no men to control us or tell us to behave! It had been such a long time that we had laughed so much and be able to forget that we had been so down for so long. It was as if dark rain clouds had lifted and the sadness had blown away with them, it was liberating. Faye's friend, Patrick, always slept on the couch because there was nowhere else for him and his long legs, and we would surface at whatever time we managed to climb out of bed. I was always first up and awake to feed the dogs and get them out in the garden for their morning business.

These celebrations went on for months and was in my opinion, well overdue!

I celebrated being accepted for my coveted job role in a lovely family's home and was working to secure an additional client to make the ends a little easier to meet every month.

My interview with the family was a success because there seemed to be an aura about us that would prove to be a friendship, as well Louise being my boss. On my arrival on a cold crisp November morning in 2015, I was greeted by the smiling face of a beautiful lady with a fantastic sense of humour! She showed me around her home that they had lovingly restored to its original beauty, with their own designs for practicality purposes. The family had two dogs with plans in future of a third! I was in my element and was praying at the time of interview that I would get it!

I had once again put on my suit and boots, and my red longline coat because it was freezing! I turned to leave as we chatted in the hallway on my way out of the house, when Louise said, "Forgive me for asking but what is your mental health state like?" I was not shocked or offended because I probably would have asked the same question.

I could only reply with the truth. "Shit happens, people get divorced all the time, but I will be okay. I just need to go with the flow and get through it."

Within a week, I had been informed by the agency that I had got the job!

Faye and I were embarking on our journey together. I knew that she would in time find another boyfriend and would perhaps want her own space and move out. But for now, I hoped that she would take the opportunity to rebuild herself a little and have a break from the boyfriend department. She had been through so much, as had I. But with age comes wisdom, and safety in numbers would mean that we were stronger together.

We had reached the end of an era. This was now our time to show the world what we were made of, our time to shine as individuals and never allow anyone to dictate to us how we lived our lives from here on. The future was to be of our own making, although there would inevitably be slip-ups and events that were beyond our control. There would be more heartbreak and sorrow to endure, most of it at the hands of one man.

I would like to hope that you would feel the need to follow our journey forward. I equipped myself with valuable tools that would allow me to move on gracefully, tools that I educated my daughter with to enable her to be able to process her emotions in a similar fashion.

I believe that we, as parents, are our children's greatest role model, and we must teach them well.

Thanks to the generosity and bottomless pit of knowledge that my new boss possessed, I found different ways with her guidance to see everything from a different perspective. Louise taught me a great deal about how to look at things from a positive instead of the negative. She and Andrew gave me a platform to allow myself to heal at my own pace. She saw me have temper tantrums and lots of tears, and she witnessed my transformation from feeling vulnerable to being empowered. I owe this lady and the whole family a debt of gratitude because they withstood a lot from me and my days of dealing with whatever mud the ex-husband was throwing at me.

The journey of Faye and I is just beginning, this is not the end!

Please stay safe and look after yourselves because I will see you in the next book, which incidentally is called:

It's My Life!

With love and pride…Elise.